HAMLYN ALL COLOUR
MICROWAVE
COOKBOOK

HAMLYN ALL COLOUR
MICROWAVE
COOKBOOK

HAMLYN

Front jacket shows, clockwise from top right, *Tropical Shortcake* (241), *Plum Duck* (73), *Leek and Bean Gratin* (165), *Shrimp-stuffed Trout* (37)

Half-title page shows, *Three Bean Salad* (137)

Title page shows, clockwise from top right, *Spaghetti with Chicken and Ham Sauce* (193), *Piquant Pork* (281), *Stuffed Globe Artichokes* (17), *Creamed Cauliflower and Watercress Soup* (1)

Back jacket shows, clockwise from top right, *Battenburg Cake* (273), *Beef Bourguignonne* (101), *Plum Jam* (225), *Paella* (181)

The publishers would like to thank the following for supplying photographs: Batchelors 213; Edward Billington (Sugar) Ltd 299; Birds Eye Wall's Limited 10, 109, 137, 142, 145, 158, 287, 297; British Cheese 5, 195, 196, 197, 198, 263, 283; British Chicken Information Service 74, 88, 89, 99, 289; British Meat 104, 115, 123; Butter Information Council 129; California Raisin Advisory Board 49, 92, 153, 265, 279; Concentrated Butter 24, 32, 46, 76, 118, 129, 210, 276, 296, 298; Creda Ltd 8, 9, 19, 102, 103, 134, 174, 205, 217, 218, 219, 223, 256, 266; Danish Dairy Board 18, 27, 41, 44, 82, 148, 190, 201, 241, 242, 243, 247, 248, 253, 255, 261, 262, 278, 285; Egg Marketing 206, 272, 280; Fresh Fruit and Vegetable Information Bureau 15; The Kellogg Company of Great Britain Ltd 48, 105, 130, 146, 182, 184, 221, 254, 271, 277, 295; Mazola 62, 79; Mushroom Growers' Association 14, 20, 23, 28, 29, 30, 35, 42, 47, 56, 60, 77, 98, 107, 120, 144, 160, 175, 199, 291; Potato Marketing Board 57, 138, 139, 143, 154, 171, 194, 214; St Ivel 1, 3, 11, 12, 40, 50, 65, 67, 69, 83, 90, 91, 106, 119, 131, 140, 152, 162, 176, 187, 216, 224, 284, 292, 293; Scottish Salmon Information Service 51; Seafish kitchen 43, 52, 68, 71, 72; Sun Pat Peanut Butter 189, 191, 200; Twining's Information Service 64; U.S. Rice Council 78, 81, 121, 192; U.S.A. Peanuts Information Service 207, 251, 258, 290; John West Foods 13, 21, 36, 39, 54, 55, 58, 59, 63, 116, 117, 124, 126, 151, 157, 161, 170, 208, 209, 244, 245, 246, 264, 282, 286, 288

Additional photography by Martin Brigdale, Chris Crofton, Philip Dowell, James Jackson, David Jordan, Paul Kemp, Graham Kirk, Vernon Morgan, James Murphy, Norman Nichols, Roger Phillips, Charlie Stebbings, Clive Streetei, Paul Williams
Line drawings by Sandra Pond and Will Giles

First published in Great Britain in 1989
by Hamlyn, an imprint of Reed Consumer Books Limited
Michelin House, 81 Fulham Road, London SW3 6RB
and Auckland, Melbourne, Singapore and Toronto

Reprinted 1994

Copyright © 1989 Reed International Books Limited

A CIP catalogue record for this book is available
from the British Library

ISBN 0 600 55799 5

Produced by Mandarin Offset
Printed and bound in China

Contents

Useful Facts and Figures

Notes on metrication

In this book quantities are given in metric and Imperial measures. Exact conversion from Imperial to metric measures does not usually give very convenient working quantities and so the metric measures have been rounded off into units of 25 grams. The table below shows the recommended equivalents.

Ounces	Approx g to nearest whole figure	Recommended conversion to nearest unit of 25	Ounces	Approx g to nearest whole figure	Recommended conversion to nearest unit of 25
1	28	25	9	255	250
2	57	50	10	283	275
3	85	75	11	312	300
4	113	100	12	340	350
5	142	150	13	368	375
6	170	175	14	396	400
7	198	200	15	425	425
8	227	225	16 (1 lb)	454	450

Note: When converting quantities over 16 oz first add the appropriate figures in the centre column, then adjust to the nearest unit of 25. As a general guide, 1 kg (1000 g) equals 2.2 lb or about 2 lb 3 oz. This method of conversion gives good results in nearly all cases, although in certain pastry and cake recipes a more accurate conversion is necessary to produce a balanced recipe.

Liquid measures The millilitre has been used in this book and the following table gives a few examples.

Imperial	Approx ml to nearest whole figure	Recommended ml	Imperial	Approx ml to nearest whole figure	Recommended ml
$\frac{1}{4}$	142	150 ml	1 pint	567	600 ml
$\frac{1}{2}$	283	300 ml	1½ pints	851	900 ml
$\frac{3}{4}$	425	450 ml	1¾ pints	992	1000 ml (1 litre)

Spoon measures All spoon measures given in this book are level unless otherwise stated.

Can sizes At present, cans are marked with the exact (usually to the nearest whole number) metric equivalent of the Imperial weight of the contents, so we have followed this practice when giving can sizes.

Oven temperatures

The table below gives recommended equivalents.

	°C	°F	Gas Mark		°C	°F	Gas Mark
Very cool	110	225	$\frac{1}{4}$	Moderately hot	190	375	5
	120	250	$\frac{1}{2}$		200	400	6
Cool	140	275	1	Hot	220	425	7
	150	300	2		230	450	8
Moderate	160	325	3	Very Hot	240	475	9
	180	350	4				

Notes for American and Australian users

In America the 8-fl oz measuring cup is used. In Australia metric measures are now used in conjunction with the standard 250-ml measuring cup. The Imperial pint, used in Britain and Australia, is 20 fl oz, while the American pint is 16 fl oz. It is important to remember that the Australian tablespoon differs from both the British and American tablespoons; the table below gives a comparison. The British standard tablespoon, which has been used throughout this book, holds 17.7 ml, the American 14.2 ml, and the Australian 20 ml. A teaspoon holds approximately 5 ml in all three countries.

British	American	Australian
1 teaspoon	1 teaspoon	1 teaspoon
1 tablespoon	1 tablespoon	1 tablespoon
2 tablespoons	3 tablespoons	2 tablespoons
3½ tablespoons	4 tablespoons	3 tablespoons
4 tablespoons	5 tablespoons	3½ tablespoons

An Imperial/American guide to solid and liquid measures

Imperial	American	Imperial	American
Solid measures		**Liquid measures**	
1 lb butter or margarine	2 cups	¼ pint liquid	$\frac{2}{3}$ cup liquid
1 lb flour	4 cups	½ pint	1¼ cups
1 lb granulated or caster sugar	2 cups	¾ pint	2 cups
1 lb icing sugar	3 cups	1 pint	2½ cups
8 oz rice	1 cup	1½ pints	3¾ cups
		2 pints	5 cups (2½ pints)

Note: When making any of the recipes in this book, only follow one set of measures as they are not interchangeable.

Introduction

The Hamlyn All Colour Microwave Cookbook has been specially created to offer you a wide variety of dishes to cook in the microwave. From soups and first courses through to desserts and snacks – there are recipes to suit special occasions as well as everyday meals. When you are looking for basic cooking times and instructions your manufacturer's handbook is the best source of information. This book aims to provide the next step in microwave cooking – a repertoire of interesting recipes that will make the most of your microwave. They rely on the microwave for the majority of the cooking operation but a few are finished under the grill or they call for a short spell of conventional cooking to complete the dish. Each recipe is illustrated to show just how good microwave-cooked food can look and to encourage you to experiment with decorative finishing touches. So if you only use the microwave for defrosting and reheating foods, read on and you will be inspired to experiment with the speed and ease of microwave cooking.

If you own a combination microwave, then you will find that this latest piece of kitchen technology has not been overlooked and a chapter of recipes cooked by microwaves and conventional heat simultaneously is included right at the end of the book (see recipes 281–300).

Before you begin to cook any of the recipes, do spare the time to read through this brief introduction. If you are a newcomer to microwave cooking, then make sure you have read the manufacturer's instructions for your appliance and follow them closely at all times. Even similar microwave ovens vary slightly. Your microwave oven's characteristics will soon become as familiar as those of your conventional cooker.

Microwave Cooking Do's and Don'ts

If you are already a keen microwave cook then you will probably know all about the advantages and pitfalls but it is just as well to remind yourself of the following main points.

How microwaves cook

The effect of this cooking method is basically very similar to steaming. Because moisture molecules in the food jostle against one another when microwaves are used to cook food, they evaporate and produce steam. The microwaves penetrate the food and the further they travel towards the centre, the less powerful they become. As they are absorbed by the food it is heated by the molecules which are jostling against each other. So the heating is from the inside rather than from the outside. If there is a large quantity of food, or if the food is very dense, then the waves will not penetrate in as far as the centre.

Unlike baking and grilling microwave is a moist, not dry, cooking method. Therefore foods do not brown and they do not form a crisp crust. It follows that certain foods cannot be cooked successfully in a microwave oven. Foods which need lengthy, slow cooking cannot be prepared in the microwave, so forget about putting tough stewing cuts and less tender meats in the microwave and cook these as you always have done. Recipes which rely on a crust for good results should not be attempted in the microwave oven. These include items made from choux pastry, batters and soufflé-type mixtures. This is not, of course, true if you have an oven which combines microwave energy with conventional heat, in which case do try the recipes in the final chapter of this book.

Cooking Utensils

You will find that much of your existing kitchen equipment is useful for microwave cooking. Ovenproof dishes made of china, glass or earthenware can all be used in the microwave. Ovenproof glass measuring jugs, basins, bowls and dishes are useful for all sorts of cooking operations, as are plates, flan dishes, pie dishes, mugs and small individual dishes. Wooden items and baskets can be used for short periods, for example to heat bread rolls, but they will absorb microwaves and are not suitable for lengthy cooking.

Plastic containers and dishes can be used for short term defrosting or heating but should be avoided for longer cooking. Specially manufactured plastic containers are also available for longer microwave cooking.

Absorbent kitchen paper, roasting bags and special microwave cling film are all useful for a base or as a covering for certain cooking operations. Ordinary cling film should be avoided.

Do not use metal containers, baking tins or any dishes that have any metal trims or decorative finishes. Shallow foil containers that are filled with food can be used in accordance with some manufacturer's instructions but if the manufacturer does not outline the details of their use then they should be avoided. Small pieces of cooking foil can be used in some cases to prevent overcooking in certain areas of food, for example to protect protruding areas on a whole chicken, but the use must be limited to small pieces of foil on large items of food. Do not use paper-covered metal ties.

Covering Food

Follow the recipe instructions when deciding whether to cover food when cooking. For the majority of microwave cooking there is no need to add a lot of liquid but to keep the food moist the dish should be covered. Look out for casserole dishes that have lids or use a plate on top of basins and bowls. Upturned plates can be used to cover shallow dishes such as flan dishes. Special microwave cling film is useful and absorbent kitchen paper can be used to loosely cover food to prevent splattering.

The Trick of Undercooking

When using a microwave do not be afraid of undercooking the food. If you are not familiar with the microwave, then cook the food for slightly less time than recommended and check on its cooking progress. You will not harm the food by undercooking it, then putting it back for a few seconds or minutes. Once you have overcooked the food it is too late so remember to check in advance.

Rearranging Food

If you are cooking several items of food or a large quantity, then rearrange the pieces or give the food a stir at least once during cooking – more often if recommended in the recipe. For best results set the individual items of food as far apart as possible on the dish or in the bowl to promote even cooking, and arrange food like chicken drumsticks with the thinnest parts towards the centre of the dish.

Cooking Times

The cooking times given are for specific quantities of food as given in the list of ingredients in the recipe. If you make a smaller quantity of food, then allow less cooking time; if the amount of food is increased, then the cooking time will have to be lengthened.

In some cases the starting temperature of the food will play a part in determining the total cooking time – for example, when heating liquids from room temperature as opposed to those taken from the refrigerator.

If a recipe calls for a large quantity of water, then it is often better to use boiling water from a kettle than to wait a long time for the microwave to bring the liquid to the boil.

Following the Recipes

The cooking times given are for a 650 watt oven.

The power levels are listed beside the ingredients list. In the method the power level is given at the start of cooking and at intervals throughout the procedure or if the power level is changed. When the power level is not repeated, then the same setting should be used throughout.

Standing time is included in the method where a period of longer than 5 minutes is necessary. At the end of the microwave cooking time the food is extremely hot and a period of about 3 minutes should be allowed to pass before the food is eaten. This is usually accounted for by removing the food from the microwave and transferring it to the plates so it is not specified in detail.

Preparation as well as cooking times are given for each recipe, to enable you to calculate accurately the time you need to set aside to produce a particular recipe successfully. Each recipe is calorie-counted, to assist in health and weight-conscious meal planning.

The recipes are numbered for quick identification and attractive colour coding highlights the chapter you are looking for as you flick through the book. The cook's tips which appear below each recipe provide further clarification of ingredients, techniques, or decoration.

Combination Microwave Cooking

The last chapter concentrates on combination microwave cooking which is a method of cooking by using microwaves and conventional heat simultaneously. In these recipes the microwave power setting and the temperature setting are both listed next to the ingredients list. The temperature is given in degrees centigrade only to conform with the settings on the ovens that are available.

All the basic rules of microwave cooking also apply to this method. Although many of the manufacturers suggest that baking tins can be used in combination ovens (a special insulating mat is sometimes provided) the microwaves do not pass through the metal so the use of ovenproof dishes is recommended for best results.

Remember that the oven does become hot when using the combination mode so always have oven gloves ready to remove dishes when the food is cooked.

If you are using the combination microwave to prepare a meal, then prepare the items that are cooked using microwaves only first, set these foods aside and they can be reheated very quickly before serving. Next cook the foods that call for conventional heat and microwaves together – this way any residual heat from the combination mode will not spoil any items (like green vegetables) that are cooked by microwaves only.

The chapter sequence of this book has been designed as a useful aid for menu planning. Soups and starters open the book, fish and shellfish and poultry recipes follow. Meat dishes complete the main course options and vegetables to accompany the fish, poultry or meat dishes come next. Vegetarian, rice dishes and suppers and snacks each have a chapter of their own – all, naturally, make the most of the virtues of microwave cooking. The recipes for sauces provide a marvellous back-up for the main course recipes and you will find the preserves in the same chapter well worth trying. Chapters on puddings and desserts and baking concentrate on the recipes that the microwave oven cooks best. The concluding chapter is directed at owners of the latest in kitchen technology, the combination microwave oven.

Whether you have a basic microwave oven or a sophisticated combination model you are sure to find this fully illustrated recipe collection with the wealth of hints and tips a boon when planning microwave meals.

Soups

There are soups for all occasions in this chapter, from light cream soups to serve hot or iced as a dinner party starter, to substantial soups and warming chowders which make delicious lunch or supper dishes. With the aid of a microwave oven one or two portions of soup can be re-heated in the soup bowl for latecomers in just a few minutes and with a saving in washing up. When freezing soups, divide into one or two portion packs, and they will defrost much more quickly in the microwave for almost instant use.

1 | Creamed Cauliflower and Watercress Soup

(Illustrated on title page)

Preparation time
15 minutes

Cooking time
20 minutes

Setting
Full power

Serves 4

Calories
165 per portion

You will need
2 tablespoons sunflower oil
100 g/4 oz onion, chopped
1 small cauliflower, cut into florets
2 cloves garlic, chopped
225 g/8 oz potatoes, chopped
100 g/4 oz watercress, chopped
600 ml/1 pint milk
300 ml/½ pint hot chicken stock
salt and pepper
4 tablespoons single cream
    (optional)

Place the oil and vegetables in a large ovenproof bowl, reserving 4 watercress leaves for garnish. Cover and cook on Full power for 15 minutes. Add the milk and hot stock. Liquidise or sieve the soup. Season to taste, then cook for 5 minutes to reheat. Garnish with a swirl of cream, if liked, and a watercress leaf.

2 | Tuna Rice Chowder

Preparation time
15 minutes

Cooking time
27–28 minutes

Setting
Full power

Serves 4

Calories
510 per serving

You will need
1 large onion, finely chopped
grated rind and juice of 1 lemon
25 g/1 oz butter
225 g/8 oz long-grain rice
2 bay leaves
900 ml/1½ pints boiling fish stock
    (see Cook's Tip)
100 g/4 oz button mushrooms,
    sliced
1 (397-g/14-oz) can chopped
    tomatoes
salt and pepper
2 tomatoes, peeled (optional)
3 tablespoons chopped parsley
1 (198-g/7-oz) can tuna in brine,
    drained and flaked
300 ml/½ pint single cream

Place the onion, lemon rind, butter, rice and bay leaves in a large bowl. Cover and cook on Full power for 3 minutes. Stir in 600 ml/1 pint boiling fish stock, cover and cook for 10 minutes. Discard the bay leaves and stir in the remaining stock, mushrooms, chopped tomatoes, lemon juice and seasoning. Cook, uncovered for 10 minutes. Cut the tomatoes into quarters (if used), add to the chowder with the parsley and flaked tuna. Cook for a further 3 minutes. Stir in the cream and heat through for 1-2 minutes without boiling. Garnish with extra parsley. Serve at once.

Cook's Tip

For chicken stock, break up a carcass and put in a large bowl with a quartered onion, bay leaf and mace blade. Cover with boiling water and cook on Full power for 15 minutes. Cool and strain.

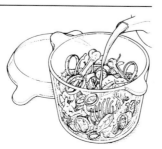

Cook's Tip

To make a good fish stock ask the fishmonger for 450 g/1 lb fish trimmings and place them in a large bowl with an onion, a carrot, a stick of celery and 2 bay leaves. Add 600 ml/1 pint boiling water and cook, covered, on Full power for 15 minutes. Leave to cool, then strain. Use the stock within 24 hours.

3 | Prawn and Haddock Bisque

Preparation time
15 minutes

Cooking time
10 minutes

Setting
Full power

Serves 4

Calories
270 per portion

You will need
225 g/8 oz haddock fillet
600 ml/1 pint milk
1 small onion, halved
1 turnip, chopped
1 small carrot, chopped
1 tablespoon brandy
1 clove garlic, crushed
salt and freshly ground pepper
pinch of cayenne
225 g/8 oz potatoes, cooked
1 tablespoon chopped parsley
225 g/8 oz peeled cooked prawns,
  defrosted if frozen
4 tablespoons cream
4 parsley sprigs to garnish

Place the haddock in a large ovenproof bowl with the milk, onion, turnip, carrot, brandy, garlic, and seasoning. Cover and cook on Full power for 5 minutes. Drain, keeping the liquid, and flake the fish. Liquidise or sieve the milk, fish, potato and parsley.

Pour the soup back into the bowl, stir in the prawns, keeping some for garnish, and cook for 5 minutes. Stir the cream into the soup. Serve garnished with the reserved prawns and parsley.

4 | Lobster Cream Soup

Preparation time
10 minutes

Cooking time
20 minutes

Setting
Full power

Serves 4-6

Calories
380–250 per portion

You will need
1 onion, finely chopped
2 sticks celery, finely chopped
grated rind and juice of 1 lemon
25 g/1 oz butter
1 bay leaf
40 g/1½ oz flour
1 egg yolk
salt and pepper
600 ml/1 pint boiling fish stock
150 ml/¼ pint double cream
3 tablespoons red wine
225 g/8 oz lobster meat (canned or
  frozen)
2 tablespoons brandy (optional)
chopped parsley to garnish

Place the onion, celery, lemon rind, butter and bay leaf in a large bowl. Cover and cook on Full power for 8 minutes until the celery is soft; discard the bay leaf. Stir in the flour, egg yolk and seasoning. Gradually add the stock and lemon juice and cook, uncovered, for 10 minutes, stirring occasionally until the soup has thickened. Mix a little soup with the cream, then stir the mixture into the soup with the wine and lobster meat. Cook for 2 minutes to heat through, without boiling. Add brandy, if used, and serve at once, garnished with parsley.

Cook's Tip

Skin the fish before using in the soup. Place the skin down on a board, rub your fingers with salt and hold the tail end. With a sharp knife, cut between the skin and flesh at an acute angle, working from tail end.

Cook's Tip

Frozen lobster should be thoroughly thawed before adding to the soup. For a less expensive soup use crab meat.
If you wish to make this soup in advance, then do not add the lobster until ready to serve.

5 | Stilton Soup

Preparation time
15 minutes

Cooking time
25½-27 minutes

Setting
Full power, Defrost

Serves 4

Calories
245 per portion

You will need
100 g/4 oz blue Stilton cheese
450 ml/¾ pint milk
a slice of onion
6 peppercorns
1 small bay leaf
25 g/1 oz butter
25 g/1 oz flour
300 ml/½ pint light chicken stock
salt and pepper
chopped parsley to garnish

Grate the cheese and put aside. Put the milk in a jug and add the onion, peppercorns and bay leaf. Heat, uncovered, on Full power for 5 minutes, then turn down to Defrost for 10 minutes to allow the flavours to infuse. Strain and keep warm.

Melt the butter on Full power for 30–60 seconds, then stir in the flour. When smooth gradually whisk in the milk then cook, uncovered, for 3–4 minutes until it boils and thickens.

Heat the stock in a jug for 3 minutes and gradually add to the sauce to make a light creamy consistency. Add the grated cheese, adjust the seasoning and serve hot or iced garnished with chopped parsley.

6 | Lancashire Warmer

Preparation time
10 minutes

Cooking time
15 minutes

Setting
Full power

Serves 4

Calories
395 per portion

You will need
1 large onion, finely chopped
2 sticks celery, finely chopped
25 g/1 oz butter
3 tablespoons cornflour
1 chicken stock cube
300 ml/½ pint boiling water
salt and pepper
300 ml/½ pint dry cider
275 g/10 oz Lancashire cheese, grated
chopped parsley to garnish (optional)

Place the onion, celery and butter in a bowl, cover and cook on Full power for 8 minutes, until the celery is just soft. Stir in the cornflour.

Dissolve the stock cube in the water, then stir into the bowl with the seasoning and cider. Cook, uncovered, for 5 minutes, stirring occasionally. Add the grated cheese and stir until it has melted.

Blend the soup in a liquidiser, return it to the bowl and reheat for 2 minutes. Serve hot with extra grated cheese and garnished with chopped parsley, if liked.

Cook's Tip

If you serve the soup iced, float a few ice cubes in each portion just before serving. Glass bowls make attractive vessels for iced soups.

Cook's Tip

The choice of cheese will determine the final flavour of the soup. 'Crumbly' cheese will not go 'stringy' when heated.

7 | Tomato Gumbo

Preparation time
15 minutes

Cooking time
25 minutes

Setting
Full power

Serves 4

Calories
255 per serving

You will need
1 medium potato
1 onion, finely chopped
2 sticks celery, finely chopped
2 cloves garlic, chopped
1 bunch spring onions
2 tablespoons oil
1 chicken stock cube
600 ml/1 pint boiling water
1 (397-g/14-oz) can chopped
  tomatoes
¼ teaspoon chilli powder
salt and pepper
225 g/8 oz gammon steak
2 tablespoons sherry (optional)

Cut the potato into small cubes and place them in a large bowl with the onion, celery and garlic. Chop the spring onions, reserve some for garnish, and add the rest to the bowl with the oil. Cover and cook for 10 minutes, stirring occasionally, until the vegetables are just tender. Dissolve the stock cube in the water, add to the bowl with the tomatoes, chilli powder and seasoning. Cook, uncovered, for 10 minutes.

Snip round the gammon steak, then place it on a rack or upturned plate. Cover with absorbent kitchen paper and cook for 5 minutes, turning the gammon once. Cut the gammon into small cubes, then add to the gumbo with the sherry, if used, and the reserved spring onions. Serve hot with crusty bread.

8 | Tomato Brew

Preparation time
5 minutes

Cooking time
12 minutes

Setting
Full power

Serves 4

Calories
125 per portion

You will need
1 (397-g/14-oz) can tomatoes
1 (435-g/15-oz) can tomato soup
2 tablespoons finely chopped
  onion
300 ml/½ pint buttermilk or 1
  tablespoon lemon juice and milk
  to make 300 ml/½ pint
1 teaspoon Worcestershire sauce
salt and pepper

Mash the tomatoes into their juices and stir in the tomato soup, onion, buttermilk or soured milk, Worcestershire sauce and salt and pepper to taste. Pour into a soup tureen, cover and cook on Full power for 12 minutes or until very hot, stirring twice during cooking. Stir again and serve with warmed French bread.

Cook's Tip

Special microwave racks are useful for cooking bacon, gammon or similar items when the fat is best drained away. They are available from any microwave stockist or cookshop.

Cook's Tip

The microwave is ideal for heating canned soups. Pour the soup into a suitable bowl, mug or jug. Heat on Full power for 2 minutes, stir well, then heat for a further 1–2 minutes, depending on the quantity. Stir well before tasting.

9 | French Onion Soup

Preparation time
10 minutes

Cooking time
30 minutes

Setting
Full power

Serves 4

Calories
315 per portion

You will need
575 g/1¼ lb onions, thinly sliced
50 g/2 oz butter
1.15 litres/2 pints hot stock
4 slices French bread, toasted and
  buttered
50 g/2 oz Gruyère cheese, grated

Place the onions and butter in a large mixing bowl. Cover and cook on Full power for 8 minutes. Stir in the stock, cover and cook for 20 minutes, stirring twice during cooking.

Top the toast with the grated cheese and float on the soup. Cook for 2 minutes to melt the cheese. Serve very hot. (The illustration above shows individual servings of soup before they are topped with the toast and cheese.)

Cook's Tip

Mixing bowls are useful for microwave cooking. To cover them use special microwave cling film or just top with a large dinner plate. If there should be room for the steam to escape, then put the plate on top at an angle.

10 | Brussels Soup

Preparation time
10 minutes

Cooking time
16–17 minutes

Setting
Full power

Serves 4–6

Calories
400–265 per portion

You will need
1 onion, sliced
225 g/8 oz potatoes, sliced
50 g/2 oz butter or margarine
2 (227-g/8-oz) packs frozen
  Brussels sprouts
600 ml/1 pint chicken stock
300 ml/½ pint milk
½ teaspoon lemon juice
salt and pepper
¼ teaspoon freshly grated nutmeg
150 ml/¼ pint single cream
50 g/2 oz flaked almonds, toasted
  (see Cook's Tip), to garnish

Place the onion and sliced potato in a large bowl with the butter or margarine. Cook on Full power for 4 minutes, stirring once.

Add the Brussels sprouts, stock, milk and lemon juice. Stir in salt and pepper to taste. Cover the bowl loosely and cook for 10 minutes.

Allow the mixture to cool slightly, then blend in a liquidiser or food processor until smooth. Return the purée to the clean bowl, stir in the nutmeg and cream and reheat, covered, for 2–3 minutes. Serve at once, garnished with almonds.

Cook's Tip

To toast almonds in a microwave oven, spread them on a flat dish and cook on Full power for 5–7 minutes, stirring frequently, until golden. It is preferable to toast 100 g/4 oz at a time, as smaller amounts may scorch.

11 | Winter Vegetable Broth

Preparation time
15 minutes

Cooking time
27–30 minutes

Setting
Full power

Serves 4–6

Calories
115–75 per portion

You will need
100 g/4 oz onions, chopped
175 g/6 oz carrots, sliced
350 g/12 oz swede, diced
100 g/4 oz parsnips, diced
3 cloves garlic, crushed
1 litre/2 pints boiling water
1 tablespoon concentrated
   tomato purée
salt and pepper
1 teaspoon dried thyme
1 teaspoon oregano
75 g/3 oz wholemeal macaroni
100 g/4 oz low-fat cottage cheese,
   drained
1 tablespoon chopped parsley

Place all the vegetables in a large ovenproof bowl, then add the water, seasonings and herbs. Cover and cook on Full power for 10 minutes, until the vegetables are tender. Add the macaroni and cook for a further 15 minutes. Heat for a few minutes, then stir in the cottage cheese and parsley before serving with wholemeal rolls.

12 | Chilled Leek and Potato Soup

Preparation time
10 minutes

Cooking time
20 minutes

Setting
Full power

Serves 4–6

Calories
320–215 per portion

You will need
1 tablespoon sunflower oil
3 leeks, washed and sliced
4 potatoes, diced
600 ml/1 pint hot chicken stock
salt and pepper
1 teaspoon dried mixed herbs
pinch of paprika
300 ml/½ pint single cream
slices of leek, separated into rings,
   to garnish

Place the oil and vegetables in a large ovenproof bowl and cook on Full power for 15 minutes. Stir in the stock, seasoning, herbs and paprika. Cook for 5 minutes, then add the single cream. Liquidise or sieve the soup. Chill before serving in individual bowls, garnished with a few leek rings.

Cook's Tip

Try using other types of pasta in this soup – small shells, broken spaghetti or a variety of shapes can be added. The vegetables can be adjusted to suit the season – leeks, cabbage, peas, new potatoes and French beans also make a good soup.

Cook's Tip

To wash leeks for use in a soup, or similar dish where they are going to be liquidised, cut them in half lengthways and hold them under running water to clean. Shake off the water and slice.

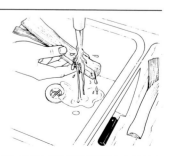

13 | Tuna and Sweetcorn Chowder

Preparation time
10 minutes

Cooking time
13–16 minutes

Setting
Full power

Serves 4

Calories
390 per portion

You will need
25 g/1 oz butter
225 g/8 oz onions, chopped
350 g/12 oz potatoes, diced
300 ml/½ pint boiling water
1 chicken stock cube
1 (326-g/11½-oz) can sweetcorn
450 ml/¾ pint milk
1 (198-g/7-oz) can tuna in brine,
   drained and roughly flaked
1 tablespoon lemon juice
salt and pepper
1 tablespoon chopped parsley
50 g/2 oz Cheddar cheese, grated

Melt the butter in a large bowl on Full power for 1 minute and sauté the onions for 2 minutes, without browning. Add the potatoes, water and crumbled stock cube and cook for 8–10 minutes until the potatoes are just tender.

Drain the sweetcorn, and make up the liquid to 600 ml/1 pint with milk. Add to the bowl with the sweetcorn, tuna and lemon juice. Adjust seasoning to taste. Heat on Full power for 2–3 minutes, then remove from the microwave and stir in the parsley and cheese. Serve at once.

14 | Cuillin Soup

Preparation time
10 minutes

Cooking time
11 minutes

Setting
Full power

Serves 6

Calories
195 per portion

You will need
450 g/1 lb button mushrooms,
   wiped
1 onion, chopped
50 g/2 oz butter or margarine
50 g/2 oz plain flour
450 ml/¾ pint milk
450 ml/¾ pint chicken stock
salt and pepper
2 tablespoons whisky
6 tablespoons single cream

Set aside six of the best mushrooms for the garnish. Slice the remaining mushrooms thinly and place in a large bowl with the onion and butter or margarine. Cook on Full power for 4 minutes, stirring once. Stir in the flour and cook for 1 minute more.

Gradually blend in the milk and stock, making sure the mixture is smooth. Add salt and pepper to taste. Cover and cook for 6 minutes, stirring once.

Meanwhile, place 1 teaspoon whisky in each of six heated soup bowls. Peel and slice the reserved mushrooms.

Ladle mushroom soup into each bowl. Add a swirl of cream to each portion and garnish with the fresh mushrooms. Serve at once.

Cook's Tip

Sweetcorn and tuna fish combine well together in a variety of dishes; however you may prefer to use peas in this recipe. If frozen peas are used, there is no need to add any extra liquid since they yield moisture as they defrost in the soup.

Cook's Tip

Stirring the soup while cooking ensures even heat distribution. Outer edges receive more microwave energy and will therefore heat more quickly, so always stir from the rim to the centre.

15 | Broccoli and Potato Soup

Preparation time
10 minutes

Cooking time
28–30 minutes

Setting
Full power

Serves 4

Calories
315 per portion

You will need
450 g/1 lb potatoes
1 small onion, chopped
25 g/1 oz butter
25 g/1 oz wholemeal flour
salt and pepper
600 ml/1 pint chicken stock
300 ml/½ pint milk
175 g/6 oz broccoli, broken into
   small florets
granary croûtons (see Cook's
   Tip) to garnish (optional)

Cut the potatoes into small cubes and place in a roasting bag with the onion and butter. Cook on Full power for 15 minutes, shaking the bag twice.

Tip the cooked vegetables into a large bowl, stir in the flour and add salt and pepper to taste. Gradually stir in the stock and milk. Cover and cook for 5 minutes, stirring once during cooking.

Add the broccoli, stir thoroughly and cook for 8–10 minutes. Serve at once, with granary croûtons, if liked.

16 | Chunky Minestrone

Preparation time
20 minutes

Cooking time
30 minutes

Setting
Full power

Serves 4

Calories
420 per portion

You will need
2 carrots, scrubbed
2 sticks celery, sliced
2 small onions, chopped
1 medium potato, cubed
2 cloves garlic, chopped
225 g/8 oz rindless back bacon
900 ml/1½ pints boiling stock
1 tablespoon tomato purée
few drops of Tabasco sauce
salt and pepper
175 g/6 oz white cabbage, finely
   shredded
1 (430-g/15-oz) can white kidney
   beans
450 g/1 lb tomatoes, peeled

Cut the carrots into 2.5-cm/1-inch lengths and quarter lengthways. Place the carrots, celery, onion, potato and garlic in a large bowl. Lay the bacon rashers on top, cover and cook for 5 minutes, rearranging the bacon once. Remove the bacon, add 300 ml/½ pint boiling stock, cover and cook for 10 minutes or until the vegetables are just soft. Stir the tomato purée, Tabasco and seasoning into the remaining stock; add to the vegetables with the cabbage. Cover and cook for 10 minutes. Roughly chop the bacon and add to the soup with the beans. Cut the tomatoes into quarters, add to the bowl and cook, uncovered, for 5 minutes. Serve with crusty bread and grated Parmesan cheese.

Cook's Tip

To make the croûtons, cut 2 thick slices of granary bread into cubes, discarding crusts. Arrange in a single layer on absorbent kitchen paper and cook on Full power for 3–4 minutes or until crisp. Melt 25 g/1 oz butter in a medium bowl, add the croûtons and stir until all the butter has been absorbed.

Cook's Tip

This is a chunky soup but don't cut the vegetables too large or the cooking times will be increased. Keep the pieces even for best results.

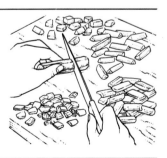

Starters

Serving a starter to a meal instead of a dessert occasionally, makes good sense in these health-conscious days, and when chosen wisely makes a saving in calories, which will please weight watchers. A wide variety of starters can be prepared with the help of a microwave oven, from pâtés and dips to marinated vegetables and hot fruit starters.

17 | Stuffed Globe Artichokes

(Illustrated on title page)

Preparation time
10 minutes

Cooking time
16–19 minutes, plus frying time

Setting
Full power

Serves 4

Calories
295 per portion

You will need
4 globe artichokes, stalks removed
3 tablespoons lemon juice
6 tablespoons olive oil
4 tablespoons fresh white breadcrumbs
2 tablespoons freshly chopped mint
2 cloves garlic, crushed
2 tablespoons chopped parsley
salt and pepper
150 ml/¼ pint dry white wine

Cut the tip off each artichoke leaf with kitchen scissors and use a small spoon to remove the hairy 'choke' in the centre. Plunge the artichokes in a bowl of cold water, with the lemon juice added. Then place the artichokes upright in a ovenproof bowl and cover. Cook on Full power for 12–15 minutes, rearranging once.

Heat 2 tablespoons of the oil in a frying pan, add the breadcrumbs stirring until golden brown. Mix in half the mint, the garlic, parsley and seasoning. Drain the artichokes and pat them dry. Ease open the leaves and spoon the seasoned mixture into the centre, pressing down firmly. Place upright in an ovenproof bowl or dish.

Combine the remaining oil and the mint with the white wine, season to taste and pour into the bowl. Cook on Full power for 4 minutes. Serve hot with the cooking liquid or melted butter, if preferred.

Cook's Tip

To test if the artichokes are cooked, gently pull away one of the leaves – it should come away easily when ready.

18 | Mackerel Pâté

Preparation time
20 minutes, plus 4 hours to chill

Cooking time
1½–2 minutes

Serves 6

Setting
Full power

Calories
265 per portion

You will need
100 g/4 oz unsalted butter, cut into cubes
150 ml/¼ pint milk
1 teaspoon gelatine
225 g/8 oz smoked mackerel fillets
1 tablespoon lemon juice
2 tablespoons horseradish sauce
black pepper

For the garnish
lemon slices
parsley sprigs

Place the butter, milk and gelatine in a large jug and cook on Full power for 1½–2 minutes or until the butter has melted, stirring once. Blend in a liquidiser for 30 seconds, pour into a bowl, cover and chill in the refrigerator for at least 3 hours.

Whip the 'cream' until it stands in soft peaks. Skin, bone and flake the mackerel. Stir in the lemon juice, horseradish sauce and pepper to taste. Fold the cream into the mackerel mixture and spoon into a serving dish or individual ramekins. Chill for 1 hour. Garnish with lemon slices and parsley and serve with crusty bread and salad.

Cook's Tip

Canned smoked mackerel fillets or other canned smoked fish make excellent speedy pâtés. If you store oily smoked fish such as mackerel in the freezer, then remember that it should be used within 2–3 months as it may turn rancid with long storage.

19 | Kipper Pâté

Preparation time
5 minutes

Cooking time
9 minutes

Setting
Defrost, Full power

Serves 4

Calories
225 per portion

You will need
225 g / 8 oz frozen kipper fillets
2 tablespoons cream
dash of anchovy essence or
   Worcestershire sauce
salt and pepper
50 g / 2 oz butter
cress to garnish (optional)

Place the kippers, still in original wrappings, on a glass plate. Cut a large cross in the wrapping and cook on Defrost for 8 minutes.

Mince the kippers and blend with the cream and seasonings. Place the butter in a glass bowl and cook on Full power for 1 minute. Add to the fish, reserving a small quantity, and beat the mixture until smooth.

Turn the pâté into small dishes and pour a little melted butter on the top. Garnish with cress, if liked. Serve with hot buttered toast or salad.

20 | Mushroom Pâté

Preparation time
15 minutes, plus
overnight to chill

Cooking time
9–10 minutes

Setting
Full power

Serves 6

Calories
150 per portion

You will need
½ teaspoon vegetable oil
450 g / 1 lb cap mushrooms,
   wiped
50 g / 2 oz butter
1 medium onion, finely chopped
50 g / 2 oz hazelnuts, roasted (see
   Cook's Tip)
100 g / 4 oz wholemeal
   breadcrumbs
1 tablespoon chopped parsley
½ teaspoon freshly grated nutmeg
salt and pepper

Line a 450-g / 1-lb loaf tin with cling film, allowing the ends of the film to overlap the tin. Lightly oil the base of the lined tin. Slice the mushrooms and arrange a row of overlapping slices down the centre of the tin.

Combine the butter and onion in a large bowl, cover and cook on Full power for 2 minutes. Stir in the remaining mushroom slices and cook for 7–8 minutes more.

Allow the mushroom mixture to cool slightly, then blend lightly to produce a chunky purée.

Chop the roasted hazelnuts finely and place them in a bowl with the breadcrumbs, parsley and nutmeg. Stir in the mushroom purée and mix well. Season to taste.

Spoon the mixture into the prepared tin and tap the tin several times on a work surface to remove any air bubbles. Chill overnight until firm.

To serve, invert the pâté on to a plate, remove the cling film and slice thickly. Serve with salad.

Cook's Tip

Boil-in-the-bag products are useful for cooking in the microwave. It is important to pierce the bag well or it will explode during cooking.

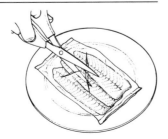

Cook's Tip

Roasting hazelnuts is child's play if you have a microwave oven. Simply place them in a small bowl and cook on Full power for 3½–4 minutes or until browned, stirring twice. Allow to cool before chopping or grinding.

21 | Citrus Liver Pâté

Preparation time
10 minutes

Cooking time
2½ minutes

Setting
Full power

Serves 4–6

Calories
325–215 (lamb's liver)
or 275–185 (chicken
liver) per portion

You will need
450 g/1 lb lamb's or chicken livers
1 onion, diced
1 (285-g/10-oz) can grapefruit
  segments in natural juice,
  reserving 2 segments to garnish
2 bay leaves
salt and pepper
50 g/2 oz butter
bay leaves to garnish (optional)

Place the liver and onions with the grapefruit, juice and bay leaves in a large bowl and cook on Full power for 2 minutes.

Remove from microwave, cool and remove bay leaves, then drain off any liquid. Blend the livers in a liquidiser with 4 tablespoons liquid, season to taste and place in small ramekin dishes or one large dish.

Melt the butter in a small jug or bowl on Full power for 30 seconds, then use to cover the pâté. Garnish with reserved grapefruit segments and bay leaves, if liked.

22 | Loaf Pâté

Preparation time
15 minutes

Cooking time
18 minutes, plus 5
minutes standing time

Setting
Full power

Serves 8

Calories
525 per serving

You will need
350 g/12 oz rindless streaky bacon
225 g/8 oz chicken livers
1 onion, chopped
1 clove garlic, chopped
675 g/1½ lb sausagemeat
1 teaspoon dried mixed herbs
1 tablespoon concentrated tomato
  purée
75 g/3 oz fresh breadcrumbs
1 egg
salt and pepper

Stretch out two-thirds of the bacon rashers with the back of a knife until they are thin. Use to line a 1-litre/2-pint loaf dish.

Mince, liquidise or purée the remaining bacon with the chicken livers, onion and garlic. Add the sausage-meat, herbs, tomato purée, breadcrumbs, egg and seasoning and mix thoroughly. Place the mixture in a bowl, cover and cook for 5 minutes, stirring occasionally.

Turn the mixture into the prepared loaf dish, cover with greaseproof paper and cook for 8 minutes repositioning the dish once. Leave to stand for 5 minutes, then cook for a further 5 minutes. Pour off the surplus fat, cover with several layers of greaseproof paper, top with weights and leave to cool; chill overnight. Turn out and serve with a salad of tomatoes, green peppers, black olives and lettuce.

Cook's Tip

This is a light pâté that makes an ideal topping for canapés. Pipe small swirls of pâté on small savoury crackers or on pieces of celery.

Cook's Tip

Vary the herbs and add chopped fresh herbs such as thyme or parsley, when available.

23 | Pâté Mushrooms

Preparation time
15 minutes

Cooking time
21–23 minutes

Setting
Full power

Serves 4

Calories
190 per portion

You will need
12 cup mushrooms, wiped
100 g/4 oz coarse pork liver pâté
25 g/1 oz butter, melted

For the sauce
1 small carrot, finely chopped
½ onion, finely chopped
1 stick celery, finely chopped
large parsley sprig
1 bay leaf
1 beef stock cube, crumbled
1 teaspoon concentrated tomato
    purée
1 teaspoon brown sugar
4 tablespoons red wine
5 tablespoons water
1 teaspoon cornflour
2 tablespoons single cream

For the sauce combine the first nine ingredients in a large bowl. Stir in 4 tablespoons water. Cover and cook on Full power for 10 minutes, stirring three times. Remove the bay leaf and parsley, then blend in a liquidiser until smooth. Return it to the clean bowl. Mix the cornflour with the remaining water, add to the sauce and stir well. Cook for 4–5 minutes, until thickened, stirring twice.

Leaving the stalks on the mushrooms, pack the cups with pâté. Arrange in a circle around the edge of two large plates. Drizzle the melted butter over and cook each dish for 3 minutes until hot. Heat the sauce on Full power for 1–2 minutes. Stir in the cream. Serve with the mushrooms.

Cook's Tip

To melt 25 g/1 oz butter in the microwave oven, place it in a small jug and cook on Full power for 20–30 seconds.

24 | Shrimps in Garlic

Preparation time
5 minutes

Cooking time
2½–3½ minutes

Setting
Full power

Serves 4

Calories
215 per portion

You will need
450 g/1 lb cooked shrimps
40 g/1½ oz concentrated butter
2–3 cloves garlic, crushed or finely
    sliced
1 tablespoon lemon juice
2 tablespoons chopped parsley
coarse sea salt
freshly ground black pepper

Divide the shrimps between four ramekins or place in one large, shallow dish. Cream the butter with the garlic in a large measuring jug and heat on Full power for 30 seconds, until melted. Stir in the lemon juice and parsley.

Pour the flavoured butter over the shrimps, sprinkle with salt and pepper and cook for 2–3 minutes to heat through thoroughly. Serve at once, with plenty of crusty bread to mop up the juices.

Cook's Tip

Prawns may be substituted for shrimps in this dish. To thaw microwave, loosely covered, on Defrost for 8–10 minutes. Prawns in a solid block should be gently eased apart as the outer area thaws.

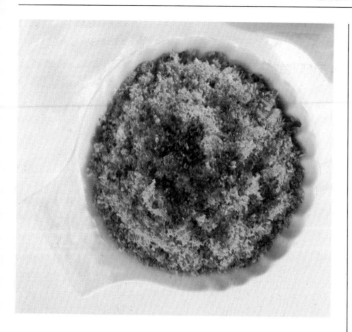

25 | Crab Creole

Preparation time
10 minutes,
plus 15 minutes to soak

Cooking time
6 minutes

Setting
Full power

Serves 4

Calories
150 per portion

You will need
2 tablespoons desiccated coconut
6 tablespoons fresh wholemeal
 breadcrumbs
6 tablespoons skimmed milk
1 onion, very finely chopped
50 g / 2 oz firm button mushrooms,
 finely chopped
1 tablespoon lemon juice
2 slices of lean ham, finely
 chopped
275 g / 10 oz white crab meat
1 egg, lightly beaten
pinch of salt
freshly ground black pepper
1 tablespoon chopped parsley
1 tablespoon grated Parmesan
 cheese
chopped parsley to garnish

Place the coconut in a small bowl with 4 tablespoons of the breadcrumbs. Stir in the milk and leave to soak for 15 minutes.

Place the onion, mushrooms and lemon juice in a bowl and cook on Full power for 3 minutes, stirring once. Stir in the ham, crab meat, soaked breadcrumb mixture, the egg, seasoning and parsley. Cover and cook for 3 minutes.

Stir well and divide between four individual dishes or scallop shells. Mix the Parmesan and remaining breadcrumbs, sprinkle over the top and grill to brown. Garnish with parsley and serve.

26 | Smoked Haddock Starter

Preparation time
8–10 minutes

Cooking time
8 minutes, plus 1–2
minutes to grill

Setting
Full power

Serves 4

Calories
245 per portion

You will need
100 g / 4 oz mushrooms, finely
 sliced
1 small onion, finely chopped
25 g / 1 oz butter or margarine,
 diced
25 g / 1 oz plain flour
250 ml / 8 fl oz milk
175 g / 6 oz cooked smoked
 haddock, skinned and flaked
salt and pepper
350 g / 12 oz cooked mashed
 potato

Combine the mushrooms, onion and butter or margarine in a large ovenproof bowl and cook on Full power for 4 minutes.

Stir in the flour, then gradually stir in the milk. Stir in the haddock and season to taste. Cover and cook for 4 minutes. Stir several times during cooking.

Pipe the mashed potato around the edges of four individual gratin dishes.

Spoon the haddock mixture into the centre of each dish and place under a preheated grill for 1–2 minutes to brown the potato.

Cook's Tip

Try using cooked and flaked white fish such as haddock, cod, coley, or whiting instead of crab meat if the latter is difficult to obtain. Cook the fish first, then flake with two forks.

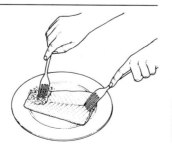

Cook's Tip

Serve with twists of lemon and thin slices of brown bread and butter

27 | Salmon Pâté

Preparation time
5 minutes, plus 2 hours
to chill

Cooking time
1 minute

Setting
Full power

Serves 6—8

Calories
270–205 per portion

You will need
150 g/5 oz Danish blue brie
50 g/2 oz butter, cubed
1 (213-g/7½-oz) can salmon,
drained and flaked
3 tablespoons mayonnaise
1 teaspoon lemon juice
2–3 tablespoons medium-dry
sherry
salt and pepper
2 teaspoons gelatine
2 tablespoons water

For the garnish
cucumber slices
watercress
slice of stuffed olive (optional)

Discard the rind from the cheese and cut it into cubes.
Place the cubes in a medium-sized bowl with the butter
and cook on Full power for 10 seconds to soften. Beat
until smooth.

Add the salmon, mayonnaise, lemon juice, sherry and
salt and pepper to taste. Mix well.

Dissolve the gelatine in the water (see Cook's Tip),
cool slightly and beat into the salmon mixture.

Pour the mixture into a lightly-oiled 600-ml/1-pint
mould and chill for 2 hours until set.

To serve, dip the mould in warm water and invert
on to a serving plate. Garnish with cucumber slices,
watercress and a slice of stuffed olive, if liked.

28 | Marinated Mushrooms

Preparation time
5 minutes, plus
overnight chilling

Cooking time
10 minutes

Setting
Full power

Serves 4

Calories
115 per portion

You will need
450 g/1 lb button mushrooms,
wiped
1 orange, peeled and cut into
segments
fennel sprigs to garnish (optional)

For the marinade
2 tablespoons sunflower oil
150 ml/¼ pint dry white wine
2 bay leaves
8 coriander seeds
grated rind and juice of 1 orange
salt and white pepper

Combine all the marinade ingredients in a large bowl,
cover and cook on Full power for 4 minutes.

Stir in the mushrooms, replace the cover and cook for
6 minutes, stirring twice during cooking.

With a slotted spoon, transfer the mushrooms to a
serving dish. Pour over the marinade, add the orange
segments and chill overnight. Garnish with fennel, if
liked.

Cook's Tip

**A microwave oven is a boon
when dissolving gelatine. Stir
the gelatine into the water in a
small bowl, stand until
spongy, then cook on Full
power for 30–45 seconds.**

Cook's Tip

**The crisp texture of Melba
toast would be the perfect foil
for the mushrooms. To make 8
slices of Melba toast, grill 4
thin slices white or wholemeal
bread (without crusts) on both
sides. Then, using a very sharp
knife, cut each slice of bread in** **half horizontally, to give 8
slices of bread toasted on one
side only. Grilling the
untoasted sides will produce
crisp, curled Melba toast,
which may be made in
advance and reheated for 1
minute on Full power.**

29 | Mushroom and Watercress Dip

Preparation time
10–15 minutes

Cooking time
6–8 minutes

Setting
Full power

Serves 4

Calories
135 per portion

You will need
1 onion, chopped
50 g/2 oz butter
1 bunch watercress, trimmed of thick stalks
2 tablespoons single cream
2 tablespoons natural yogurt
salt and pepper
225 g/8 oz small button mushrooms, wiped and finely chopped
watercress to garnish

Cook the onion with half the butter in a bowl on Full power for 3 minutes.

Put the onion, watercress, cream, yogurt and seasonings into a food processor or liquidiser and blend until smooth. Transfer to a serving dish. Cook the mushrooms with the remaining butter on Full power for 3–5 minutes, stirring once. Serve the hot mushrooms with the dip, using watercress sprigs as a garnish.

30 | Gnocchi Mushrooms

Preparation time
20 minutes,
plus 4 hours to chill

Cooking time
10–13 minutes, plus deep frying

Setting
Full power

Serves 6

Calories
380 per portion

You will need
300 ml/½ pint milk
4 button mushrooms, chopped
3 tablespoons semolina
2 tablespoons grated cheese
2 tablespoons grated Parmesan cheese
1 egg yolk
salt and pepper
24 mushrooms, stalks removed
25 g/1 oz butter
2 tablespoons lemon juice
oil for deep frying

For the coating
50 g/2 oz fresh white breadcrumbs
50 g/2 oz ham, finely diced
1 teaspoon chopped fresh herbs
50 g/2 oz vermicelli, crushed
25 g/1 oz plain flour
1 egg beaten with 1 egg white

Cook the milk and mushrooms on Full power for 3–4 minutes. Whisk in the semolina. Cook for 4 minutes, then beat well. Beat in the cheeses, egg yolk and seasonings; cool. Arrange the mushrooms on dishes, dot with butter and sprinkle with lemon juice. Cover lightly and cook each dish for 3–5 minutes. Sandwich the mushrooms in pairs with the gnocchi mixture. Combine the breadcrumbs, ham, herbs and vermicelli. Coat the mushrooms in flour, egg and the breadcrumb mixture; chill well. Deep fry the mushrooms until golden brown. Drain and serve.

Cook's Tip

This delicious dip is versatile; it can double up as a piquant sauce to serve with fish steaks.

Cook's Tip

Tomato sauce is a good accompaniment for this recipe: see recipe 236. Alternatively you could serve Hollandaise Sauce (recipe 235) flavoured with peeled, diced, deseeded tomato stirred in (as shown).

31 | Mushroom Croustades

Preparation time
10 minutes

Cooking time
11 minutes

Setting
Full power

Serves 4

Calories
270 per portion

You will need
4 (5-cm/2-in) thick slices bread
oil for deep frying
2 tablespoons plain flour
25 g/1 oz butter
150 ml/¼ pint milk
salt and black pepper
350 g/12 oz button mushrooms, sliced
2 tablespoons chopped parsley
lemon wedges to garnish

Trim the bread into neat squares about 7.5 cm/3 in. in size or slightly larger. Hollow out the middle, leaving an even, neatly shaped case. Heat the oil for deep frying to 190 C/375 F, then fry the bread until golden brown. Drain thoroughly on absorbent kitchen paper, blotting the insides of each bread case.

Place the flour, butter and milk in a large basin and whisk thoroughly. Cook on Full power for 3 minutes, then whisk well. Whisk in the seasoning to taste, then stir in the mushrooms and cook for a further 3 minutes. Stir in the parsley.

Arrange the croustades on individual plates, then spoon the mushroms into them. Add a garnish of lemon wedges.

32 | Vegetable Platter

Preparation time
20 minutes

Cooking time
40–41 minutes

Setting
Full power

Serves 4

Calories
440 per portion

You will need
8 small new potatoes, scrubbed
100 g/4 oz broccoli or cauliflower florets
100 g/4 oz baby carrots
225 g/8 oz French beans
40 g/1½ oz concentrated butter
1 small onion, finely chopped
1 tablespoon chopped mixed herbs
150 ml/¼ pint hot vegetable stock
6 tablespoons dry white wine
300 ml/½ pint whipping cream
2 egg yolks · salt and pepper

Prick the potatoes and cook, covered, with 4 tablespoons water on Full power for 10 minutes, stirring once. Using a slotted spoon, transfer the potatoes to a serving platter and keep warm. Add the broccoli or cauliflower and carrots to the remaining water, cover and cook for 6 minutes, stirring once. Add to the potatoes.

Add the beans to the bowl with 2 tablespoons water, cover and cook for 8 minutes, stirring once. Drain and add to the vegetable platter.

Place a little of the butter in a large bowl. Cut the rest into cubes. Add the onion and herbs to the bowl and cook for 4 minutes. Stir in the stock, wine and cream and cook for 8 minutes. Every 2 minutes for the first 6 minutes, stir in a third of the butter. Beat the egg yolks in a small bowl. Mix in 2 tablespoons of the hot sauce, stir into the sauce and cook for 2 minutes, stirring frequently. Season and serve with the vegetables, reheating them for 2–3 minutes first.

Cook's Tip

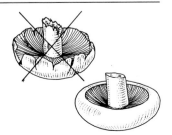

Choose mushrooms with care, avoiding any that are limp or discoloured, and they will reward you with excellent flavour when cooked in a microwave oven.

Cook's Tip

Vary the vegetables used for the platter according to the season, but be sure to consult the manual for your microwave oven for the appropriate cooking times. In addition to the vegetables suggested here, try any young seasonal vegetables, such as fennel, mange-tout peas, leek, beetroot or asparagus. A seasonal fresh herb garnish, such as the mint sprig shown, may be added for extra flavour.

33 | Celebration Asparagus on Toast

Preparation time
5 minutes

Cooking time
2 minutes

Setting
Full power

Serves 4

Calories
335 per portion

You will need
450 g / 1 lb cooked asparagus
   spears
4 thick slices white bread
40 g / 1½ oz butter
4 slices cooked ham
4 slices Gouda cheese
2 tomatoes, thickly sliced
salt and freshly ground black
   pepper
few basil leaves

Cut the asparagus spears in half, if large. Toast the bread lightly on both sides and spread with the butter. Place a slice of ham on each piece of toast and cover with the asparagus spears. Lay the cheese slices on the asparagus and top with the tomato slices. Season with the salt and pepper to taste. Chop a few of the basil leaves and sprinkle over the tomatoes.

   Place on a plate or shallow dish and cook on Full power for 2 minutes. Serve immediately, garnished with the remaining basil.

Cook's Tip

Asparagus on Toast makes a filling hors d'oeuvre or light supper dish if served with a green salad.

34 | Cauliflower and Apple Salad

Preparation time
10–15 minutes

Cooking time
6 minutes

Setting
Full power

Serves 4

Calories
95 per portion

You will need
350 g / 12 oz cauliflower florets
6 tablespoons water
2 carrots, scraped and coarsely
   grated
2 tomatoes, chopped
watercress sprigs, shredded
1 dessert apple, cored and diced
50 g / 2 oz raisins
2 tablespoons olive oil
1 tablespoon lemon juice
salt and pepper

Place the cauliflower florets in a bowl. Add the water, cover and cook on Full power for 6 minutes, until lightly cooked but still firm. Drain, refresh in iced water and drain again. Pat dry on absorbent kitchen paper and transfer to a salad bowl.

   Add the carrots, tomatoes and watercress, with the diced apple (see Cook's Tip). Sprinkle over the raisins.

   Combine the oil, lemon juice, salt and pepper in a small jug. Whisk together, then pour over the salad. Toss gently and serve immediately.

Cook's Tip

If making the salad ahead of time, toss the apple in lemon juice, cover with cling film and chill separately to prevent browning. Add to salad just before serving.

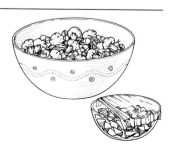

35 | Boozy Grapefruit

Preparation time
5 minutes

Cooking time
3 minutes

Setting
Full power

Serves 4

Calories
65 per portion

You will need
2 ruby or pink grapefruit
4 teaspoons ginger wine or ginger ale
4 teaspoons light brown sugar
50 g/2 oz crystallised ginger, finely chopped

Cut both grapefruit in half, remove the pips and loosen the segments with a grapefruit knife. Place in four individual bowls.

Pour 1 teaspoon of ginger wine or ale over each, then sprinkle with sugar and crystallised ginger.

Arrange the grapefruit halves around the edge of a shallow dish and cook on Full power for 3 minutes, turning the grapefruit around, if necessary, after 1½ minutes. Serve at once.

36 | Mexican Dip

Preparation time
10 minutes

Cooking time
7 minutes

Setting
Full power

Serves 4

Calories
190 calories per portion

You will need
25 g/1 oz butter
1 large onion, chopped
2 teaspoons (canned) minced chilli
1 teaspoon concentrated tomato purée
3 tablespoons chicken stock
100 g/4 oz cream cheese
150 ml/¼ pint natural yogurt

Melt the butter on Full power for 1 minute, add the onion and cook for 4 minutes. Add the chilli, tomato purée and the chicken stock and cook for a further 2 minutes.

Remove from the microwave, add the cream cheese and yogurt and serve with fresh vegetables or crackers.

Cook's Tip

Citrus fruits, such as oranges, lemons and grapefruit, will yield more juice if the skin is lightly pricked and the fruit is warmed in the microwave oven for a few seconds on Full power before halving and squeezing.

Cook's Tip

Jars of minced chilli are available from some supermarkets and good delicatessens. The minced chilli keeps well in a cool place and is useful for all sorts of spicy dishes. It saves buying a whole packet of chillies when you only need one. If you cannot obtain the product, then use 1 small chopped fresh chilli, seeds removed.

Fish and Shellfish

The microwave oven is really at its best when cooking fish and shellfish; the naturally moist and tender flesh requires only a short cooking time. Don't be tempted to cook fish any longer than stated in the recipe even if it appears slightly translucent in the centre, it will continue to cook after removal from the oven. These recipes include all the popular fresh fish as well as making use of canned and frozen varieties.

37 | Shrimp-stuffed Trout

(Illustrated on front jacket)

Preparation time
10 minutes

Cooking time
15–18 minutes

Setting
Full power

Serves 4

Calories
310 per portion

You will need
4 (225-g/8-oz) trout, gutted with heads on

For the stuffing
1 spring onion, finely chopped
1 stick celery, finely chopped
1 tablespoon finely chopped red pepper
1 tablespoon lemon juice
50 g/2 oz butter
salt and pepper
100 g/4 oz shrimps, chopped
100 g/4 oz fresh breadcrumbs
1 egg, beaten

For the garnish
lime or lemon wedges (optional)
parsley sprigs (optional)

Make sure the trout are clean and pat dry with absorbent kitchen paper if necessary.

To make the stuffing, place the onion, celery, red pepper, lemon juice, butter, and salt and pepper in a dish. Cook on Full power for 3–4 minutes, or until vegetables are partly cooked. Stir in shrimps, breadcrumbs and egg and mix well. Spoon stuffing into trout and close cavities with string or wooden cocktail sticks.

Arrange the trout in a shallow dish. Cover and cook for 12–14 minutes or until the trout flakes. Leave to stand, covered with foil, for 3 minutes before serving. If liked garnish as shown.

Cook's Tip

To chop a celery stick, first cut it lengthways into thin sticks, then hold them all together and slice across to make fine dice.

38 | Plaice Paupiettes

Preparation time
15–20 minutes

Cooking time
20–21 minutes

Setting
Full power

Serves 4

Calories
590 per portion

You will need
100 g/4 oz butter, diced
1 medium onion, finely chopped
1 clove garlic, crushed
4 button mushrooms, wiped and thinly sliced
300 ml/½ pint dry white wine
8 plaice fillets
300 ml/½ pint milk
50 g/2 oz plain flour
salt and pepper
1 tablespoon double cream
75 g/3 oz flaked almonds, toasted (Cook's Tip 10)

Place half the butter in a large quiche dish with the onion, garlic, mushrooms and wine. Cover and cook on Full power for 4 minutes, stirring twice.

Skin the fish fillets (see Cook's Tip 3). Season lightly, roll up from the head and add to the dish. Baste with the wine sauce and arrange the fish rolls around the edge of the dish so that none touches the other. Replace the cover and cook for 9 minutes, rearranging the fish rolls and turning them over halfway through cooking. With a slotted spoon, transfer the fish rolls to a shallow serving dish and set aside.

Strain the cooking liquid into a large jug and add the milk. Whisk in the flour and add the remaining butter. Cook for 6–7 minutes until the sauce thickens, stirring thoroughly every minute. Season to taste.

Whisk the cream into the sauce, spoon it over the fish and reheat for 1 minute. Sprinkle the almonds on top and serve immediately.

Cook's Tip

Small paper cartons and tins of wine are good if you want a small quantity of inexpensive wine for cooking. It saves opening a bottle or using a wine that is of better quality than is necessary. For a cheaper alternative, use dry cider.

39 | Cod with Loganberry Sauce

Preparation time
5 minutes

Cooking time
14–16 minutes

Setting
Full power

Serves 4

Calories
120 per portion

You will need
4 frozen pre-formed cod steaks
salt and pepper
2 tablespoons water
1 (285-g/10½-oz) can loganberries
   in fruit juice
4 pickled cucumbers, diced
2 teaspoons arrowroot

Place the cod steaks in a deep dish, season with salt and pepper, add 1 tablespoon water and cook, covered, on Full power for 5 minutes. Turn the steaks over and cook for a further 5–7 minutes.

Put the loganberries and cucumber in a medium bowl and heat on Full power for 3 minutes. Blend the arrowroot with the remaining water and stir into the loganberry sauce. Heat on Full power for 1 minute.

Drain the cod and serve with the sauce poured over.

Cook's Tip

Frozen pre-formed fish steaks are a useful freezer item. Look out for haddock and plaice steaks as well as the usual cod and coley. They are ideal for pies, fish cakes and other recipes that require skinned, boneless fish. For a really quick snack, just cook them in the microwave, then top with cheese and brown under the grill.

40 | Orange and Watercress Plaice

Preparation time
10 minutes

Cooking time
15 minutes

Setting
Full power

Serves 4

Calories
390 per portion

You will need
4 plaice fillets, skinned and cut
   lengthways

For the sauce
400 g/14 oz tomatoes, peeled and
   roughly chopped
1 tablespoon granulated sugar
2 teaspoons wine vinegar
pinch of paprika
salt and pepper
juice of 1 orange
150 ml/¼ pint double cream

For the stuffing
50 g/2 oz fresh wholemeal
   breadcrumbs
2–3 tablespoons chopped
   watercress
grated rind of 1 orange
1 large egg, beaten

Place all the sauce ingredients, except for the cream, in a large ovenproof bowl. Cover and cook on Full power for 5 minutes. Sieve the sauce, then stir in the cream.

Mix the stuffing ingredients together and divide the mixture equally between the plaice fillets. Roll each one up and secure with a cocktail stick. Arrange the plaice rolls in an ovenproof dish and pour the sauce round them. Cover and cook for 10 minutes.

Cook's Tip

When using cocktail sticks for cooking make sure they are wooden or the plastic will melt! Stick them right into the middle of the rolls to keep the fish neatly in place.

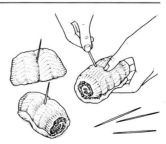

41 | Plaice with Mushrooms

Preparation time
10 minutes

Cooking time
14½ minutes

Setting
Full power

Serves 4

Calories
470 per portion

You will need
175 g/6 oz mushrooms
50 g/2 oz butter
50 g/2 oz fresh breadcrumbs
¼ teaspoon tarragon
salt and pepper
1 egg, beaten
8 small plaice fillets, skinned

For the sauce
175 g/6 oz Danish Dania cheese
  with mushrooms
2 tablespoons single cream

Slice two of the mushrooms, place in a basin with half the butter and cook on Full power for 1 minute. Remove, drain on absorbent kitchen paper and reserve. Finely chop the remaining mushrooms and cook in the remaining butter for 2 minutes. Add the breadcrumbs, tarragon, salt and pepper and enough beaten egg to bind the mixture. Divide the stuffing between the fillets and roll up. Secure with wooden cocktail sticks. Place in a large dish, as far apart as possible, and cover. Cook on Full power for 10 minutes.

To make the sauce, remove the rind from the cheese, cut it into cubes and place in a bowl. Cook for 45 seconds, stir, cook for a further 30–60 seconds until melted and smooth. Stir in the cream. Serve the fish garnished with the sliced mushrooms with a little of the sauce poured over and the remainder served separately.

Cook's Tip

When cooking items like these fish rolls in the microwave a flan dish is ideal as it allows plenty of space to set the rolls well apart. To cover, simply invert a large dinner plate over the top. Remember to avoid all plates and dishes with metal trims and decorations.

42 | Cod and Mushroom Pie

Preparation time
20–30 minutes

Cooking time
31–33 minutes, plus
grilling topping

Setting
Full power

Serves 4

Calories
525 per portion

You will need
675 g/1½ lb potatoes, sliced
150 ml/¼ pint water
275 g/10 oz closed cup
  mushrooms, wiped and sliced
2 tablespoons vegetable oil
25 g/1 oz plain flour
300 ml/½ pint milk
½ teaspoon paprika
salt and pepper
1 (198-g/7-oz) can sweetcorn
  kernels, drained
40 g/1½ oz butter
4 spring onions, finely chopped
450 g/1 lb cod fillets, skinned
25 g/1 oz Cheddar cheese, grated
  (optional)

Place the potatoes in a large bowl with the water. Cover loosely and cook on Full power for 15 minutes, stirring once. Cover the bowl with foil and prepare the filling.

Place the mushrooms in a bowl with the oil, cover and cook for 2½ minutes. Stir in the flour, then gradually beat in the milk, paprika, salt and pepper. Cover and cook for 3½ minutes, stirring three times during cooking. Stir in the sweetcorn.

Drain the potatoes and mash with the butter. Stir in the spring onions and seasoning. Cut the cod into even-sized chunks and place in a large pie dish. Pour the mushroom sauce over and cook for 10–12 minutes, stirring once. Top with the potato. If liked, sprinkle with cheese and brown under a hot grill.

Cook's Tip

When fish is cut into even-sized chunks for microwave cooking, there is no danger that some portions will be overcooked while others are underdone.

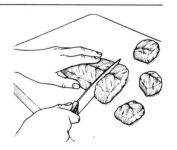

43 | Hake with Oranges and Dill

Preparation time
5 minutes

Cooking time
10–10½ minutes

Setting
Full power

Serves 4

Calories
175 per portion

You will need
300 ml / ½ pint fish or chicken
  stock
1 tablespoon chopped fresh dill
salt and pepper
4 (175-g/6-oz) hake steaks
1 tablespoon cornflour
6 tablespoons concentrated
  orange juice
2 oranges, peeled and cut into
  segments
fresh dill to garnish

Place the stock, dill, salt and pepper in a large shallow dish. Cover and cook on Full power for 3 minutes.

Add the hake steaks, spooning the liquid over the fish, replace the cover and cook for 6 minutes. With a slotted spoon transfer the hake to a serving dish.

In a measuring jug, mix the cornflour with the orange juice. Add to the stock remaining in the shallow dish and mix well. Stir in the orange segments. Cook for 1–1½ minutes, stirring every 30 seconds until the sauce thickens.

Pour a little of the sauce over the fish, garnish with fresh dill and serve. Hand the remaining orange sauce separately.

44 | Crunchy Fish Bake

Preparation time
10 minutes

Cooking time
13½–14½ minutes

Setting
Full power

Serves 4

Calories
390 per portion

You will need
350 g / 12 oz smoked haddock,
  skinned
300 ml / ½ pint milk
25 g / 1 oz butter
25 g / 1 oz plain flour
2 hard-boiled eggs, chopped
salt and pepper

For the topping
4 slices bread
40–50 g / 1½–2 oz butter

Place the fish in a suitable serving dish with 150 ml / ¼ pint of the milk, cover and cook on Full power for 10 minutes. Reserve the cooking juices and make them up to 300 ml / ½ pint with the remaining milk. Flake the fish. Place the butter in a basin and cook for 30 seconds, stir in the flour and whisk in the milk mixture. Cook for 2–3 minutes, whisking twice during cooking, until thick and smooth. Add the chopped eggs to the sauce and stir in the fish. Add salt and pepper to taste. Pour into the serving dish already used. To make the topping, toast the bread, butter it and cut into triangles. Arrange butter side up over the fish and cook for 1 minute before serving.

Cook's Tip

A wooden spoon may be left in the measuring jug for the short time it takes to cook the orange sauce, making frequent stirring simple.

Cook's Tip

This recipe illustrates a good point when using the microwave. Do not isolate the microwave oven in your kitchen – use it for the foods it cooks best, then turn to traditional methods for making crunchy toppings, for *browning crusts and for cooking foods like pasta in pints of boiling water. You will still save time by bringing the microwave oven into action to cook the main ingredients, vegetables and sauces.*

45 | Colourful Kebabs

Preparation time
10 minutes

Cooking time
6 minutes

Setting
Full power

Serves 4

Calories
180 per portion

You will need
4 smoked haddock fillets, skinned
    and quartered
2 large courgettes, trimmed with a
    cannelle knife or potato peeler
    and cut into 24 slices
24 button mushrooms
1 tablespoon grapeseed oil or
    vegetable oil
1 tablespoon white wine vinegar
1 teaspoon chopped fresh thyme
    or ½ teaspoon dried thyme
freshly ground black pepper

For the garnish
½ lemon, cut into wedges
watercress sprigs

Thread the fish, courgette slices and mushrooms on to eight skewers, alternating the various ingredients as you thread them.

Mix the oil and vinegar together, then brush the mixture over the kebabs. Finally, sprinkle them with the thyme and pepper.

Place the kebabs on a large plate and cover with absorbent kitchen paper. Cook on Full power for 6 minutes, turning the kebabs with their cooking juices halfway through the cooking.

Garnish with lemon wedges and watercress and serve with brown rice or noodles.

Cook's Tip

Grapeseed oil is a useful ingredient for healthy cooking as it contains virtually no cholesterol. As an alternative to the smoked haddock, try using cod or halibut as a change.

46 | Shepherd of the Sea

Preparation time
20 minutes

Cooking time
17½ minutes, plus
grilling topping

Setting
Full power

Serves 6

Calories
370 per portion

You will need
50 g / 2 oz concentrated butter
225 g / 8 oz leeks, washed,
    trimmed and thinly sliced
25 g / 1 oz plain flour
200 ml / 7 fl oz fish stock
3 tablespoons white wine
200 ml / 7 fl oz milk
2 tablespoons chopped parsley
350 g / 12 oz cod fillets, skinned
    and cut into chunks
100 g / 4 oz canned smoked
    mussels, drained
100 g / 4 oz peeled cooked prawns
100 g / 4 oz Cheddar cheese, grated
2 eggs, separated
1 kg / 2 lb potatoes, cooked
2 eggs, separated
salt and pepper

Place half the butter in a large bowl with the leeks, cover and cook for 4 minutes. Stir in the flour, then gradually add the stock, wine and milk. Mix well, cover and cook for 3½ minutes, stirring three times. Stir in the parsley, cod, mussels and prawns. Mix in the cheese, cover and cook for 8 minutes, stirring once. Place the fish mixture in a heatproof dish.

Mash the potatoes with the remaining butter and beat the egg yolks in. Whisk the egg whites until stiff and fold in. Top the fish with potato. Cook for 2 minutes, then grill to brown.

Cook's Tip

To cook potatoes for mashing, dice them, place in a bowl with 150 ml / ¼ pint water and cover. Cook 1 kg / 2 lb on Full power for 15–20 minutes, stirring once. Stand 5 minutes, then mash.

47 | Fish Tumble

Preparation time
10 minutes

Cooking time
13 minutes

Setting
Full power

Serves 4

Calories
195 per portion

You will need
1 (397-g/14-oz) can tomatoes
50 g/2 oz green pepper, chopped
1 stick celery, sliced
1 tablespoon finely chopped onion
50 g/2 oz cucumber, finely diced
450 g/1 lb button mushrooms,
   wiped and quartered
salt and pepper
4 large plaice fillets
1 teaspoon lemon juice
1 tablespoon chopped parsley to
   garnish

Place the tomatoes, pepper, celery, onion and cucumber. Cover loosely and cook on Full power for 8 minutes, stirring twice. Add the mushrooms and seasoning.

Arrange the plaice fillets in a large shallow dish, sprinkle with lemon juice and pour over the tomato mixture. Cover loosely and cook for 5 minutes. Sprinkle with parsley and serve at once.

48 | Trout with Ginger and Avocado

Preparation time
15 minutes

Cooking time
12–14 minutes

Setting
Full power

Serves 4

Calories
415 per portion

You will need
4 (225-g/8-oz) trout, gutted, with
   heads on
25 g/1 oz butter or margarine
1 small onion, chopped
1 clove garlic, crushed
50 g/2 oz Nutri-grain rye and oats
   with hazelnuts, crushed
finely grated rind and juice of 2
   limes
25 g/1 oz fresh root ginger, peeled
   and grated
1 avocado, stoned, peeled and
   chopped
6 tablespoons white wine

For the garnish
watercress
lime slices
avocado slices

Rinse and dry the body cavities of the trout, then trim off any fins. Place the butter or margarine in a bowl with the onion and garlic. Cook on Full power for 4 minutes. Stir in crushed cereal, lime rind and juice and ginger. Fold in avocado chunks.

Fill each fish with this stuffing and slash the skins in two places. Arrange the stuffed fish in a large oval or rectangular dish, alternating heads and tails. Pour over the wine. Cover and cook for 8–10 minutes, turning the fish over halfway through cooking. Garnish with watercress and slices of lime and avocado. Serve at once.

Cook's Tip

For even cooking in the microwave oven, arrange the fish fillets in a single layer, thinner portions to the centre. Leave a little space between the fillets if possible and do not double them over.

Cook's Tip

To remove the stone from an avocado cleanly, strike it with the blade of a sharp knife. The blade will penetrate the stone, which may then be lifted out easily.

49 | Stuffed Trout

Preparation time
20–30 minutes

Cooking time
17–21 minutes

Setting
Full power

Serves 4

Calories
545 per portion

You will need
300 ml/½ pint milk
1 bay leaf
1½ medium onions
50 g/2 oz butter or margarine
75 g/3 oz fresh breadcrumbs
50 g/2 oz raisins
2 tablespoons chopped parsley
grated rind and juice of 1 lemon
salt and pepper
4 (225-g/8-oz) trout, gutted, with
    heads on
25 g/1 oz plain flour
50 g/2 oz cucumber, finely diced
½ teaspoon chopped tarragon

Place the milk in a measuring jug with the bay leaf and half an onion. Cook on Full power for 2 minutes. Chop the remaining onion and place in a bowl with half the butter or margarine. Cook on Full power for 4–5 minutes until soft. Stir in the breadcrumbs, raisins, parsley, lemon rind and juice. Season and mix well.

Fill each fish with this stuffing and slash the skins in two places. Arrange the fish in a large dish, alternating heads and tails. Cover loosely and cook for 8–10 minutes, turning the fish over halfway through cooking.

Strain the flavoured milk into a clean bowl. Whisk in the flour gradually, add the remaining butter and cook for 3–4 minutes until the sauce thickens, stirring thoroughly every minute and making certain that any flour at the base of the bowl is incorporated. Add the cucumber and tarragon, with salt and pepper to taste, stir well and serve with the trout. Garnish as shown.

Cook's Tip

Always check foods after the minimum suggested cooking time has elapsed. It is easy to extend the cooking time but impossible to rescue dishes that have been overcooked.

50 | Chilled Trout and Horseradish Cheese

Preparation time
20 minutes

Cooking time
6 minutes

Setting
Full power

Serves 4

Calories
405 per portion

You will need
1 large pink trout, cleaned
salt and pepper
25 g/1 oz butter
parsley sprig
1 bay leaf
6 peppercorns
1 carrot, sliced
1 tablespoon lemon juice

For the garnish
5-cm/2-inch cucumber, thinly
    sliced
20 whole cooked prawns (optional)
parsley sprig

For the horseradish cheese
150 g/6 oz soft cheese
1 teaspoon lemon juice
pinch of caster sugar
pinch of tarragon
6 teaspoons horseradish sauce
150 ml/¼ pint double cream

Place the trout in a large dish. Season the inside and dot with butter. Add the remaining ingredients, cover and cook on Full power for 6 minutes. Skin the fish, decorate with 'scales' of cucumber and garnish. Cover and chill. Beat the cheese, lemon juice, sugar and tarragon together. Stir in the horseradish. Lightly whip the cream and fold into the cheese. Season and serve chilled.

Cook's Tip

To check if cooked, gently insert the point of a knife into the back of the fish. The flesh should be slightly undercooked when ready. Stand for 2–3 minutes to finish cooking.

51 | Cold Poached Salmon

Preparation time
15 minutes

Cooking time
12 minutes,
plus 5 minutes
standing time

Serves 6—8

Calories
375—280 per portion,
for the mayonnaise
360—270 per portion

You will need
1 (2.25-kg/5-lb) salmon or salmon
trout, cleaned
2 bay leaves
a few peppercorns
a few parsley sprigs
4 tablespoons water
juice of ½ lemon
25 g/1 oz butter

For the garnish
lemon wedges (optional)
salad ingredients
300 ml/½ pint mayonnaise
crisp lettuce or chicory

Descale the fish and tie the mouth shut. Put the bay leaves, peppercorns and parsley into the body cavity, curl the fish inside a 25-cm/10-inch flan dish. Pour the water and lemon juice into the dish. Cover with a *double* thickness of microwave cling film, wrapping it tightly over the fish and around the dish to keep the fish in shape. Pierce the film. Cook on Full power for 12 minutes. Stand, still covered, for 5 minutes. Before cooling check that the fish is completely cooked: insert a pointed knife straight down into the thick part of the body so that you can see that the flesh is not opaque. Remove flavourings from cavity and untie mouth. Garnish and serve.

52 | Herring Kebabs

Preparation time
15 minutes, plus
1 hour to marinate

Cooking time
5—6 minutes

Setting
Full power

Serves 4

Calories
455 per portion

You will need
4 herring, filleted
1 large red pepper, cored,
deseeded and cut into chunks
salt and pepper

For the marinade
3 tablespoons sunflower oil
1 clove garlic, crushed
grated rind and juice of 1 orange
2 tablespoons soy sauce
2 tablespoons chopped parsley

For the garnish
4 orange wedges
parsley sprigs

Rub the scales off the herring and remove the fins. Cut each herring into four pieces. Combine all the ingredients for the marinade in a large bowl. Mix well and stir in the herring. Set aside to marinate for 1 hour.

Drain the herring, discarding the marinade, and thread on to four wooden skewers, alternating with chunks of red pepper. Sprinkle with salt and pepper to taste.

Place the skewers on a double thickness of absorbent kitchen paper around the rim of a large plate or dish. Cook on Full power for 5—6 minutes, turning the skewers over once.

Serve garnished with orange wedges and parsley and accompanied by saffron rice, if liked.

Cook's Tip

It is important to pierce the skin of the fish before cooking. This will happen if the fins are removed. Microwave cling film is vital to keep the fish in place, so do not skimp on its use.

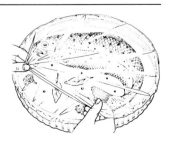

Cook's Tip

Remember to use only wooden skewers in the microwave oven; metal ones can cause arcing and flashing which will damage the appliance.

53 | Mustard Herring

Preparation time	**You will need**
10 minutes	25 g/1 oz butter
	2 tablespoons lemon juice
Cooking time	salt
8 minutes	1½ tablespoons coarse-grained
	mustard
Setting	4 (350-g/12-oz) herring, cleaned
Full power	and gutted
	2 tablespoons plain flour
Serves 4	lemon twists to garnish

Calories
525 per portion

Place the butter in a shallow dish large enough to hold all the herring in a single layer, and melt on Full power for about 45 seconds. Stir in the lemon juice, salt and mustard.

Coat the herring in the flour, add them to the dish and turn to coat in the lemon butter.

Arrange the fish, head to tail in the dish, cover and cook for 7–8 minutes. Rearrange the fish and turn them over once during cooking. Serve immediately, garnished with lemon twists.

54 | Mackerel 'Dolmades'

Preparation time	**You will need**
10–15 minutes	2 (125-g/4.4-oz) cans mackerel
	fillets in brine, drained
Cooking time	2 tablespoons chopped red pepper
5–6 minutes	1 tablespoon concentrated tomato
	purée
Setting	1 teaspoon grated lemon rind
Full power	salt and pepper
	8 large cabbage leaves
Serves 4	4 tablespoons water
	300 ml/½ pint fish stock
Calories	1 tablespoon cornflour
155 per portion	

For the garnish
lemon twists
dill sprigs

Mash the mackerel fillets and mix well with the pepper, tomato purée, lemon rind and seasoning.

Place the whole cabbage leaves in a large bowl with the water, cover and cook on Full power for 1–2 minutes until soft. Drain the leaves and lay on a tea towel. Divide the mackerel mixture between the cabbage leaves, then fold up each one into a parcel shape to enclose the filling. Place the cabbage parcels in a shallow bowl and pour over the stock. Cook for 4 minutes on Full power, turning the dish after 2 minutes. Transfer the dolmades to a serving dish. Blend the cornflour with a little water, stir into the juices and cook on Full power for 3–4 minutes, until thickened. Serve the parcels with the sauce poured over and garnished as shown.

Cook's Tip

To serve 2, use 15 g/½ oz butter, 1 tablespoon lemon juice, 1 tablespoon mustard, 2 herring and 1 tablespoon flour. Cook the fish for 3–4 minutes.

Cook's Tip

Instead of the cabbage you may like to try vine leaves – available in packets or cans from delicatessens and good supermarkets. You will need a few extra as they are smaller than cabbage leaves.

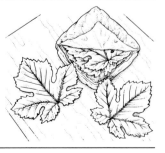

55 | Spinach and Mackerel Mould

Preparation time
15 minutes

Cooking time
8–10 minutes

Setting
Full power

Serves 6

Calories
220 per portion

You will need
450 g / 1 lb spinach, trimmed
1 (425-g/15-oz) can mackerel
    steaks in brine
about 150 ml / ¼ pint fish stock
25 g / 1 oz butter
1 large onion, finely chopped
grated rind of 1 lemon
4 teaspoons gelatine
175 g / 6 oz sweetcorn, cooked
2 tomatoes, peeled, deseeded and
    chopped
salt and pepper

For the garnish
lemon slices
tomato slices

Cook the spinach on Full power for 1 minute, drain and pat dry. Use to line a 1.15-litre / 1-pint ring mould.

Drain the mackerel steaks and make up the liquid to 300 ml / ½ pint with the stock. Melt the butter in a small bowl for 1 minute on Full power, add the onion and cook for 3 minutes until soft. Add the lemon rind. Heat the fish stock in a small bowl until just boiling for 3–5 minutes, add the gelatine, then stir until dissolved. Mash the fish, add to the onion with the remaining ingredients and the stock. Pour into the mould, chill until set, then turn out and garnish.

56 | Mushroom Mackerel

Preparation time
10 minutes

Cooking time
18–19 minutes

Setting
Full power

Serves 4

Calories
370 per portion

You will need
25 g / 1 oz butter
1 small onion, finely chopped
2 teaspoons caster sugar
1 tablespoon concentrated tomato
    purée
salt and pepper
3 tablespoons red wine
225 g / 8 oz button mushrooms,
    wiped
4 small (225-g/8-oz) mackerel,
    gutted, with heads removed

For the garnish
rosemary sprigs
cucumber slices

Place the butter and onion in a bowl and cook, covered, on Full power for 3 minutes. Stir in the sugar, tomato purée and seasoning. Make the wine up to 150 ml / ¼ pint with water and stir into the bowl. Cook, uncovered, for 5 minutes. Add mushrooms, cover and cook for a further 2 minutes, stirring once. Place the mackerel on a large dish, alternating tails and thick ends of the fish. Brush with the sauce, cover and cook on Full power for 4 minutes. Rearrange fish, brush again with sauce, re-cover and cook a further 4–5 minutes, until cooked. Garnish and serve.

Cook's Tip

Soft cod's roe can be used to make a light, savoury fish mould. Follow the recipe but substitute 3 (100-g / 3½-oz) cans soft cod's roe for the mackerel.

Cook's Tip

The small mackerel with heads removed should fit into a large flan dish (about 25 cm / 10 in). Place them neatly, cover with a plate and rearrange halfway through cooking if necessary.

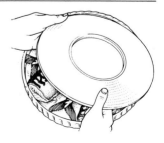

57 | Tuna Tomatoes

Preparation time
10 minutes

Cooking time
5–6 minutes

Setting
Full power

Serves 4

Calories
260 per portion

You will need
225 g/8 oz potatoes, diced
1 (198-g/7-oz) can tuna, drained
  and flaked
225 g/8 oz cottage cheese
¼ green pepper, cored, deseeded
  and chopped
salt and pepper
4 large tomatoes

Place the potatoes with 2 tablespoons water in a dish, cover and cook on Full power for 5–6 minutes. Leave to cool.

Mix together the tuna, cottage cheese, green pepper, salt and pepper and potato. Slice the tops off the tomatoes and scoop out the seeds carefully. Fill with the potato mixture. Replace tomato top. Chill. Serve on a bed of lettuce leaves.

58 | Spaghetti with Tuna Sauce

Preparation time
10 minutes

Cooking time
8 minutes, plus 8–12
minutes to cook pasta

Setting
Full power

Serves 4

Calories
385 per portion

You will need
225 g/8 oz spaghetti
salt and pepper
1 clove garlic, crushed
1 onion, chopped
4 teaspoons vegetable oil
2 tablespoons plain flour
300 ml/½ pint chicken stock
2 tablespoons white wine
1 tablespoon concentrated tomato
  purée
1 (400-g/14-oz) can tuna chunks in
  brine, drained
chopped parsley to garnish
  (optional)

Cook the spaghetti conventionally in boiling salted water for 8–12 minutes, until cooked, stirring occasionally.

Meanwhile, cook the garlic and onion in a medium bowl in the oil on Full power for 3 minutes. Add the flour, stock, wine, tomato purée and cook for a further 5 minutes. Add the tuna and adjust seasoning.

Serve the sauce hot, poured over the spaghetti and garnish with parsley, if liked.

Cook's Tip

There are a variety of low-fat soft cheese in the shops now – you may prefer the texture of the smooth ones to the cottage cheese in this recipe. Try plain soft cheese or any of those flavoured with garlic and herbs if you like.

Cook's Tip

If you are cooking a lot of pasta, then boil it in advance on the hob, drain and turn into a bowl. Dot with butter when ready (do not mix), cover and heat for a few minutes in the microwave. Stir and serve.

59 | Creamy Pilchard Pasta

Preparation time
15 minutes

Cooking time
11 minutes, plus 15
minutes to cook pasta

Setting
Full power

Serves 2

Calories
945 per portion

You will need
175 g/6 oz pasta shapes
salt and pepper
50 g/2 oz butter or margarine
1 medium onion, sliced
1 red pepper, cored, deseeded and
   chopped
50 g/2 oz mushrooms, thinly sliced
2 tablespoons plain flour
150 ml/¼ pint milk
1 tablespoon lemon juice
3 tablespoons chopped parsley
1 (425-g/15-oz) can pilchards in
   brine
red pepper rings to garnish

Cook the pasta conventionally in boiling salted water in a medium saucepan for about 15 minutes, or until tender. Drain and keep warm.

Place the butter in a medium bowl and cook for 1 minute on Full power, until melted. Add the onion and pepper and cook for 4 minutes. Add the mushrooms and cook for a further minute. Stir in the flour and then blend in the milk, lemon juice and parsley, reserving a small quantity for garnish. Season to taste. Cook for 5 minutes until thickened and boiling.

Drain and flake the pilchards and stir into the sauce, cook for a further minute. Serve hot, poured over the pasta, garnish with the reserved parsley and pepper rings.

60 | Scallop and Mushroom Shells

Preparation time
10 minutes

Cooking time
13 minutes

Setting
Medium, Full power

Serves 6

Calories
110 per portion

You will need
225 g/8 oz scallops, sliced
   if large
150 ml/¼ pint white wine
100 g/4 oz broccoli
1 tablespoon vegetable oil
1 onion, finely chopped
225 g/8 oz mushrooms, wiped and
   sliced
3 tablespoons plain flour
150 ml/¼ pint milk
100 g/4 oz peeled cooked prawns
2 tablespoons lemon juice
salt and pepper
6 lemon wedges to garnish

Place the scallops in a dish with the wine. Cover and cook on Medium power for 4–5 minutes, until the scallops are opaque and just firm to the touch.

Separate the broccoli florets from the stalk. Slice the stalk thinly. Combine the oil, broccoli stalk and onion in a bowl and cook on Full power for 3 minutes, stirring once. Stir in the mushrooms and broccoli florets, cover and cook for 3 minutes, stirring once.

Stir in the flour and cook for 1 minute. Drain the cooking juices from the scallops and gradually add them to the onion mixture, with the milk. Stir well. Cook for 3 minutes, stirring every minute until the mixture is thick and creamy. Add the reserved scallops, prawns, lemon juice and salt and pepper to taste. Mix gently and heat through for 2 minutes. Divide between six individual dishes and garnish.

Cook's Tip

**When cooking in the
microwave, select a dish that
is bigger than necessary to
hold the food – this prevents
any spillage and allows plenty
of room for stirring. Big
casseroles and bowls are
great!**

Cook's Tip

**To thaw 225 g/8 oz frozen
scallops in the microwave
oven, place in a single layer in
a shallow dish, cover and
microwave on Defrost for 4–5
minutes, separating and
turning during thawing.**

61 | Seafood Curry

Preparation time
10 minutes

Cooking time
15 minutes

Setting
Full power, Medium

Serves 4

Calories
170 per portion

You will need
1 small onion, chopped
2 tablespoons oil
1 teaspoon curry powder
1 small dessert apple, cored and diced
2 tomatoes, peeled, deseeded and chopped
225 g/8 oz peeled cooked prawns, defrosted if frozen
2 teaspoons plain flour
150 ml/¼ pint natural yogurt
salt and pepper
4 lemon wedges to garnish

Place the onion, oil and curry powder in a large bowl. Stir, then cook on Full power for 4 minutes, stirring once during cooking.

Stir in the apple and cook for 4 minutes more, stirring once. Add the tomatoes and prawns and cook for 3 minutes.

Combine the flour and yogurt in a small bowl, whisking the mixture thoroughly. Add a little of the cooking liquid from the prawn mixture and stir. Gradually add the yogurt mixture to the seafood curry, stirring gently. Season to taste.

Cover the bowl, reduce the power to Medium and cook for 4 minutes, stirring twice. Garnish with lemon wedges and serve at once, with brown rice, if liked.

62 | Chilli Prawn Stir-fry

Preparation time
10 minutes

Cooking time
10–11 minutes

Setting
Full power

Serves 4

Calories
190 per portion

You will need
2 tablespoons light sunflower oil
1 chilli, deseeded and chopped
3 spring onions, chopped
100 g/4 oz canned bamboo shoots, sliced
3 tablespoons wine vinegar
1½ tablespoons concentrated tomato purée
2 tablespoons oyster sauce
6 tablespoons chicken stock
1½ tablespoons cornflour
350 g/12 oz peeled cooked prawns

For the garnish
spring onion curls (see Cook's Tip)
4 whole cooked prawns

Place the oil, chilli, spring onions and bamboo shoots in a dish. Cook on Full power for 3 minutes, stirring once.

Stir in the vinegar, tomato purée and oyster sauce. Add half the stock and mix well. Cook for 2–3 minutes, until the liquid boils.

In a cup, mix the cornflour with the remaining stock. Add to the vegetable mixture and stir well. Cook for 3 minutes, stirring every minute. Stir in the prawns and cook for 2 minutes more, stirring once. Transfer to a serving dish, garnish with spring onion curls and whole prawns in shells and serve at once.

Cook's Tip

Yogurt may be made in the microwave oven. Place 600 ml/1 pint milk in a large bowl. Cover and cook on Full power for 6 minutes. Cool over iced water to 46 C/115 F. Beat in 1 tablespoon natural yogurt and 2 tablespoons milk powder. Reduce power to Low and cook for 1–1¼ hours, until thick and creamy. Whisk well, cover and chill in the refrigerator.

Cook's Tip

To make spring onion curls, top and tail each spring onion. Place on a wooden board and, with a sharp knife, form strips by making numerous small cuts in each stem, starting about 2.5 cm/1 in from the bulb. Soak in iced water to curl.

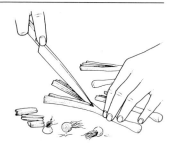

63 | Prawn Curry

Preparation time
15 minutes

Cooking time
11½–12½ minutes

Setting
Full power

Serves 2

Calories
410 per portion

You will need
25 g/1 oz butter
1 small onion, finely chopped
1 tablespoon curry powder
1 tablespoon plain flour
300 ml/½ pint stock
2 teaspoons concentrated tomato
    purée
2 teaspoons lemon juice
1 teaspoon brown sugar
1 teaspoon marmalade
1 (100-g/4-oz) can prawns in brine
2 tablespoons single cream
100 g/4 oz cooked long-grain rice

Melt the butter in a medium bowl on Full power for 1 minute. Add the onion and cook for 3 minutes until soft.

Stir in the curry powder and cook for 1 minute. Add the flour, stock, tomato purée, lemon juice, sugar and marmalade. Cook for 3 minutes, stirring occasionally. Add the prawns and cook for 1–2 minutes until the sauce is thick, then add the cream and cook for a further 30 seconds.

Reheat the rice for 2 minutes until hot. Serve the curry over the rice, and accompany with side dishes of coconut, peach slices, tomato wedges and sliced cucumber.

64 | Oriental Prawns

Preparation time
10 minutes

Cooking time
7 minutes

Setting
Full power

Serves 4

Calories
170 per portion

You will need
2 tablespoons oil
2 cloves garlic, crushed
2.5-cm/1-inch piece fresh root
    ginger, peeled and finely sliced
1 (225-g/8-oz) can bamboo shoots,
    drained
2 teaspoons soy sauce
2 tablespoons freshly made tea
2 teaspoons lemon juice
1 teaspoon chives
salt and pepper
350 g/12 oz peeled cooked prawns

Place the oil, garlic and ginger in a bowl and cook, uncovered, on Full power for 3 minutes, stirring occasionally. Add bamboo shoots, soy sauce, tea, lemon juice, chives and seasoning. Cook, uncovered, for 2 minutes. Stir in the prawns, cook for a further 2 minutes, stirring once, until the prawns are heated through. Serve with rice.

Cook's Tip

The strength of curry powders varies enormously. If you favour hot food buy a hot powder, for a mild result buy mild powder. If the item is simply curry powder then it may well be quite hot. When making any dish with hot spices, add a little less than recommended if you are unused to the ingredients.

Cook's Tip

The best way to peel ginger is to break off the knobs and then use a small, sharp knife to peel the pieces separately. Remember it does freeze well, so why not prepare a lot and freeze in small packets?

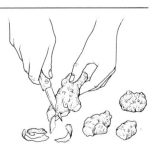

65 | Malay Prawns

Preparation time
15 minutes

Cooking time
10 minutes

Setting
Full power

Serves 4

Calories
370 per portion

You will need
1 onion, finely chopped
1 tablespoon oil
2 teaspoons curry powder
2 tablespoons plain flour
300 ml / ½ pint fish stock
2 teaspoons concentrated tomato purée
1 tablespoon mango chutney
juice of ½ small lemon
150 ml / ¼ pint double cream
450 g / 1 lb peeled cooked prawns
fresh coriander leaves to garnish

Put the onion and the oil in a medium bowl and cook on Full power for 5 minutes. Remove, add the curry powder, flour, stock, tomato purée, chutney and lemon juice. Cover and cook on Full power for 4 minutes. Remove and stir in cream and prawns. Cook for 1 minute. Serve hot garnished with coriander.

66 | King Prawn Skewers

Preparation time
10 minutes, plus
1 hour to marinate

Cooking time
5 minutes

Setting
Full power

Serves 4

Calories
115 per portion

You will need
12 uncooked king prawns, peeled
1 tablespoon lemon or lime juice
½ teaspoon ground coriander
1 teaspoon chilli powder
1 tablespoon concentrated tomato purée
1 tablespoon natural yogurt
freshly ground black pepper
1 small green pepper
1 large mango, stoned, peeled and cut into 8 slices

For the garnish
lime wedges
parsley sprigs

Place the prawns in a bowl and sprinkle with the lemon or lime juice. Mix the coriander, chilli powder, tomato purée, yogurt and black pepper into the prawns and marinate for 1 hour.

Cut the end off the green pepper and remove the pith and seeds. Cut into 8 squares and blanch in boiling water for 2 minutes.

Thread the prawns, mango and green peppers on to four wooden skewers, alternating 3 prawns with 2 slices of mango and 2 squares of green pepper on each skewer. Place on a single layer of absorbent kitchen paper and cook on Full power for 5 minutes, turning them once. Serve garnished with lime wedges and parsley.

Cook's Tip

Fresh coriander leaves resemble flat-leaf parsley but they are sold with roots on. Keep the bunch in a cool place in a jug of water. It can also be chopped and frozen.

Cook's Tip

Be careful not to overcook as this will toughen the flesh of the shellfish. If you cannot obtain king prawns you could substitute a firm white fish such as cod or hake.

67 | *Moules Au Gratin*

Preparation time
15–20 minutes

Cooking time
5 minutes, plus 5 minutes to grill

Setting
Full power

Serves 2

Calories
330 per portion

You will need
1 litre/2 pints live mussels, scraped and cleaned
150 ml/¼ pint hot fish stock
1 tablespoon sunflower oil
4 tablespoons freshly grated Parmesan cheese
50 g/2 oz wholemeal breadcrumbs
5 tablespoons chopped parsley
¼–½ teaspoon garlic salt
freshly ground black pepper

Place the mussels and stock in a large ovenproof bowl and cook on Full power for 5 minutes, until they have opened. Remove the mussels, reserving the stock, and discard half of each shell. Transfer to an ovenproof serving dish, spoon oil over the mussels and keep warm. Mix the cheese, breadcrumbs, parsley, garlic salt and pepper. Sprinkle over the mussels. Strain the fish stock and pour over the mussels. Heat under a hot grill for 5 minutes until crisp and golden. Serve immediately.

68 | *Moules Marinière*

Preparation time
20 minutes, plus overnight soaking

Cooking time
11 minutes

Setting
Full power

Serves 4

Calories
210 per portion

You will need
2.25 litres/4 pints live mussels
25 g/1 oz butter
1 onion, finely chopped
1 clove garlic, crushed
300 ml/½ pint white wine
2 tablespoons lemon juice
3 bay leaves
salt and pepper
3 tablespoons chopped parsley

Prepare the mussels (see Cook's Tip). Set aside.

Combine the butter, onion and garlic in a large bowl. Cook on Full power for 3 minutes.

Stir in the wine, lemon juice, bay leaves and half the mussels. Cover loosely and cook for 4 minutes, stirring once.

Using a slotted spoon, transfer the mussels to a serving dish, discarding any that have not opened.

Stir the remaining mussels into the liquid in the bowl and cook for 4 minutes, stirring once. Again, discard any unopened mussels together with the bay leaves. Add the mussels and their cooking juices to the serving dish, season to taste and sprinkle with parsley. Serve at once.

Cook's Tip

Scrape the mussels clean with a small sharp knife and pull away the black hairs known as the 'beard' with a small tug. It is important to discard any mussels which are not shut tightly or which do not shut quickly if given a tap.

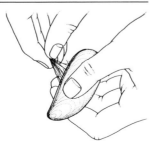

Cook's Tip

Make the most of fresh mussels by careful preparation: remove any grit by immersing the mussels overnight in a bucket of water to which a handful of oatmeal has been added. Drain and wash the mussels, scrub thoroughly and remove the beard. The mussels are now ready for use. Any that are not tightly shut (and which do not shut quickly when tapped firmly) should be thrown away.

69 | Dorset Scallops

Preparation time
15 minutes

Cooking time
18–19 minutes, plus grilling time

Setting
Full power

Serves 4

Calories
290 per portion

You will need
4 scallops, quartered
2 sticks celery, chopped
100 g/4 oz mushrooms, chopped
1 bay leaf
slice of lemon
150 ml/¼ pint dry white wine
450 g/1 lb potatoes
1 large egg
3 tablespoons double cream
salt and pepper

For the sauce
40 g/1½ oz butter
40 g/1½ oz plain flour
150 ml/¼ pint hot fish stock
3 tablespoons cream
1 large egg yolk

Put the scallops, celery, mushrooms, bay leaf, lemon and wine in an ovenproof dish and cover. Cook on Full power for 3 minutes. Then cook the potatoes in 4 tablespoons of water in a roasting bag for 10 minutes, drain and beat with the egg and cream. Season and pipe around the edge of four scallop shells. Drain the scallops and reserve fish liquor. Remove the bay leaf and lemon.

Whisk together the butter, flour and fish liquor, made up to 300 ml/½ pint with the fish stock. Cook on Full power for 4 minutes. Whisk well, then stir in the cream and egg. Cook for 1–2 minutes. Add the scallops. Brown the potato under a hot grill and spoon hot scallop sauce into the centre of the dishes.

70 | Fish Salad

Preparation time
10 minutes

Cooking time
6 minutes

Setting
Full power

Serves 4

Calories
310 per portion

You will need
675 g/1½ lb cod fillet
25 g/1 oz butter
5-cm/2-in piece cucumber, sliced
4 spring onions, chopped
salt and pepper
150 ml/¼ pint soured cream
2 generous tablespoons
    mayonnaise

For the salad
½ small Chinese cabbage or lettuce
2 tomatoes, sliced
2 teaspoons capers, drained

Place the cod in a dish with the butter. Cover and cook for 6 minutes, rearranging the fish once during cooking. Discard the skin and bones, flake the fish and leave to cool.

Reserve 4 slices of cucumber for the garnish and quarter the rest. Place cucumber, onions and seasoning in a bowl with the fish. Mix the soured cream and mayonnaise together, then carefully fold into the fish.

Shred the Chinese cabbage or lettuce and arrange on four individual plates. Divide the fish mixture between the plates and garnish with halved tomato slices. Top each salad with a slice of cucumber and a few capers. Serve at once.

Cook's Tip

To clean scallops, prize open any closed shells with a strong knife. Cut away the white flesh and the red coral, discarding the grey outer flesh and all the other parts. Rinse thoroughly. Scrub the scallop shells clean, dry and use as dishes.

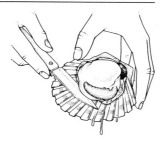

Cook's Tip

Try other types of fish in this salad – white fish like plaice, halibut or hake all work well. Smoked haddock or smoked cod can also be used for a stronger flavour. Crisp toast or crusty bread is a good accompaniment.

71 | Prawn and Huss Salad

Preparation time
5 minutes

Cooking time
8–10 minutes

Setting
Full power

Serves 4

Calories
260 per portion

You will need
225 g/8 oz huss fillet, skinned and
 cubed
25 g/1 oz butter
1 tablespoon lemon juice
1 bay leaf
450 g/1 lb small potatoes, cooked
 in their skins
100 g/4 oz peeled cooked prawns
¼ cucumber, thinly sliced
whole cooked prawns to garnish
 (optional)

For the dressing
2 tablespoons crunchy peanut
 butter
pinch of mustard powder
3 tablespoons boiling water

Place the fish in a dish, dot with the butter and pour over the lemon juice. Add the bay leaf, cover and cook on Full power for 8–10 minutes, turning the dish once. Discard bay leaf and cool the fish.

Meanwhile, mix together the potatoes, prawns and cucumber. To make the dressing, blend the peanut butter with the mustard and gradually whisk in the boiling water. Gently stir the fish into the potato mixture and spoon over the sauce just before serving. Garnish with prawns in shells, if liked.

72 | Skate and Spinach Salad

Preparation time
10 minutes

Cooking time
8 minutes, plus
4 minutes frying time

Setting
Full power

Serves 4

Calories
365 per portion

You will need
225 g/8 oz skate wing
25 g/1 oz butter
1 tablespoon lemon juice
1 tablespoon butter
1 tablespoon sunflower oil
4 slices wholemeal bread
175 g/6 oz small spinach leaves,
 washed
1 avocado pear, peeled, stoned,
 sliced and dipped in lemon juice

For the dressing
3 tablespoons oil
1 tablespoon wine vinegar
¼ teaspoon mustard powder
salt and pepper

Place the skate in a shallow dish, cut the butter into pieces and place on top, pour over the lemon juice, cover and cook on Full power for 8 minutes or until fish comes easily off the bones. Turn the dish once. Drain, cool slightly and flake flesh away from the bones. Chill fish.

In a large frying pan heat the butter and oil. Cut the bread into small cubes and cook in the hot fat until crisp and golden.

In a bowl, mix together the fish, spinach and avocado slices. Whisk together the oil, vinegar, mustard and seasoning, and pour over the salad. Sprinkle the croûtons on top just before serving.

Cook's Tip

To cook small new potatoes, scrub them and place in a roasting bag or dish with 2 tablespoons water. Cover or secure the end with a rubber band. Cook on Full power for 8–10 minutes, rearranging once.

Cook's Tip

Skate must be absolutely fresh. It should be a nice clean colour and have a fresh tangy smell. Skate that is slightly old will smell strongly of ammonia and it should be avoided as the flavour will also be unpleasantly tainted. Buy from *a good, busy fishmonger and the skate will be fresh.*

Poultry

Chicken, turkey and duck are tender meats, so cook well in the microwave oven; cut into cubes or shredded, or in even pieces like boneless breast or thighs, poultry cooks evenly and quickly. Chicken joints can be cooked successfully but need more care to prevent the ends from overcooking. Whole chickens are best served with a sauce as they cook before they brown satisfactorily, but the longer cooking time of turkey enables the fat to get hot enough to brown the skin.

73 | Plum Duck

(Illustrated on front jacket)

Preparation time
15 minutes

Cooking time
40 minutes, plus
10–15 minutes
standing time

Setting
Full power

Serves 4

Calories
700 per portion

You will need
1 (2-kg/4-lb) duckling, defrosted completely if frozen
2 tablespoons plum jam, sieved

For the garnish
watercress sprigs (optional)
potato sticks (optional)

Remove giblets and use in another recipe. Wash and dry the duckling and truss in the usual way to make a neat shape. Prick the skin all over with a fork. Brush the skin with half the plum jam. Place breast-side down on a microwave roasting rack (or upturned saucer) in a glass dish. Cook on Full power for 20 minutes. Turn breast-side up. Drain away any excess fat from the dish. Brush with the remaining jam. Cook for a further 20 minutes or until a thermometer registers 82–85 C/180-185 F when inserted in the thickest part of the thigh, and the juices run clear.

Cover with a 'tent' of foil (shiny side next to meat) and stand for 10–15 minutes. Serve garnished as shown, if you like.

Cook's Tip

It is quite surprising what can be done with a few tablespoons of jam. Tart preserves like plum jam and marmalade, can be mixed with savoury ingredients to make tangy sweet and sour sauces for poultry, pork or oily fish like mackerel. Try mixing a little garlic, cooked onion and vinegar with plum jam or orange marmalade for brushing on pork chops. Cherry preserve can be used with duck to make a delicious sauce.

74 | Chicken with Redcurrants

Preparation time
15 minutes

Cooking time
39–40 minutes

Setting
Full power

Serves 4–6

Calories
615–410 per portion

You will need
1 (1.5-kg/3-lb) oven-ready chicken
1 medium orange
200 ml/7 fl oz chicken stock
2 tablespoons redcurrant jelly
3 tablespoons red wine
salt and pepper
175 g/6 oz redcurrants
about 1 tablespoon sugar
2 teaspoons cornflour
2 tablespoons water

For the garnish
watercress sprigs
orange segments

Place the chicken in a large roasting bag. Thinly pare the rind from the orange and squeeze the juice. Cut half the rind into matchstick strips and add to the chicken with the juice, stock, redcurrant jelly and red wine. Add salt and pepper to taste. Secure the end of the bag with an elastic band and pierce the top in several places. Cook on Full power for 25 minutes, turning the chicken over and around once. Transfer the chicken to a serving dish and cover in a foil tent.

String the redcurrants (see Cook's Tip), reserving a few for garnish, if liked. Add to the cooking juices in the dish, stir in sugar to taste, cover and cook for 10 minutes.

In a cup, mix the cornflour with the water to a cream. Add to the sauce, stir and cook for 4–5 minutes, stirring several times. Spoon the sauce over the chicken, garnish and serve.

Cook's Tip

Redcurrants can be readily persuaded to part from their stems if the tines of a fork are used to isolate them. If the currants are to be frozen, leave them on the stalks. When solid, they will be very easy to remove.

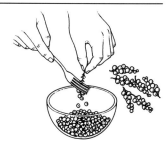

75 | Chicken in Orange Sauce

Preparation time
10–15 minutes

Cooking time
10 minutes

Setting
Full power

Serves 4

Calories
205 per portion

You will need
1 small onion, chopped
4 dried apricots, chopped
8 walnut halves, chopped
8 grapes, halved
4 teaspoons bran
8 tablespoons fresh wholemeal
  breadcrumbs
4 teaspoons chopped parsley
salt and black pepper
8 tablespoons orange juice
4 boneless chicken breasts,
  skinned
1 chicken stock cube
300 ml/½ pint hot water
1 tablespoon cornflour
strips of orange peel to garnish

Mix the onion, apricots, walnuts and grapes with the bran, breadcrumbs, parsley and seasoning. Mix in 1 tablespoon orange juice. Place the stuffing on the chicken, roll up and secure with a wooden cocktail stick. Put into an ovenproof dish. Dissolve the stock cube in the hot water, add the remaining orange juice and pour around the chicken. Cover and cook on Full power for 5 minutes.

Remove the chicken and make up the cooking liquid with water to 300 ml/½ pint, if necessary. Blend the cornflour with a little water until smooth. Pour into the cooking liquid, then pour the sauce over the chicken again. Cover and cook for a further 5 minutes. Garnish with the orange strips.

Cook's Tip

Bran and other high-fibre breakfast cereals can be useful for mixing with stuffings and other savoury dishes. With the addition of a little liquid, they bind all the flavouring ingredients and at the same time absorb tasty cooking juices. In addition they provide essential fibre for the diet.

76 | Apricot Chicken

Preparation time
20 minutes

Cooking time
14½–15½ minutes

Setting
Full power

Serves 4

Calories
350 per portion

You will need
40 g/1½ oz concentrated butter
75 g/3 oz no-need-to-soak dried
  apricots
1 small onion, finely chopped
1 teaspoon finely grated orange
  rind
1 egg, beaten
100 g/4 oz ground almonds
4 (100-g/4-oz) boneless chicken
  breasts, skinned
tarragon sprigs to garnish
  (optional)

Place half the butter in a bowl with the apricots, onion and orange rind. Cover and cook on Full power for 5 minutes, stirring once. Set aside to cool slightly.

Meanwhile, beat the egg in a shallow bowl. In a second bowl, spread the almonds. Coat the chicken in the egg, then the almonds.

Beat the chicken breasts flat with a meat mallet or rolling pin. Divide the apricot filling between them, roll up and secure with wooden cocktail sticks.

Place the remaining butter in a shallow dish and cook on Full power for 30 seconds to melt. Add the chicken rolls to the dish and turn to coat in butter. Cover loosely and cook for 9–10 minutes, turning and rearranging once.

Remove the strings from the chicken rolls and garnish each roll with a sprig of tarragon if liked. Serve at once with salad ingredients.

Cook's Tip

When grating oranges or lemons, work on a sheet of greaseproof paper, using a pastry brush to remove all the rind from the grater. It is then a simple matter to brush the rind from the paper into the bowl or casserole.

77 | Chicken and Cider Casserole

Preparation time
10 minutes

Cooking time
27 minutes

Setting
Full power

Serves 4

Calories
205 per portion

You will need
4 chicken thighs or drumsticks, skinned
2 tablespoons oil
225 g/8 oz closed cup mushrooms, wiped and sliced
2 tablespoons chopped tarragon
1 small onion, finely chopped
4 sticks celery, thinly sliced
4 tablespoons cider
pinch of garlic powder
salt and pepper

Place the chicken portions in a casserole, thinner ends to the centre. Brush with the oil, cover and cook on Full power for 14 minutes, turning the chicken over and rearranging the portions halfway through cooking.

Place the remaining ingredients in a bowl and cook for 8 minutes, stirring twice. Pour over the chicken and cook for 5 minutes. Stand, covered, for 2–3 minutes before serving.

78 | Chicken Provençale

Preparation time
10 minutes

Cooking time
32 minutes, plus 5 minutes standing time

Setting
Full power

Serves 4

Calories
370 per portion

You will need
1 large onion, sliced in rings
1 (397-g/14-oz) can chopped tomatoes
150 g/5 oz concentrated tomato purée
6 tablespoons white wine
1 clove garlic, crushed
1 teaspoon oregano
salt
4 (100-g/4-oz) boneless chicken breasts, skinned
225 g/8 oz American long-grain rice
600 ml/1 pint boiling water

For the garnish
1 lemon, sliced
chopped parsley

Combine the onion rings, chopped tomatoes, tomato purée and wine in a casserole. Stir in the garlic and oregano and add salt to taste. Cover and cook on Full power for 5 minutes, stirring several times. Add the chicken breasts to the casserole and cook for a further 12 minutes, turning the breasts over and rearranging them halfway through. Set aside while cooking the rice.

Mix the rice and water in a large deep bowl. Stir in 1 teaspoon salt, cover and cook for 15 minutes. Allow to stand for 5 minutes, covered. To serve, arrange the chicken on a bed of rice and garnish with lemon slices and parsley.

Cook's Tip

Never wash cultivated mushrooms. It is quite unnecessary and leaches out valuable nutrients. Simply wipe with a clean damp cloth before use.

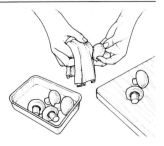

Cook's Tip

Use a deep bowl such as a mixing bowl or soufflé dish to cook the rice. The bowl should not be so wide that the water is spread too thinly to cover the rice, but must be deep enough to prevent the water boiling over.

79 | Milano Chicken

Preparation time
5 minutes

Cooking time
19 minutes

Setting
Full Power

Serves 4

Calories
285 per portion

You will need
1 green pepper
1 large onion, sliced
2 tablespoons pure corn oil
1 packet cream of tomato
   no-simmer soup
pinch of oregano
450 ml/¾ pint water
100 g/4 oz button mushrooms,
   sliced
4 chicken portions, skinned

Trim the stalk end off the pepper, then remove the core and seeds from inside. Slice the flesh thinly and place in a casserole with the onion and oil. Cover loosely and cook on Full power for 5 minutes.

Stir in the soup mix and oregano. Gradually add the water, stirring constantly. Cook for 2 minutes, stirring once.

Add the mushrooms and chicken portions to the casserole, turning them in the sauce to coat them completely. Place meaty side down, cover and cook for 12 minutes, turning and rearranging the chicken once during cooking. Allow to stand for 2–3 minutes before serving.

80 | Pomegranate Chicken

Preparation time
10 minutes

Cooking time
17 minutes

Setting
Full Power

Serves 4

Calories
480 per portion

You will need
25 g/1 oz butter
3 onions, chopped
175-225 g/6–8 oz walnuts,
   chopped
900 ml/1½ pints water
salt and pepper
10 tablespoons pomegranate
   syrup or juice
4 tablespoons sugar
4 chicken pieces

Place the butter, onion and walnuts in a large ovenproof bowl and cook on Full power for 5 minutes, stirring halfway through the cooking time.

Add the water and season to taste, then stir in the pomegranate syrup or juice and sugar. Add the chicken and cover. Cook for 12 minutes, rearranging the chicken pieces halfway through the cooking time.

Transfer the chicken to a heated serving dish, pour over the sauce and serve the Pomegranate Chicken immediately.

Cook's Tip

Because the chicken will continue to cook by conduction of heat after it has been removed from the microwave oven, it is important to observe standing times. Cover the dish with foil during this period.

Cook's Tip

As an alternative to the chicken above, try replacing it with duck as originally used in Iran. Use duck joints or cut a whole duck into four pieces using kitchen scissors. A heavy knife or meat cleaver are also useful for this.

81 | Spanish Chicken with Rice

Preparation time
15–20 minutes

Cooking time
22 minutes

Setting
Full Power

Serves 4

Calories
555 per portion

You will need
2 tablespoons vegetable oil
12 chicken drumsticks
1 onion, sliced
1 green pepper, cored, deseeded
  and sliced
1 clove garlic, crushed
225 g/8 oz long-grain rice
600 ml/1 pint hot chicken stock
2 tablespoons concentrated
  tomato purée
3 tomatoes, peeled and quartered
75 g/3 oz stuffed green olives
2 tablespoons chopped parsley to
  garnish (optional)

Heat a browning dish according to the manufacturer's instructions (see Cook's Tip). Without removing it from the microwave oven, add 1 tablespoon of the oil with the drumsticks and cook on Full power for 4 minutes, turning and rearranging the drumsticks once. Cover with foil and allow to stand.

Combine the remaining oil with the onion, green pepper and garlic in a casserole and cook for 1 minute. Stir in the rice and cook for 2 minutes, then add the stock, tomato purée and drumsticks. Stir well, cover and cook for 10 minutes, stirring once.

Finally stir in the tomatoes and olives and cook for 5 minutes more. Allow to stand for 2–3 minutes before serving, garnished with parsley, if liked.

Cook's Tip

Starting the chicken off in a browning dish improves the colour, but is not essential. If preferred, brown the drumsticks in a frying pan, or eliminate this step, and use skinned drumsticks.

82 | Chicken with Blue Brie Sauce

Preparation time
5 minutes

Cooking time
9–10 minutes

Setting
Full power

Serves 4

Calories
395 per portion

You will need
75 g/3 oz butter
4 (100-g/4-oz) boneless chicken
  breasts, skinned
1 small cucumber, peeled
150 g/5 oz Danish blue brie
  cheese, rind removed
2 teaspoons cornflour
1 tablespoon milk
salt and pepper
pinch of freshly grated nutmeg
about 1 teaspoon lemon juice

Heat a browning dish according to the manufacturer's instructions, add 50 g/2 oz of the butter and chicken, cover and cook for 4–5 minutes. Cut the cucumber in half lengthways and scoop out the seeds. Dice the flesh. Chop the cheese.

Place the remaining butter in a jug and melt for 30 seconds. Add the cucumber and cook for 2 minutes. Stir in the cheese until melted. Mix the cornflour with the milk. Add to the sauce and mix well. Cook for 2½ minutes, stirring twice. Add seasoning, nutmeg and lemon juice and serve with the chicken.

Cook's Tip

You may like to remove the skin from chicken which is to be cooked in a sauce in the microwave. Not only will the appearance be better, but flavour will be improved as the sauce is able to penetrate the chicken.

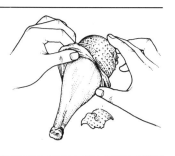

83 | Chicken and Mushroom Cheese Loaf

Preparation time
30–40 minutes

Cooking time
20 minutes, plus 5 minutes standing time

Setting
Full power

Serves 6

Calories
240 per portion

You will need
225 g/8 oz uncooked chicken meat, finely diced
225 g/8 oz lean gammon or bacon, diced
100 g/4 oz button mushrooms, chopped
1–2 tablespoons chopped parsley
1 large onion, chopped
1 clove garlic, crushed
100 g/4 oz fresh wholemeal breadcrumbs
1 egg, beaten
salt and black pepper
100 g/4 oz cheese, cubed

Mix together the diced chicken, gammon or bacon, mushrooms, parsley, onion, garlic, breadcrumbs and egg. Season well with salt and pepper. Spoon half the mixture into a 15 × 10-cm/6 × 4-inch loaf dish and press down firmly. Spread the cheese over the top and cover with the remaining meat mixture. Press down well. Cover loosely with greaseproof paper and cook on Full power for 20 minutes. If you do not have a turntable, turn the dish three times during cooking. Remove paper after 15 minutes. Leave to stand for 5 minutes before serving. Serve hot, in slices, with boiled or new potatoes and a green vegetable, or cold with salad and wholemeal bread.

84 | Yogurt Chicken Bake

Preparation time
10 minutes

Cooking time
19 minutes, plus 5 minutes standing time

Setting
Full power

Serves 4

Calories
335 per portion

You will need
1 small onion, finely chopped
2 sticks celery, finely chopped
1 tablespoon oil
100 g/4 oz button mushrooms, wiped and sliced
350 g/12 oz cooked chicken, finely diced
1 tablespoon chopped parsley
salt and pepper

For the topping
100 g/4 oz cream cheese
150 ml/¼ pint natural yogurt
2 egg yolks, lightly beaten
1 teaspoon prepared mustard

Combine the onion, celery and oil in a casserole and cook on Full power for 2 minutes. Stir in the mushrooms and cook for 2 minutes more. Add the chicken and parsley with salt and pepper to taste and mix well.

Make the topping by mixing the cream cheese, yogurt and egg yolks in a bowl. Beat in the mustard and season to taste.

Spoon the cream cheese mixture gently over the chicken and cook for 15 minutes. Allow to stand for 5 minutes before serving.

Cook's Tip

If you have a food processor or liquidiser then making breadcrumbs is easy. If not, use a large grater and rub chunks of bread on the coarse blade, holding it over a large bowl.

Cook's Tip

Make the mustard for the topping as late as possible before use to prevent it drying. If mustard must be prepared ahead, use milk rather than water and it will stay creamy.

85 | Barbecue Beans with Chicken

Preparation time
5–10 minutes

Cooking time
21 minutes

Setting
Full power

Serves 4

Calories
420 per portion

You will need
40 g/1½ oz butter
1 small onion, chopped
1 tablespoon caster sugar
1 tablespoon vinegar
½ teaspoon chilli powder
2 teaspoons paprika
3 tablespoons tomato ketchup
4½ tablespoons natural yogurt
4 large chicken legs
1 (439-g/15½-oz) can red kidney
　beans
parsley sprigs to garnish

Place the butter and onion in a large ovenproof bowl and cook on Full power for 4 minutes. Add the sugar and stir until dissolved, then add the vinegar, chilli powder and paprika. Mix the tomato ketchup with the yogurt and add to the bowl, stirring well to combine.

Skin the chicken legs and place in the bowl, coating well with the sauce. Drain the kidney beans and mix into the casserole.

Cover and cook for 10 minutes. Stir the casserole before cooking for a further 7 minutes. Serve garnished with parsley.

86 | Chicken with Tarragon

Preparation time
15–20 minutes

Cooking time
25 minutes, plus 15 minutes standing time

Setting
Full power

Serves 6

Calories
450 per portion

You will need
1 (1.5-kg/3-lb) chicken
salt and pepper
2 teaspoons chopped fresh
　tarragon

For the mayonnaise
1 egg yolk
¼ teaspoon mustard powder
150–300 ml/¼–½ pint olive oil
4 teaspoons tarragon vinegar

For the garnish
50 g/2 oz green grapes, peeled,
　halved and deseeded
50 g/2 oz black grapes, peeled,
　halved and deseeded
fresh tarragon sprigs

Place the chicken in a roasting bag. Secure the end of the bag with an elastic band and pierce the top in several places. Cook on Full power for 25 minutes, turning once. Wrap the chicken in foil and allow to stand for 15 minutes, then remove the skin and slice the flesh neatly. Arrange on a serving platter, season and sprinkle with the tarragon; cool.

Whisk the egg yolk with seasoning and mustard in a small bowl. Beat in the oil drop by drop until thick, then beat in the tarragon vinegar. Spoon the mayonnaise over the chicken and garnish with grapes and tarragon.

Cook's Tip

When cooking chicken thighs, legs or breasts in a sauce in the microwave, remove the skin and any fat before cooking otherwise the sauce could become greasy. Removing the skin also ensures that the flavour of the sauce penetrates the flesh of the chicken more successfully.

Cook's Tip

Chill the reserved juices overnight in the refrigerator. Remove the layer of fat and use the stock to add flavour to a soup or sauce.

87 | *Chinese Chicken*

Preparation time
10–15 minutes

Cooking time
26–29 minutes

Serves 4

Setting
Full power

Calories
250 per portion

You will need
8 chicken drumsticks, skinned
8 spring onions, finely chopped
½ green pepper, cored, deseeded
  and diced
½ red pepper, cored, deseeded and
  diced
2 cloves garlic, crushed
25 g/1 oz butter, diced
1 tablespoon cornflour
¼ teaspoon five spice powder
about 300 ml/½ pint hot chicken
  stock
2 tablespoons red wine vinegar
1 tablespoon dark soy sauce
grated rind of 1 orange
50 g/2 oz soft light brown sugar

Place the chicken in an ovenproof dish, cover and cook on Full power for 13–15 minutes, rearranging halfway through the cooking. Set aside, covered.

Place the spring onions, peppers and garlic in a bowl, then cover and cook for 5 minutes, stirring halfway through the cooking time. Stir in the butter, cover and cook for 2 minutes.

Stir in the cornflour and five spice powder. Make the chicken juices up to 300 ml/½ pint with the stock, then stir in the remaining ingredients. Cover as before and cook for 3 minutes, stirring halfway through the cooking time. Add the chicken, cover as before and cook for 3–4 minutes.

88 | *Chicken with Lentils*

Preparation time
15–20 minutes

Cooking time
29 minutes

Setting
Full power

Serves 4

Calories
270 per portion

You will need
1 medium onion, finely chopped
2 tablespoons oil
2 cloves garlic, finely chopped
½ teaspoon mild chilli powder
½ teaspoon ground cumin
½ teaspoon turmeric
100 g/4 oz green lentils
600 ml/1 pint hot chicken stock
4 chicken wings
75 g/3 oz shredded fresh spinach
  (see Cook's Tip)

Place the onion, oil and garlic in a large casserole and cook on Full power for 3 minutes. Stir in the spices and cook for 1 minute more.

Add the remaining ingredients, cover and cook for 25 minutes, stirring and rearranging the chicken wings once.

Serve with hot crusty wholemeal bread and a bowl of thick natural yogurt, if liked.

Cook's Tip

Five spice powder is a strongly flavoured condiment used in a variety of Chinese dishes. It is made up of pepper, star anise, fennel, cloves and cinnamon. It has a strong smell and should be used by the pinch not by the spoonful!

Cook's Tip

When fresh spinach is not obtainable, use thoroughly defrosted and drained frozen leaf spinach. Press the water out of the vegetable in a fine sieve. Add to the chicken and lentils for the final 3 minutes cooking time.

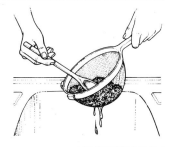

89 | Red Chicken Curry

Preparation time
15 minutes, plus 20 minutes to steep coconut and 4 hours to chill

Cooking time
21–22 minutes

Setting
Full power

Serves 4

Calories
245 per portion

You will need
50 g/2 oz desiccated coconut
300 ml/½ pint boiling water
2 teaspoons tandoori paste
½ teaspoon ground ginger
½ teaspoon ground cinnamon
½ teaspoon cumin seeds
salt and pepper
4 chicken thighs, skinned
1 medium onion, finely chopped
2 chillies, deseeded and finely chopped
1 tablespoon oil
1 large clove garlic, crushed
1 tablespoon cornflour
3 tablespoons cold water
1 tablespoon chopped fresh coriander (optional)

Prepare coconut milk by steeping the coconut in the boiling water in a bowl for 20 minutes. Strain and squeeze out the coconut to extract all the milk. Stir in the tandoori paste, spices and seasoning. Place the chicken portions in a large shallow dish. Spoon over the coconut mixture. Cover closely and chill for 4 hours.

Combine the onion, chillies, oil and garlic in a large shallow dish. Cook on Full power for 3 minutes. Add the chicken and marinade. Cover and cook for 15 minutes, rearranging the chicken once. Mix the cornflour with the water. Add to the chicken and stir. Cook for 3–4 minutes, until thickened, stirring twice. Serve sprinkled with coriander.

Cook's Tip

Pappadums make a good accompaniment for this curry and they will crisp in the microwave oven, though they will not have their characteristic golden colour. Place 2 pappadums on the floor of the microwave and cook on Full power for about 1 minute until puffed. Stand on a wire rack to cool and become crisp.

90 | Chicken and Asparagus Salad

Preparation time
30 minutes

Cooking time
10–12 minutes

Setting
Full power

Serves 4

Calories
968 per portion

You will need
2 chicken breast joints
1 (340-g/12-oz) can asparagus pieces, drained
50 g/2 oz low-fat soft cheese
4 tablespoons mayonnaise
4 tablespoons natural yogurt
½ teaspoon paprika
pinch of cayenne
½ cucumber, sliced
paprika to garnish (optional)

Place the chicken joints in a dish, cover and cook on Full power for 10–12 minutes. Pierce the joints at the thickest point to check that they are cooked – the meat should be just slightly pink when ready. Leave to cool completely. Discard all skin and bone, and cut the chicken into cubes.

Place the asparagus and chicken in a bowl. Blend the soft cheese, mayonnaise and yogurt together and add the peppers. Pour over the chicken. Arrange the cucumber on the base of the serving dish and spoon the chicken mixture in the centre. Garnish with paprika, if you like.

Cook's Tip

When cooking individual foods in the microwave, place them as far apart as possible in a dish or on a plate to promote even cooking. Turn and re-position several times during cooking.

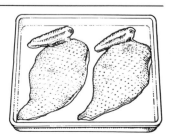

91 | Curried Chicken and Apricot Salad

Preparation time
30 minutes

Cooking time
7–10 minutes, plus 15 minutes to cook pasta

Setting
Full power

Serves 6

Calories
235 per portion

You will need
2 (350-g/12-oz) boneless chicken breasts
175 g/6 oz pasta shells
6 fresh apricots, stoned and sliced
½ bunch watercress, trimmed

For the dressing
150 ml/¼ pint natural yogurt
2 tablespoons mayonnaise
½ teaspoon concentrated tomato purée
½ teaspoon caster sugar
salt and pepper
3 tablespoons single cream
1 teaspoon curry paste

Skin the chicken breasts, place them in a dish and cover. Cook on Full power for 7–10 minutes, then leave to cool. When cool enough to handle cut the chicken meat into small cubes. Cook the pasta in a saucepan of boiling water for 15 minutes. Drain and rinse under cold water.

Toss the chicken, pasta, apricots and watercress together in a salad bowl. Mix the dressing ingredients together and pour over the salad. Serve chilled.

92 | Siesta Salad

Preparation time
15–20 minutes

Cooking time
35 minutes

Setting
Full Power

Serves 4

Calories
375 per portion

You will need
2 oranges
4 (100-g/4-oz) boneless chicken breasts, skinned
450 ml/¾ pint chicken stock
175 g/6 oz brown rice
½ teaspoon salt
1 (198-g/7-oz) can sweetcorn kernels, drained
1 green pepper, cored, deseeded and diced
½ red pepper, cored, deseeded and diced
50 g/2 oz raisins
watercress to garnish

Grate one of the oranges. Peel the remaining orange. Separate both into segments, removing all the pith. Reserve the segments and orange rind.

Arrange the chicken breasts in a shallow dish, taking care that the portions do not overlap. Pour over the chicken stock, cover and cook on Full power for 10 minutes, turning once. Drain off most of the stock, leaving just enough to moisten the chicken. Set aside. Make the stock up to 450 ml/¾ pint with water.

Place the rice in a large deep bowl, add the measured stock and water and stir in the salt and orange rind. Cook, covered, for 25 minutes.

Drain the chicken, dice the flesh and add to the rice. Mix well. Set aside several of the reserved orange segments for garnish and add the remainder to the salad, with the sweetcorn, peppers and raisins. Garnish and serve.

Cook's Tip

To stone apricots, cut them in half and remove the stone. Alternatively, cut down one side of the apricots, then ease the fruit apart and remove the stone. The fruit will still appear whole.

Cook's Tip

When segmenting oranges, always work over a bowl to catch the juice. Peel the orange, remove pith, then cut between the segments to separate them.

93 | Roast Turkey

Preparation time
20 minutes

Cooking time
100–106 minutes, plus
15 minutes standing
time

Setting
Full power

Serves 12–15

Total calories
400–320

You will need
1 (4.5-kg/10-lb) turkey
vegetable oil for brushing

For the stuffing
50 g/2 oz butter
2 medium onions, chopped
2 sticks celery, chopped
450 g/1 lb pork sausagemeat
1 cooking apple, chopped
225 g/8 oz fresh breadcrumbs
1 tablespoon chopped parsley
1 teaspoon dried mixed herbs
salt and pepper
1 egg, beaten

Place the butter, onions and celery in a bowl, cover and
cook on Full power for 3 minutes. Add the sausagemeat
and apple. Cover and cook for a further 2–3 minutes.
Stir in the breadcrumbs, parsley, herbs, salt and pepper
and egg and mix well. Use to stuff turkey. Tie drumsticks and wings close to body with string. Brush all
over with oil. Place bird on an up-turned dish (or microwave roasting rack) in a glass dish, breast-side down.
Cook for 25 minutes. Turn breastside up. Cook for 25
minutes, turn breast-side down. If some areas are cooking too quickly cover them with small pieces of foil.
Cook for 20–25 minutes, turn breast-side up. Cook for
25 minutes or until a microwave thermometer registers
82–85 C/180–185 F, juices run clear and joints are flexi-
ble. Cover with a 'tent' of foil (shiny side inwards) and
stand for 15 minutes.

94 | Spinach-Wrapped Turkey Parcels

Preparation time
10–20 minutes

Cooking time
13 minutes, plus 5
minutes standing time

Setting
Full power

Serves 4

Calories
190 per portion

You will need
1 small onion, finely chopped
1 tablespoon water
225 g/8 oz fresh spinach, trimmed,
  blanched and chopped
2 tablespoons fresh wholemeal
  breadcrumbs
pinch of freshly grated nutmeg
2 tablespoons flaked almonds
salt and pepper
4 thick turkey breast fillets
radicchio leaves to garnish

To wrap
8 large spinach leaves, trimmed
  and blanched
a little sunflower oil

Place the onion and water in a bowl and cook on Full
power for 3 minutes. Drain the spinach thoroughly and
squeeze to extract as much water as possible. Add to
the onion and mix in the breadcrumbs, nutmeg, flaked
almonds and seasoning. Make a slit in each turkey fillet
and fill with stuffing. Wrap in spinach. Brush with oil,
place in a single layer in a shallow dish and cover loosely
with greaseproof paper. Cook on Full power for 10
minutes, rearranging once. Stand, covered, for 5 minutes
then garnish and serve.

Cook's Tip

**The reason for covering a
whole bird, meatloaf or similar
item with a tent of foil is so
that the heat that is given off is
reflected back inwards. It is
important to put the shiny side
inwards.**

Cook's Tip

**To blanch spinach leaves in the
microwave, trim and wash
well, then place (wet) in a large
bowl. Cover and cook on Full
power for 2–3 minutes. Drain
and use. For the above recipe
frozen chopped spinach can be
used in the filling.**

95 | Turkey Rolls with Garlic Butter

Preparation time
5 minutes

Cooking time
7 minutes

Setting
Defrost, Full power

Serves 4

Calories
540 per portion

You will need
100 g/4 oz butter
2 cloves garlic, crushed
4 (175-g/6-oz) boneless turkey
    breasts, skinned
8 rashers rindless streaky bacon,
    stretched
parsley sprigs to garnish

Place the butter in a bowl and soften on Defrost for 1 minute. Add the garlic and mix well.

Flatten the turkey breast fillets between two sheets of greaseproof paper. Divide the garlic butter between them and roll up. Wrap 2 bacon rashers around each roll, securing with wooden cocktail sticks.

Arrange the turkey rolls in a circle around the edge of a large pie dish. Cover and cook on Full power for 6 minutes, rearranging the rolls and turning them over halfway through cooking. Allow to stand for 3 minutes, then transfer the rolls to a platter with a slotted spoon. Pour any garlic butter remaining in the dish into a small jug and offer separately. Garnish the turkey rolls with parsley and serve with brown rice or noodles, if liked.

96 | Sherried Turkey

Preparation time
15 minutes, plus 30
minutes to marinate

Cooking time
8–11 minutes

Serves 4

Setting
Full power

Calories
305 per portion

You will need
6 tablespoons chicken stock
1 tablespoon hazelnut or
    sunflower oil
3 tablespoons dry sherry
2 boneless turkey fillets (about
    350 g/12 oz each), cut into
    1-cm/½-inch strips
1 medium onion, sliced
1 green pepper, cored, deseeded
    and cut into 1-cm/½-inch strips
50 g/2 oz flaked almonds
1 teaspoon cornflour

Place the 4 tablespoons of the stock, oil and sherry in a large dish. Add the turkey strips and marinate for 30 minutes. Stir in the onion and pepper and cook on Full power for 6–8 minutes, stirring every 2 minutes, until cooked. Stir in the almonds. Mix the cornflour to a paste with the remaining stock and stir into turkey mixture. Cook for 2–3 minutes, stirring once, to thicken. Serve with plain boiled rice.

Cook's Tip

Try varying the filling by using a parsley butter (4 tablespoons chopped parsley to 100 g/4 oz butter) or use a mixture of 50 g/2 oz butter and 50 g/2 oz crumbled Stilton cheese.

Cook's Tip

A good way of removing the middle from peppers is to cut around the stalk end with a long pointed knife. Cut deep down into the middle of the pepper, then you will be able to pull out most of the core in one go.

97 | Turkey Salad with Grapes

Preparation time
10–15 minutes,
plus 1 hour to
cool chicken

Cooking time
12 minutes

Setting
Full power

Serves 6

Calories
185 per portion

You will need
4 (175-g/6-oz) turkey breasts
1 small onion, finely chopped
finely grated rind and juice of 1 lemon
1 slice fresh root ginger, peeled and chopped
2 parsley sprigs
1 bay leaf
salt and pepper
450 ml/¾ pint chicken stock
150 ml/¼ pint natural yogurt
1 head curly endive, separated into leaves
100 g/4 oz green grapes, halved and deseeded
50 g/2 oz flaked almonds

Skin the turkey breasts and place them in a shallow dish with the onion, lemon rind and juice, ginger and herbs. Add salt and pepper to taste and pour over the chicken stock. Cover and cook on Full power for 12 minutes. Set the turkey aside at room temperature for 1 hour to cool in the cooking liquid.

Remove the turkey breasts from the liquid and cut them into neat pieces. Reserve. Strain 150 ml/¼ pint of the chicken stock into a jug and stir in the yogurt, with salt and pepper to taste. Mix well.

Arrange the endive around the edge of a serving platter. Fill the centre with the turkey and grapes. Pour over the yogurt sauce and sprinkle with almonds. Serve cold (see Cook's Tip).

Cook's Tip

Serve the salad cold, but do not chill in the refrigerator as this would blunt the delicate flavours.

98 | Warm Mushroom Salad

Preparation time
15 minutes

Cooking time
8–9 minutes

Setting
Full power

Serves 4

Calories
200 per portion

You will need
225 g/8 oz turkey livers
½ small head curly endive
25 g/1 oz pine nuts
2 tablespoons vegetable oil
225 g/8 oz cup mushrooms, wiped and cut into quarters
2 tablespoons red wine vinegar
salt and pepper

Rinse and dry the livers, then halve or quarter them. Arrange the endive on four individual serving plates. Place the nuts in a small bowl with 1 tablespoon of the oil. Cover and cook on Full power for 2–3 minutes or until golden brown. Pour the remaining oil into a large shallow dish. Add the liver, coat in oil and spread out so that they do not overlap. Cover and cook for 3 minutes, turning once.

With a slotted spoon, remove the livers from the dish. Add the mushrooms to the juices remaining in the dish and cook for 2 minutes, stirring once. While the mushrooms are cooking, slice the livers thinly (they should still be pink inside).

Return the liver slices to the dish with the reserved pine nuts and vinegar. Season and heat through for 1 minute, then serve on the endive. Serve at once.

Cook's Tip

If turkey or chicken livers are to be cooked whole in the microwave oven, they should first be pricked or slashed to prevent the surrounding membranes from bursting. This rule applies to all types of offal.

99 | Rosemary Chicken with Orange

Preparation time
10 minutes

Cooking time
19 minutes

Setting
Full power

Serves 4

Calories
240 per portion

You will need
4 (100-g/4-oz) chicken breasts, skinned
4 sprigs rosemary
1 orange, cut into 8 slices
salt and pepper
2 tablespoons oil
12 button onions
12 button mushrooms, wiped
2 tablespoons coarse-cut marmalade
6 tablespoons chicken stock
rosemary sprigs to garnish

Slit one side of each chicken breast to form a pocket. Tuck a sprig of rosemary and two slices of orange into each. Add salt and pepper to taste.

Place the oil and onions in a shallow dish. Cook on Full power for 5 minutes. Add the prepared chicken breasts and cook for 2 minutes.

Stir in the mushrooms, marmalade and stock. Cover and cook for 12 minutes, turning and rearranging the chicken once during cooking. Stand, covered, for 2–3 minutes before serving, garnished with rosemary sprigs.

100 | Duck in Mustard Sauce

Preparation time
10 minutes

Cooking time
26–27 minutes, plus
5 minutes
standing time

Setting
Full power

Serves 4

Calories
685 per portion

You will need
4 (350-g/12-oz) duck portions or cut a 1.8-kg/4-lb oven-ready duckling into 4 pieces
salt and pepper
25 g/1 oz butter
1 medium onion, chopped
6 tablespoons dry red wine
juice of ½ lemon
2 teaspoons coarse-grain French mustard
watercress to garnish

Remove and reserve the giblets if using a whole duckling. Clean the pieces and pat dry with absorbent kitchen paper. Season generously and place pieces, skin side down, in a large casserole on a roasting rack or an up-turned saucer. Cover and cook on Full power for 23 minutes, turning skin side up halfway through the cooking time. Stand for 5 minutes. Place the butter, onion and, if using, the duck liver, in a basin and cook for 2–3 minutes. Remove liver and mash to a paste. Add the wine, lemon juice, mustard and duck liver, if using, to the bowl and stir well. Cook for 1 minute. Place the duck portions on a serving dish, pour over a little of the sauce and garnish with the watercress. Serve the remaining sauce separately.

Cook's Tip

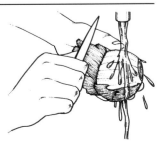

If close encounters with onions make you cry, work under running water or, if time permits, chill the onions in the freezer for 10–15 minutes before peeling.

Cook's Tip

Duck cooks very well in the microwave to yield tender moist results. At the end of the cooking time you may like to brown the outside under a very hot grill or in a very hot oven for a few minutes. Once tried you will never cook duck conventionally again!

Meat Dishes

Not all meats cook well in the microwave oven, and joints are best in a combination oven. When cooking casseroles use good quality meat as the quick cooking method of a microwave is not suitable for tougher cuts. When defrosting casseroles and stews, break up the frozen meat as it begins to defrost and stir frequently to prevent the outer meat overcooking before the centre is defrosted.

101 | Beef Bourguignonne

(Illustrated on back jacket)

Preparation time
10 minutes

Cooking time
50–62 minutes

Setting
Full power, Low

Serves 4

Calories
400 per portion

You will need
575 g/1¼ lb sirloin steak
100 g/4 oz rindless streaky bacon, chopped
150 ml/¼ pint red wine
7 tablespoons hot beef stock
1 clove garlic, crushed
4 small onions, quartered or 175 g/6 oz silver-skin onions
2 tablespoons deseeded chopped green pepper
100 g/4 oz button mushrooms, sliced
salt and pepper
1 teaspoon dried mixed herbs
1 tablespoon cornflour

Cut the steak into 5-mm × 5-cm/¼ × 2-inch strips, cutting with the grain of the meat.

Place bacon in a large casserole and cook on Full power for 2–3 minutes. Add the meat, wine, 4 tablespoons stock, garlic, onions, green pepper, mushrooms, seasoning and herbs. Cover and cook for 5 minutes or until boiling. Cook on Low for about 40–50 minutes or until tender.

Mix cornflour to a smooth paste with the remaining stock and stir into the meat mixture. Cover and cook on Full power for 3–4 minutes, stirring after 2 minutes, to thicken meat juices. Add a little more wine or stock, if necessary. Serve very hot.

102 | Carbonnade of Beef with Mushrooms

Preparation time
15 minutes

Cooking time
63 minutes, plus 5 minutes standing time

Setting
Full power, Low, Defrost

Serves 4

Calories
400 per portion

You will need
575 g/1¼ lb good braising or frying steak, cut into 1-cm/½-in cubes
40 g/1½ oz butter
25 g/1 oz plain flour
1 (213-g/7½-oz) can mushrooms, drained
salt and pepper
½ teaspoon brown sugar
½ teaspoon vinegar
300 ml/½ pint brown ale
300 ml/½ pint stock
1 medium onion, thinly sliced
¼ teaspoon freshly grated nutmeg

Place the meat and butter in a large, round casserole. Cover and cook on Full power for 8 minutes. Mix together the flour, mushrooms, salt and pepper, sugar, vinegar, ale, stock, onion and nutmeg. Add to the meat, stir well and re-cover. Cook on Low power for 35 minutes, stirring twice during cooking. Cook on Defrost for 20 minutes, or until the meat is tender. Stir well and stand, covered, for 5 minutes.

Cook's Tip

If you want to speed up the cooking time on casseroles in the microwave, then use frying steak and cut the meat across the grain into slices, then again into strips.

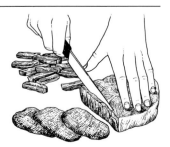

Cook's Tip

Instead of the beef in this recipe you could use lamb or pork. Select lean pieces, discarding any gristle and fat. Cut small dice as above and cook in the same way. Pork will take less time to become tender.

103 | One-dish Macaroni Beef

Preparation time
5 minutes

Cooking time
33 minutes, plus
5 minutes standing
time

Setting
Full power, Defrost

Serves 3–4

Calories
390–295 per portion

You will need
225 g/8 oz minced beef
1 small onion, finely chopped
100 g/4 oz macaroni (uncooked)
250 ml/8 fl oz tomato juice
350 ml/12 fl oz water
4 tablespoons tomato ketchup
1 (198-g/7-oz) can sweetcorn
2 teaspoons brown sugar
½ teaspoon salt
black pepper
chilli powder

Place the mince and onion in a large casserole. Cover and cook on Full power for 3 minutes. Drain off excess liquid. Stir in the macaroni, tomato juice, water, ketchup, sweetcorn, sugar, salt, pepper and chilli powder to taste. Cover and cook on Defrost for 30 minutes, stirring at 10-minute intervals. Stir and stand for 5 minutes. Serve hot.

104 | Meatballs in Chilli Sauce

Preparation time
10–15 minutes

Cooking time
38 minutes

Setting
Full power, Medium

Serves 4

Calories
390 per portion

You will need
450 g/1 lb minced beef
1 small onion, finely chopped
50 g/2 oz porridge oats
1 tablespoon concentrated tomato
  purée
½ teaspoon celery salt
1 teaspoon chopped parsley
1 egg, beaten

For the sauce
1 small onion, chopped
1 tablespoon oil
½ small green pepper, cored,
  deseeded and chopped
1 (397-g/14-oz) can chopped
  tomatoes
2 tablespoons vinegar
1 tablespoon sugar
1 teaspoon mild chilli powder
300 ml/½ pint beef stock

Mix the beef thoroughly with the remaining ingredients, then shape into 16 meatballs. Arrange in a single layer in a shallow dish. Cover with absorbent kitchen paper and cook on Full power for 4 minutes, turning once. Cook on Medium for 6 minutes.

Place the onion, oil and pepper in a large bowl. Cover and cook on Full power for 3 minutes. Stir in all the remaining sauce ingredients and cook for 5 minutes more, stirring once. Add the meatballs, and coat them in the sauce. Cover and cook on Medium for 20 minutes.

Cook's Tip

Before you embark on a shopping trip for microwave cookware check the dishes you have. Many are ideal – large casseroles, soufflé dishes, jugs, basins and mixing bowls can all be used. Avoid metal trims.

Cook's Tip

When cooking meatballs, or any similar-sized items, in the microwave, turn and rearrange them during cooking, moving pieces from the outside of the dish towards the middle. If time is short, finish this dish on Full power for 14 minutes rather than Medium.

105 | Bran Meat Loaf

Preparation time
10 minutes

Cooking time
20–25 minutes

Setting
Full power, Medium

Serves 4

Calories
370 per portion

You will need
50 g/2 oz All-bran breakfast cereal
150 ml/¼ pint water
225 g/8 oz minced beef
225 g/8 oz pork sausagemeat
1 large onion, finely chopped
pinch of dried mixed herbs
salt and pepper
1 egg, beaten

Place the All-bran in a large bowl. Add the water, mix well and set aside for 4–6 minutes, until the cereal has absorbed all the liquid.

Add the minced beef and sausagemeat with the onion and herbs. Mix well and add salt and pepper to taste. Stir in the egg.

Press the mixture into a greased loaf dish measuring about 11.5 × 21 cm/4½ × 8½ inches. Cover loosely and cook on Full power for 5 minutes. Reduce the power to Medium and cook for 15–20 minutes more.

Allow the meat loaf to stand in the dish for 2–3 minutes, then turn it out on to a serving platter. Serve hot or cold. A salad makes a good accompaniment.

106 | Steak with Creamed Pepper Sauce

Preparation time
15 minutes

Cooking time
14 minutes

Setting
Full power

Serves 4

Calories
390 per portion

You will need
675 g/1½ lb rump steak
1 large onion, sliced
1–2 cloves garlic, crushed
1 tablespoon oil
1 green pepper, cored, deseeded
  and cut into strips
100 g/4 oz button mushrooms,
  sliced
pinch of dried sage
salt and freshly ground black
  pepper
50 g/2 oz low-fat soft cheese
2 tablespoons milk
1 tablespoon lemon juice
grated lemon rind to garnish

Trim the fat off the steak and cut into thin strips. Put the onion and garlic in a medium casserole and cook on Full power for 3 minutes. Add the meat and cook on Full for 7 minutes, stirring once. Add the pepper, mushrooms, sage and seasoning. Cook for 2 minutes. Blend the soft cheese with the milk and lemon juice. Stir into the meat and cook for 2 minutes before sprinkling with lemon rind and serving with pasta.

Cook's Tip

Browning a meat loaf under a hot grill improves both the colour and the flavour. When microwave cooking is complete, turn the meat loaf out on to a Swiss roll tin and brown under the grill for about 10 minutes.

Cook's Tip

A quick way to cut pepper into strips: quarter it lengthways, cut away all core, then holding four pieces together cut into thin strips.

107 | Beef and Mushroom Kebabs

Preparation time
15–20 minutes, plus 2
hours to marinate

Cooking time
14 minutes

Setting
Medium, Full power

Serves 6

Calories
375 per portion

You will need
675 g/1½ lb steak, cubed
225 g/8 oz button mushrooms
1 green and 1 red pepper, cored
    deseeded and cut into squares
12 bay leaves
1 teaspoon cornflour
1 tablespoon cold water
salt and pepper

For the marinade
2 tablespoons clear honey
6 tablespoons red wine
6 tablespoons olive oil
1 clove garlic, crushed
4 drops of chilli sauce

Thread the beef, vegetables and bay leaves on to six wooden skewers and place in a large shallow dish. Place the honey in a bowl. Cook on Medium for 1 minute, then stir in the remaining marinade ingredients. Brush over the kebabs and set aside for 2 hours. Drain the kebabs (reserve the marinade) and arrange on a large plate. Cook on Medium for 5 minutes, turning and rearranging once. Baste with marinade and cook for 5 minutes more, turning once.

In a large jug, mix the cornflour with the water. Pour in the remaining marinade and any cooking juices. Cook on Full power for 3 minutes, stirring once. Season and serve at once, with the kebabs.

Cook's Tip

Use good-quality beef for the kebabs – rump steak, frying steak or fillet if you can afford it. Avoid tough cuts. Cooking on Medium will help to keep the meat tender. Arrange kebabs as far apart as possible for even cooking. If space allows, position them like the spokes of a wheel on a large plate.

108 | Mince Hot Pot

Preparation time
15 minutes

Cooking time
20 minutes, plus grilling
time

Setting
Full power

Serves 4

Calories
415 per portion

You will need:
1 medium onion, chopped
50 g/2 oz carrots, grated
3 tablespoons sunflower oil
225 g/8 oz very lean mince or
    ground beef
1 (227-g/8-oz) can tomatoes
1 tablespoon concentrated tomato
    purée
½ teaspoon curry powder
½ beef stock cube
salt and pepper
1 (227-g/8-oz) can butter or
    canellini beans, drained
225 g/8 oz cooked potatoes, thinly
    sliced

Place the onion, carrot and 2 tablespoons of the oil in a large ovenproof bowl. Stir well, then cook on Full power for 5 minutes.

Add the beef, tomatoes, tomato purée, curry powder, the crumbled stock cube and seasoning to taste and mix all the ingredients together well. Cover and cook for a further 10 minutes.

Stir well, then add the drained butter or cannellini beans, mixing in gently. Re-cover and cook for a final 5 minutes. Remove to a heatproof serving dish. Place the potatoes on top of the meat and brush with the remaining oil, then brown under a hot grill before serving.

Cook's Tip

If you like, use a special crinkle cutter to slice the potatoes decoratively.

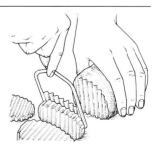

109 | *Chinese Beef*

Preparation time
15–20 minutes, plus 15 minutes to marinate beef

Cooking time
9–11 minutes

Setting
Full power

Serves 4

Calories
185 per portion

You will need
175 g/6 oz steak, cut into strips
2 tablespoons oil
2 spring onions, cut into strips
$\frac{1}{4}$ teaspoon ground ginger
75 g/3 oz frozen cut green beans, defrosted (see Cook's Tip)
75 g/3 oz frozen cauliflower, defrosted and cut into small florets
50 g/2 oz frozen petits pois
50 g/2 oz bean sprouts, washed
$\frac{1}{2}$ red pepper, cored, deseeded and cut into strips
salt and pepper

For the marinade
2 tablespoons soy sauce
1 tablespoon sherry
2 teaspoons cornflour

Combine the marinade ingredients, mix in the steak and set aside for 15 minutes.

Drain the meat, add to a dish with the oil, spring onions and ginger. Reserve the remaining marinade. Cook on Full power for 3 minutes, stirring once. Transfer to a plate and cover with foil.

Add the vegetables and seasoning to any juices in the dish and cook for 3 minutes. Stir in the marinade and steak and cook for 3–5 minutes.

Cook's Tip

It is seldom necessary to thaw frozen vegetables before cooking in the microwave oven. It is recommended for this recipe as additional water would alter the nature of the stir fry, producing steamed rather than crisply cooked vegetables. To thaw the beans and cauliflower, mix them together in a large bowl, cover and allow 3–4 minutes on Defrost.

110 | *Meatballs in Tomato and Cumin Sauce*

Preparation time
10 minutes

Cooking time
21 minutes, plus 5 minutes standing time

Setting
Full power

Serves 4

Calories
435 per portion

You will need
5 tablespoons fresh wholemeal breadcrumbs
1 tablespoon bran
4 tablespoons skimmed milk
1 large onion, finely chopped
1 clove garlic, crushed
2 tablespoons water
450 g/1 lb lean minced lamb
1 tablespoon chopped parsley
salt and pepper
600 ml/1 pint Tomato sauce (recipe 236)
$\frac{1}{2}$ teaspoon cumin seeds

Place the breadcrumbs and bran in a bowl, stir in the milk and leave to stand.

Place the onion and garlic in a large ovenproof bowl with the water and cook on Full power for 4 minutes. Stir in the meat, parsley, breadcrumbs and bran. Season with salt and pepper and mix thoroughly. Shape into 12–16 firm small balls.

Pour the tomato sauce into a large bowl or casserole and stir in the cumin seeds. Cover and cook for 5 minutes, stirring halfway through cooking. Drop in the meatballs. Stir lightly, cover and cook for 12 minutes, stirring two or three times during cooking. Allow to stand, covered, for 5 minutes before serving. Serve with tagliarini (puréed spinach is added to the basic dough to make the pasta green) or a variety of pasta of your choice.

Cook's Tip

When cooking meatballs place them as far apart as possible in the dish. Stir the sauce over them evenly so that they will all cook in the same time.

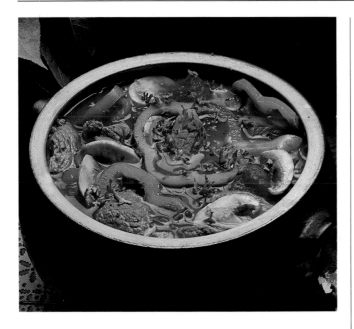

111 | Lamb Provençale

Preparation time
10 minutes

Cooking time
21 minutes

Setting
Full power

Serves 4

Calories
400 per portion

You will need
1 large onion, sliced
1 clove garlic, crushed
2 tablespoons vegetable oil
675 g/1½ lb lamb fillet
1 (397-g/14-oz) can chopped
  tomatoes
1 tablespoon concentrated tomato
  purée
150 ml/¼ pint white wine
bouquet garni
salt and pepper
100 g/4 oz button mushrooms,
  wiped and sliced
1 green pepper, cored, deseeded
  and sliced
2 tablespoons chopped parsley to
  garnish

Combine the onion, garlic and oil in a casserole and cook on Full power for 4 minutes.

Meanwhile, trim the meat and cut it into small even-sized cubes. Add to the onion mixture with the tomatoes, tomato purée and wine. Stir in the bouquet garni (see Cook's Tip) and season to taste. Cover and cook for 12 minutes, stirring once during cooking.

Add the mushrooms and green pepper and cook for 5 minutes more, stirring halfway through cooking and again when cooking is complete. Remove the bouquet garni. Allow to stand for 3 minutes, then garnish with chopped parsley and serve.

112 | Mediterranean Mince

Preparation time
10 minutes

Cooking time
15 minutes, plus
15 minutes to cook
pasta

Setting
Full power

Serves 4

Calories
580 per portion

You will need
225 g/8 oz macaroni
salt and pepper
1 small green pepper, cored,
  deseeded and finely diced
1 medium onion, finely chopped
25 g/1 oz butter
2 tomatoes, peeled and chopped
1 tablespoon concentrated tomato
  purée
2 cloves garlic, crushed
½ teaspoon ground cinnamon
½ teaspoon freshly grated nutmeg
450 g/1 lb minced beef
50 g/2 oz Cheddar cheese, grated
watercress to garnish

Cook the macaroni conventionally, on the hob. Add it to a saucepan of boiling salted water and cook for about 15 minutes, until tender but not soft.

Meanwhile place the green pepper, onion, butter, tomatoes, tomato purée and garlic in a very large bowl. Season to taste and add the spices. Cover and cook on Full power for 7 minutes, stirring once.

Stir in the meat, replace the cover and cook for 8 minutes, stirring halfway through cooking.

Drain the macaroni, add it to the meat sauce and toss well. Spoon the mixture into a warm shallow serving dish, sprinkle with grated cheese and serve at once, garnished with watercress.

Cook's Tip

To make a bouquet garni, tie together a bay leaf, 2 fresh parsley sprigs and 1 sprig of thyme. A sprig of leaf celery may be added if liked. Bouquets garnis are also available in pouches and sachets.

Cook's Tip

If preferred, the dish may be finished under a hot grill. The mince can be placed in individual ovenproof dishes.

113 | Lamb and Coriander Kebabs

Preparation time
15 minutes

Cooking time
9 minutes, plus 5 minutes standing time

Setting
Full power

Serves 4

Calories
310 per portion

You will need
1 onion, finely chopped
1 clove garlic, crushed
2 tablespoons water
350 g/12 oz lean minced lamb
½ teaspoon ground coriander
1 tablespoon chopped fresh coriander or parsley
2 tablespoons fresh wholemeal breadcrumbs
1 egg
salt and pepper
6 tablespoons sesame seeds, toasted
1 green and 1 yellow pepper, cored and deseeded
8 button mushrooms, halved
lemon wedges to garnish

Put the onion, garlic and water in a bowl and cook on Full power for 3 minutes. Mix in the lamb, ground coriander, herbs, breadcrumbs, egg and seasoning. Shape into 16 small balls, then roll in the sesame seeds. Cut the peppers into squares. Thread the meatballs, peppers and mushrooms on eight wooden skewers. Arrange on a large plate and cook for 3 minutes. Turn the skewers and cook for a further 3 minutes. Wrap the kebabs in foil and allow to stand for 5 minutes before serving, garnished with lemon wedges.

114 | Lamb Garbanzo

Preparation time
15 minutes

Cooking time
16–21 minutes

Setting
Full power

Serves 4

Calories
595 per portion

You will need
8 lean lamb noisettes
1 large onion, finely chopped
1 clove garlic, crushed
1 tablespoon oil
225 g/8 oz carrots, sliced
1 teaspoon oregano
1 (397-g/14-oz) can tomatoes
1 (415-g/14½-oz) can chick peas, drained
salt and pepper
2 tablespoons chopped fresh parsley

If you like, quickly brown the fat on the noisettes by holding betwen thumb and forefinger and rolling across a hot frying pan on the conventional hob (see Cook's Tip). Place the onion and garlic in a dish with the oil and cook on Full power for 2 minutes. Arrange the lamb in the dish, add the carrots, oregano and tomatoes, cover and cook for 9–12 minutes until lamb and vegetables are cooked, rearrange once during cooking. Add the chick peas and season to taste. Cook for a further 5–8 minutes, stirring twice.

Leave to stand for 3 minutes before serving, garnished with the parsley.

Cook's Tip

Minced lamb is available from many supermarkets. If you cannot find any, then ask your butcher to trim and mince a shoulder of lamb for you. Any extra can be frozen. Some supermarkets have a butcher on the premises so do not be afraid to ask for special items – they are often very helpful.

Cook's Tip

To brown the fatty edge of noisettes, chops or any similar meat, first heat a frying pan on the hob. Unless the pan is likely to stick do not add fat. Hold a piece of meat on end and brown the fat on the hot pan for a few seconds.

115 | Pork with Lemon

Preparation time
5 minutes , plus 1 hour
to marinate

Cooking time
16 minutes

Setting
Full power

Serves 4

Calories
350 per portion

You will need
675 g/1½ lb pork tenderloin, cut
into 1-cm/½-inch slices
2 teaspoons cornflour
1 teaspoon prepared mustard
150 ml/¼ pint single cream

For the marinade
4 tablespoons oil
6 tablespoons white wine
4 tablespoons lemon juice
salt and pepper
1 bay leaf

Combine all the marinade ingredients in a large shallow dish. Add the pork and stir until well coated. Set aside to marinate for 1 hour.

Heat a browning dish according to the manufacturer's instructions. Drain the slices of pork, reserving 2 tablespoons of the marinade, and pat dry on absorbent kitchen paper. Without removing the browning dish from the microwave oven, add the pork, taking care that the slices do not overlap. Cook on Full power for 3 minutes, turn the slices over and cook for 3 minutes more.

Meanwhile mix the cornflour with the mustard and reserved marinade in a 600-ml/1-pint jug. Stir in the cream and add seasoning to taste. Pour the mixture over the pork, stir thoroughly and cook for 10 minutes more, stirring once to rearrange the meat in the dish. Allow the pork to stand for 2–3 minutes before serving.

Cook's Tip

For two people, use 350 g/
12 oz pork tenderloin and 6
tablespoons cream. Divide all
other quantities by half.
Follow the same cooking
times for searing the pork, but
reduce the final cooking time
to 6 minutes.

116 | Sweet n' Sour Pork

Preparation time
15–20 minutes

Cooking time
21–22 minutes

Setting
Full power

Serves 4–6

Calories
270–180 per portion

You will need
4 teaspoons butter or margarine
2 cloves garlic, crushed
1 onion, cut into wedges
350 g/12 oz lean boneless pork,
cut into 1-cm/½-inch cubes
2 carrots, cut into 1-cm/½-inch
slices
½ cucumber, cut lengthways into
3-mm/⅛-inch strips
1 (440-g/15½-oz) can pineapple
rings, juice reserved
4 teaspoons plain flour
3 tablespoons vinegar
3 tablespoons soy sauce

Melt the butter in a large bowl on Full power for 1 minute. Add the garlic and onion and cook for 3 minutes until soft. Add the pork, carrots, cucumber, and pineapple juice. Cover and cook for 15 minutes, stirring once.

Blend the flour with the vinegar and add the soy sauce, then add to the pork mixture with the pineapple rings, cut into pieces. Cook for a further 2–3 minutes and serve hot.

Cook's Tip

Place cooled pork and sauce in
microwave/freezer container,
seal, label and freeze. To use
reheat from frozen on Full
power for 10–15 minutes.

117 | Pork Chops with Peaches

Preparation time
10 minutes

Cooking time
9 minutes

Setting
Full power

Serves 4

Calories
505 per portion

You will need
1 medium onion, chopped
2 tablespoons vegetable oil
1 (285-g/10-oz) can peach slices, juice reserved
1 teaspoon ground cinnamon
salt and pepper
4 pork chops

Place the onion in a medium bowl with the oil and cook on Full power for 3 minutes until soft. Add the peach juice, cinnamon, seasoning and the chops, cover and cook on Full power for 5 minutes, turning once. Add the peaches and cook for another minute. Serve hot.

118 | Pork Malay

Preparation time
15–20 minutes, plus overnight to marinate

Cooking time
20 minutes

Setting
Full power

Serves 4—6

Calories
485–325 per portion

You will need
675 g/1½ lb pork steaks, diced
3 large cloves garlic, crushed
2.5-cm/1-inch piece fresh root ginger, chopped
2 tablespoons ground coriander
1 tablespoon soy sauce
4 tablespoons crunchy peanut butter
600 ml/1 pint vegetable or chicken stock
25 g/1 oz concentrated butter
1 medium onion, chopped
4 small dried chillies (optional)
50 g/2 oz creamed coconut
parsley or coriander sprigs to garnish

Place the pork in a shallow dish. Blend the garlic, ginger, coriander, soy sauce, peanut butter and stock in a liquidiser or food processor. (It may be necessary to do this in two batches.) Do not overblend (see Cook's tip). Pour the mixture over the meat, cover and allow to stand in a cool place for at least two hours, preferably overnight.

Combine the butter and onion in a casserole. Cook on Full power for 3 minutes, stirring once. Add the pork, with its marinade. Stir in the chillies, if used, and cook for 15 minutes, stirring twice to rearrange the meat in the dish.

Break the creamed coconut into small cubes. Stir these into the casserole and cook for 2 minutes, stirring frequently to make a smooth sauce.

Allow to stand for 2—3 minutes before serving with a garnish of parsley or coriander.

Cook's Tip

If you prefer, brown the chops first in a browning dish, following the manufacturer's instructions for heating the dish. Remove the chops, then add the onion and remaining ingredients and cook as above.

Cook's Tip

Watch the marinade mixture carefully while blending. It should not be too finely processed as a chunky texture adds interest to the sauce.

119 | Pork Korma with Coconut

Preparation time
15 minutes

Cooking time
43 minutes

Setting
Full Power, Medium, Low

Serves 4

Calories
290 per portion

You will need
450 g / 1 lb lean pork
1 onion, chopped
1 tablespoon oil
2 teaspoons madras curry powder
1 clove garlic, crushed
300 ml / ½ pint chicken stock
25 g / 1 oz creamed coconut
salt and black pepper
2 tablespoons soft cheese, such as Shape
1 tablespoon plain flour
1 tablespoon milk
1 tablespoon concentrated tomato purée
100 g / 4 oz fresh or canned pineapple, diced

Trim all the fat from the pork and cube the meat. Put the onion and oil in a medium casserole with the spices and garlic. Cover and cook on Full power for 3 minutes. Add the pork, stock and creamed coconut. Season, cover and cook on Medium for 20 minutes. Blend the soft cheese with the flour, milk and tomato purée. Add to the pork with the pineapple. Cook on Low for 20 minutes. Serve with pilau or basmati rice and a tomato or cucumber salad.

Cook's Tip

Pork cooks well in the microwave because it is usually fairly tender. Look out for lean cuts like leg steaks, shoulder, fillet or knuckle end of leg. Sparerib pork tends to be marbled with plenty of fat.

120 | Veal Escalopes with Mushrooms

Preparation time
20 minutes

Cooking time
16 minutes

Setting
Full power

Serves 4

Calories
300 per portion

You will need
1 small onion, finely chopped
100 g / 4 oz mushrooms, chopped
1 tablespoon oil
2 tablespoons chopped parsley
salt and pepper
4 (100-g / 4-oz) veal escalopes

For the sauce
2 tablespoons cornflour
50 g / 2 oz butter
150 ml / ¼ pint chicken stock
150 ml / ¼ pint dry sherry
finely pared rind and juice of 1 orange
225 g / 8 oz mushrooms, sliced
1 teaspoon mushroom ketchup

Place the onion and mushrooms in a bowl with the oil. Cook on Full power for 3 minutes. Stir in parsley and seasoning to taste. Flatten the veal between greaseproof paper. Divide the mushroom filling between them, roll up and secure with string.

Place the cornflour and butter in a large jug. Gradually whisk in the stock, sherry, orange rind and juice. Cook for 6 minutes, whisking once during cooking and again when cooking is complete. Place mushrooms and ketchup in a large shallow dish. Arrange the veal on top, spooning over a little sauce. Cover and cook for 7 minutes, rearranging once. Re-heat sauce for 3 minutes, pour over veal rolls.

Cook's Tip

Chop parsley the French way by placing sprigs in a small bowl and snipping them with scissors.

121 | Pork Chops with Orange

Preparation time
15 minutes

Cooking time
36 minutes, plus 5 minutes standing time

Setting
Full power

Serves 4

Calories
455 per portion

You will need
1 tablespoon oil
4 pork chops, trimmed of excess fat
1 large onion, sliced
1 clove garlic, crushed
1 tablespoon cornflour
300 ml/½ pint orange juice
1 green pepper, cored, deseeded and sliced
225 g/8 oz long-grain rice
600 ml/1 pint boiling stock
salt (optional)
orange slices to garnish

Heat a browning dish according to the manufacturer's instructions. Add the oil and pork chops and cook on Full power for 2 minutes on each side. Add onion and garlic and cook for 2 minutes more.

In a jug, mix the cornflour with the orange juice. Stir well, add the green pepper and pour over the pork chops. Cover and cook for 10 minutes, turning the chops over and rearranging them once. Cover with foil and allow to stand while cooking the rice.

Combine the rice and stock in a large deep bowl. Add salt if necessary (see Cook's Tip). Cover and cook for 15 minutes. Allow to stand for 5 minutes, until all the water has been absorbed and the rice grains are separate. Use the standing time to finish the pork chops: top each chop with orange slices and cook for 5 minutes. Transfer to a serving dish and serve with the rice.

Cook's Tip

Home-made stocks may need extra salt. If, however, you have used a stock cube, this may prove unnecessary.

122 | Pickle Loaf

Preparation time
20 minutes

Cooking time
18 minutes, plus 10 minutes standing time and grilling time

Setting
Full power

Serves 8

Calories
290 per portion

You will need
225 g/8 oz pig's liver, trimmed
675 g/1½ lb boneless pork
1 large onion, finely chopped
1 clove garlic, crushed
75 g/3 oz fresh breadcrumbs
1 egg
1 teaspoon ground coriander
1 teaspoon oregano
few drops of Tabasco sauce
salt and pepper
watercress to garnish

For the filling
1 dessert apple, grated
50 g/2 oz Wensleydale cheese, grated
3 tablespoons sweet pickle

For the topping
75 g/3 oz Wensleydale cheese, grated
2 tablespoons cider

Dice the liver and pork and place in a bowl with the onion and garlic. Cover and cook on Full power for 10 minutes, stirring once. Mince until smooth. Mix with the remaining ingredients and place half in a 1-litre/2-pint loaf dish. Mix the apple and cheese. Spread half the pickle over the meat, top with the apple mixture, then add the remaining pickle. Spread the remaining meat on top. Cover and cook for 8 minutes. Stand for 10 minutes before turning out. For the topping, mix the cheese and cider to a paste, spread over the loaf and grill until melted. Garnish with watercress.

Cook's Tip

This loaf is good hot, with baked potatoes and salad. It also makes an ideal pâté-style dish to serve cold. It can be served as a platter with salad ingredients as a garnish and plenty of fresh crusty bread as an accompaniment.

123 | Spare Ribs Barbecue-style

Preparation time
5 minutes

Cooking time
25–30 minutes

Setting
Full power

Serves 3–4

Calories
875–655 per portion

You will need
675 g/1½ lb pork spare ribs
2 tablespoons soft brown sugar
3 tablespoons soy sauce
6 tablespoons tomato ketchup
few drops of Tabasco sauce

Place the spare ribs, bone side up, in a single layer in a large shallow dish.

Mix all the remaining ingredients in a jug and pour over the ribs. Cook on Full power for 25–30 minutes, turning the ribs over and rearranging them several times. Serve at once with a green salad.

Cook's Tip

Save time and effort at a barbecue by cooking spare ribs as suggested above, then finishing them off over the coals for the authentic char-grilled appearance.

124 | Pork and Ham Loaf

Preparation time
15 minutes

Cooking time
21 minutes, plus
5 minutes standing time

Setting
Full power

Serves 6–8

Calories
210–155 per portion

You will need
1 tablespoon oil
1 small onion, finely chopped
½ green pepper, cored, deseeded and finely chopped
225 g/8 oz cooked ham, minced
225 g/8 oz minced pork
50 g/2 oz wholemeal breadcrumbs
2 teaspoons mustard powder
½ teaspoon salt
¼ teaspoon pepper
1 egg
watercress sprigs to garnish

For the sauce
1 (440-g/15½-oz) can pineapple rings, juice reserved
2 tablespoons brown sugar
1 tablespoon cornflour
1 tablespoon vinegar

Place the oil in a small bowl, add the onion and pepper and cook on Full power for 3 minutes until soft. Mix with all the remaining ingredients, place in a 450-g/1-lb loaf dish and cook on Full power for 12 minutes. Stand for 5 minutes.

Mix all the ingredients for the sauce using the pineapple juice but reserving the fruit. Turn out the meatloaf and add any juices to the sauce. Cook the sauce for 3–4 minutes. Garnish the loaf with pineapple rings, spoon a little sauce over and cook for 2 minutes before serving, garnished with watercress sprigs.

Cook's Tip

If you are concerned that the meatloaf may stick to the dish, then simply place a piece of greaseproof or non-stick paper in the base before greasing the dish.

125 | Apple-stuffed Pork

Preparation time
10 minutes

Cooking time
12–14 minutes

Setting
Full power

Serves 4

Calories
445 per portion

You will need
450 g/1 lb pork steak or boneless chops
100 g/4 oz apple sauce
1 clove garlic, crushed
150 ml/¼ pint white wine or apple juice
300 ml/½ pint stock
1 (415-g/14½-oz) can red kidney beans, drained
1 tablespoon soy sauce
chopped coriander or parsley to garnish

Using a very sharp knife, slice into the pork steaks to make a pocket. Mix the apple sauce and garlic together and fill the pork pockets. Make sure the stuffing is well pushed into the pork.

Place the pork in a shallow dish, add the white wine or apple juice and stock, cover, and cook for 10–12 minutes on Full power. Add the beans and soy sauce and cook for a further 2 minutes. Serve hot garnished with coriander or parsley.

126 | Ham in Cider

Preparation time
10 minutes

Cooking time
13–15 minutes

Setting
Full power

Serves 4

Calories
335 per portion

You will need
25 g/1 oz butter
225 g/8 oz baby onions
25 g/1 oz cornflour
300 ml/½ pint dry cider
150 ml/¼ pint stock
1 (454-g/16-oz) can cooked ham, diced
1 (397-g/14-oz) can tomatoes
1 (326-g/11-oz) can sweetcorn, drained
1 teaspoon dried mixed herbs
salt and pepper
chopped parsley to garnish

Melt the butter in a large bowl on Full power for 1 minute. Add the onions and cook for 3 minutes until soft.

Blend the cornflour with a little of the cider and add to the bowl with the rest of the cider and stock. Stir well and cook on Full power for 7 minutes until thickened. Stir in the ham, tomatoes, sweetcorn, herbs and salt and pepper to taste and cook for a further 2–4 minutes. Serve hot garnished with chopped parsley.

Cook's Tip

Select fairly thick chops for stuffing. When you cut into them use a small, sharp pointed knife and make sure you do not cut through completely.

Cook's Tip

When they are in season, prepare and freeze a large batch of pickling onions for use in casseroles and stews. Wrap them in a heavy bag and secure the end with a metal tie. They are then ready to use as and when you need them, **without any fuss over peeling them.**

127 | Bacon with Pineapple

Preparation time
10 minutes, plus 1 hour to marinate

Cooking time
20–25 minutes

Setting
Full power

Serves 6

Calories
380 per portion

You will need
1-1.5 kg/2–3 lb rindless bacon joint
cloves
2 (439-g/15½-oz) cans pineapple rings, drained with the syrup reserved
2 tablespoons soft light brown sugar
1 teaspoon French mustard
¼ teaspoon ground ginger
maraschino cherries

Score the fat surface of the bacon diagonally, to make a trellis pattern, and stud with cloves.

Place the bacon in a roasting bag. Combine the pineapple syrup, sugar, mustard and ginger and pour into the bag. Leave to marinate for 1 hour.

Place the bacon in the bag in a dish and loosely fold over the top of the bag.

Cook on Full power for 20–25 minutes, or until tender. Place the bacon on a heated serving plate, pour over the juices and serve surrounded by the pineapple rings and cherries.

Cook's Tip

Serve with potatoes cooked in their jackets and sliced green beans or Cauliflower Cheese.
Instead of pineapple, try substituting canned peach or apricot halves for a change.

128 | Gammon with Peaches

Preparation time
5 minutes

Cooking time
22 minutes, plus
10–15 minutes standing time

Setting
Full power, Low

Serves 6

Calories
335 per portion

You will need
1 kg/2¼ lb unsmoked gammon joint
1 (395-g/14-oz) can peach halves in natural juice
2 tablespoons clear honey
lettuce or watercress to garnish

Place gammon in a roasting bag, tie open end with string and pierce bag three times. Place on a microwave roasting rack (or upturned saucer) in a glass dish. Cook for 10 minutes on Full power, turning meat over after 5 minutes. Cook on Low for 10 minutes or until internal temperature reaches 70 C/160 F on a microwave thermometer. Cover with a 'tent' of foil (shiny side inwards) and stand for 10–15 minutes. Drain peaches and place halves around the edge of the serving dish. Cook on Full power for 1 minute. Put honey in a small dish and cook for 1 minute. Place bacon on serving dish and brush both meat and peaches with the honey. Garnish with lettuce or watercress.

Cook's Tip

Using a microwave rack or upturned saucer for cooking joints of meat prevents the food from sitting in the fat as it cooks and promotes a lighter, less greasy result.

129 | Special Stir Fry

Preparation time
15 minutes

Cooking time
8–10 minutes

Setting
Full power

Serves 4

Calories
215 per portion

You will need
2 tablespoons sunflower oil
knob of butter
2.5-cm/1-in piece fresh root
  ginger, grated
225 g/8 oz lean pork or beef,
  trimmed of fat and sliced into
  thin strips
1 tablespoon soy sauce
225 g/8 oz sliced vegetables (see
  Cook's Tip)

Place the oil and butter in a large shallow dish. Add the ginger and meat and toss until thoroughly mixed. Cook on Full power for 4–5 minutes. Add the soy sauce and mix well. Stir in the prepared vegetables, then cook for 4–5 minutes, stirring every minute. Serve immediately.

130 | Stuffed Cabbage Leaves

Preparation time
15 minutes

Cooking time
21–24 minutes, plus
3–4 minutes
conventional cooking

Setting
Full power

Serves 4

Calories
350 per portion

You will need
8 large cabbage leaves
1 medium onion, chopped
1 tablespoon oil
225 g/8 oz minced beef
50 g/2 oz mushrooms, sliced
1 teaspoon dried mixed herbs
1 tablespoon concentrated tomato
  purée
½ teaspoon salt
black pepper
75 g/3 oz All-bran cereal
1 tablespoon milk

For the sauce
25 g/1 oz margarine
25 g/1 oz plain flour
300 ml/½ pint milk
2 tablespoons tomato ketchup
50 g/2 oz mushrooms, sliced

Cook the cabbage leaves in a large pan of boiling water for 3–4 minutes. Drain. Whisk together the margarine, flour, milk and ketchup in a jug and cook on Full power for 5–6 minutes. Cook onion and oil in a bowl for 3 minutes. Add meat and cook for 4 minutes. Stir in the mushrooms, herbs, purée, seasoning, cereal and milk and cook for 6–8 minutes, stirring once. Stir in 2 tablespoons of the sauce. Place the meat mixture in the centre of the cabbage leaves and fold sides in, then roll up. Place in a round dish. Add the mushrooms to the remaining sauce and pour on top. Cook for 3 minutes.

Cook's Tip

Careful preparation is the key to a successful stir fry. Suitable vegetables include cauliflower, carrots, red and green pepper, spring onions, baby corn and bean sprouts. All the vegetables should be cut to more or less the same size and meat should be sliced as thinly as possible. This is easier to achieve if the meat is sliced while semi-frozen.

Cook's Tip

The trick to remember when stuffing any type of leaves is to avoid adding too much filling. Make sure that when you fill the leaves there is enough green to enclose the meat.

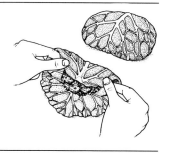

131 | Devilled Liver with Yogurt Dressing

Preparation time
15 minutes

Cooking time
11–12 minutes

Setting
Full power

Serves 4

Calories
235 per portion

You will need
25 g/1 oz flour
1 teaspoon cumin seeds
½ teaspoon turmeric
½ teaspoon cayenne
salt and pepper
225 g/8 oz lamb's liver
50 g/2 oz onion, sliced
1 clove garlic, crushed
50 g/2 oz butter
grated rind and juice of 1 lemon
1 tablespoon chopped parsley
3 tablespoons natural yogurt

For the garnish
lemon wedge
natural yogurt
grated lemon rind

Mix the flour, spices and seasoning. Cut the liver into small pieces and coat in the flour. Cook the onion, garlic and butter in a dish on Full power for 3 minutes. Add the liver and lemon rind and cook covered, for 7–8 minutes, stirring once. Stir in the remaining ingredients, heat for 1 minute. Garnish with lemon wedge, natural yogurt and grated lemon rind. Serve with rice.

132 | Cottage Pie

Preparation time
30 minutes

Cooking time
38–40 minutes plus grilling time

Setting
Full power

Serves 4

Calories
545 per portion

You will need
1 kg/2 lb potatoes, cut in chunks
4 tablespoons water
knob of butter
3 tablespoons milk
salt and pepper
1 large onion, chopped
1 tablespoon oil
450 g/1 lb minced beef
1 tablespoon concentrated tomato purée
300 ml/½ pint boiling beef stock
100 g/4 oz mushrooms, chopped

Place the potatoes in a large bowl with the water and cook on Full power for 20 minutes, stirring once. Drain the potatoes and mash with the butter, milk and seasoning.

Place the onion and oil in a casserole dish and cook for 3 minutes. Stir in the remaining ingredients and cook, covered, on Full power for 12–15 minutes, stirring once. Top the mince with the potatoes, heat on Full power for 3 minutes, then brown under the grill.

Cook's Tip

Liver cooks well in the microwave but be careful not to overcook or the liver could become hard and grainy.

Cook's Tip

Use a hand-held electric mixer to mash the potato and achieve a light fluffy texture without lumps.

133 | Liver and Bacon Savoury

Preparation time
5 minutes, plus 1
hour soaking time

Cooking time
18 minutes, plus 4–5
minutes standing
time

Setting
Full power, Low

Serves 6

Calories
275 per portion

You will need
450 g/1 lb liver, sliced and soaked
in milk for 1 hour
1 large onion, chopped
25 g/1 oz margarine
salt and pepper
1 (397-g/14-oz) can tomatoes
2 tablespoons concentrated
tomato purée
6 rashers rindless bacon, halved
and rolled

Drain the liver. Place the onion and margarine in a large, round glass casserole. Cover and cook on Full power for 3 minutes. Add the liver, salt and pepper, tomatoes and their juices, and tomato purée and place the bacon rolls on top. Cover and cook on Low for about 15 minutes or until the liver is cooked. Stand, covered for 4–5 minutes.

134 | Kidney and Mushroom Pudding

Preparation time
10 minutes

Cooking time
12 minutes,
plus 5 minutes
standing time

Setting
Medium

Serves 4

Calories
405 per portion

You will need
350 g/12 oz lambs' kidneys, cored
and cut into small pieces
1 tablespoon flour seasoned with
salt and pepper
1 (213-g/7½-oz) can mushrooms,
reserving brine

For the suet pastry
175 g/6 oz plain flour
75 g/3 oz shredded suet
salt and pepper
1 teaspoon baking powder
4–5 tablespoons cold water

Mix together the flour, suet, salt and pepper and baking powder. Add enough water to make a soft dough. Roll out on a lightly floured surface, reserving about a third for the lid, and line a 750-ml/1¼-pint pudding basin. Toss the kidneys in the seasoned flour. Mix with the mushrooms and pile into basin. Pour in sufficient mushroom brine to come just three quarters of the way up the dough. Roll out remaining dough to make the lid and dampen edges to seal. Place inside a roasting bag, allowing room for the pastry to rise, and secure end with an elastic band. Cook on Medium for 12 minutes, turning once. Stand for 5 minutes.

Cook's Tip

**Soaking the liver in milk gives
it a mild flavour. This
procedure may not be
necessary if you use good-
quality lamb's liver.**

Cook's Tip

**The simplest way to remove
the cores from kidneys is to
cut the kidneys in half, then
snip out the cores with a pair
of kitchen scissors.**

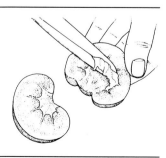

135 | Kidneys Milanese

Preparation time
20 minutes

Cooking time

Setting
Full power

Serves 4

Calories
410 per portion

You will need
1 onion, chopped
1 tablespoon oil
1 clove garlic, crushed
225 g/8 oz rindless streaky bacon, diced
450 g/1 lb lambs' kidneys, cored and diced
1 tablespoon flour
salt and pepper
1 (397-g/14-oz) can chopped tomatoes
150 ml/¼ pint red wine
½ teaspoon marjoram
chopped parsley to garnish

Place the onion, oil and garlic in a large casserole dish and cook on Full power for 3 minutes. Add the bacon and kidneys and cover the dish. Cook on Full power for 3 minutes, then stir in the flour, seasoning, tomatoes, wine and marjoram. Cover and continue to cook for a further 10–12 minutes, stirring once, until the kidneys are all cooked. Serve with pasta and sprinkle with chopped parsley.

136 | Kidney Ragoût

Preparation time
15 minutes

Cooking time
17½ minutes

Setting
Full power

Serves 4

Calories
245 per portion

You will need
1 medium onion, chopped
½ red pepper, cored, deseeded and diced
1 courgette, sliced
1 teaspoon chopped fresh rosemary
1 clove garlic, crushed
25 g/1 oz butter
25 g/1 oz cornflour
150 ml/¼ pint red wine
175 ml/6 fl oz hot beef stock
12 lambs' kidneys, cored and halved
50 g/2 oz button mushrooms, wiped and sliced
1 tablespoon concentrated tomato purée
salt and pepper
fresh rosemary to garnish

Place the onion, red pepper, courgette, rosemary, garlic and butter in a large bowl. Cover and cook on Full power for 5½ minutes, stirring once.

Stir in the cornflour and gradually add the wine, stock, kidneys, mushrooms, tomato purée and salt and pepper to taste. Replace the cover and cook for 12 minutes, stirring at 4 minute intervals and removing the cover after 10 minutes.

Spoon into a warm serving dish and garnish with fresh rosemary.

Cook's Tip

For a delicious starter or light supper dish, pile the kidney mixture on hot toast and garnish with chopped parsley.

Cook's Tip

If fresh rosemary is not available, use ½ teaspoon dried rosemary in the ragoût and garnish with fresh parsley.

Vegetables

Many vegetables, particularly the moister ones like leeks, courgettes and marrows cook better in a microwave oven than they do by conventional methods. The quick cooking in little additional water ensures that fresh and frozen vegetables retain their colour and texture. But don't salt the vegetables before cooking as this tends to draw out the moisture. Some salad recipes using cooked vegetables are included in this chapter as vegetables cooked in a microwave have a really superb flavour.

137 | Three Bean Salad

(Illustrated on half-title page)

Preparation time
5 minutes

Cooking time
8½–10 minutes

Setting
Full power

Serves 3–4

Calories
200–150 per portion

You will need
3 rashers rindless streaky bacon
100 g/4 oz frozen whole green beans
100 g/4 oz frozen broad beans
2 tablespoons water
175 g/6 oz canned kidney beans
25 g/1 oz flaked almonds, browned

For the dressing
1 tablespoon clear honey
grated rind and juice of ½ orange
½ teaspoon tarragon
salt and pepper

Place bacon on absorbent kitchen paper and cook on Full power for 3½–4 minutes or until crisp. Cut into small pieces. Place the green and broad beans in a dish with the water. Cover and cook for 5–6 minutes, stirring once. Stand for 2–3 minutes. Stir in the kidney beans.

To make the dressing, mix together the honey, orange rind and juice, tarragon and seasoning. Pour the dressing over the warm vegetables and toss lightly. Chill. Just before serving mix in the bacon and almonds.

138 | Ham Jackets

Preparation time
5–10 minutes

Cooking time
20 minutes

Setting
Full power

Serves 4

Calories
400 per portion

You will need
4 (225-g/8-oz) potatoes, scrubbed
75 g/3 oz butter
1 clove garlic, crushed
225 g/8 oz lean cooked ham, diced
1 teaspoon dried mixed herbs
salt and pepper
chopped parsley to garnish

Place the potatoes on absorbent kitchen paper on the turntable and cook on Full power for 19 minutes, turning once.

Cut each potato in half lengthways and scoop out the flesh into a bowl. Add the remaining ingredients to the potato. Blend until smooth and pile back into the shells.

Return the eight halves to the microwave and reheat for 1 minute. Serve hot, garnished with the parsley.

Cook's Tip

Honey crystallised in a wide-necked jar? Clarify it by placing the open jar in the microwave oven and warm on Full power for 1–2 minutes. Stir.

Cook's Tip

To crush garlic, without a crusher, place a peeled clove on a chopping board and sprinkle with a little salt. Then crush with the flat, wide blade of a knife, pressing hard with the palm of your hand.

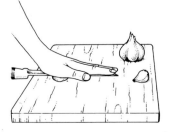

139 | Rosemary Bake

Preparation time
15 minutes

Cooking time
9 minutes

Setting
Full power

Serves 4

Calories
335 per portion

You will need
575 g/1¼ lb potatoes, thinly sliced
1 onion, thinly sliced
100 g/4 oz Cheddar cheese, grated
½ teaspoon freshly grated nutmeg
1 teaspoon rosemary
150 ml/¼ pint milk
40 g/1½ oz butter
salt and pepper

In a large casserole dish, layer the sliced potatoes, alternating with the onion, cheese, nutmeg and rosemary. Pour on the milk and dot with butter. Season well.

Cover and cook on Full power for 9 minutes and then leave to stand for a further 2–3 minutes. Serve hot.

140 | Cheese and Corn Potato Cake

Preparation time
20 minutes

Cooking time
21–22 minutes, plus
3 minutes to grill

Setting
Full power

Serves 4

Calories
350 per portion

You will need
450 g/1 lb potatoes, cubed
3 tablespoons water
25 g/1 oz butter
100 g/4 oz lean unsmoked back
   bacon, chopped
1 (326-g/11.5-oz) can sweetcorn
   kernels, drained
225 g/8 oz cottage cheese
1 tablespoon chopped parsley
salt and black pepper
parsley sprigs to garnish

Put the potatoes in a dish with the water, cover and cook on Full power for about 12 minutes, until tender. Drain off the water, then mash the potatoes with the butter. Place the bacon in a basin and cook, uncovered, on Full power for 2–3 minutes. Reserve some bacon for a garnish.

Stir the sweetcorn, cheese, bacon and parsley into the mashed potato. Season. Spoon into a casserole and cook on Full power for 7 minutes. Press down well, then brown under a hot grill for 3 minutes. Garnish with the reserved bacon and parsley. Serve with a green salad.

Cook's Tip

A nutmeg grater – a tiny version of a cheese grater, often with a compartment to store whole nutmegs – is one of the most useful pieces of kitchen equipment.

Cook's Tip

Ham may be used instead of back bacon, if preferred. Alternatively, try thinly sliced spiced sausage or frankfurter. Or omit the meat altogether and serve with salami cornets.

141 | Potato and Egg Mayonnaise

Preparation time
20 minutes

Cooking time
10–12 minutes

Setting
Full power

Serves 4

Calories
325 per portion

You will need
450 g / 1 lb waxy (salad) potatoes
2 tablespoons water
2 tablespoons French Dressing (see below)
4 spring onions, sliced
4 hard-boiled eggs, chopped
2 dill pickles, chopped
3 tablespoons mayonnaise
3 tablespoons natural yogurt
1 tablespoon chopped fennel to garnish

Cook the potatoes in their skins with the water in a roasting bag on Full power for 10–12 minutes, until tender. Drain, chop roughly and place in a bowl. Pour over the dressing while still warm, toss thoroughly and leave to cool. Add the spring onions, eggs and dill pickles.

Mix together the mayonnaise, yogurt and 2 tablespoons juice from the dill pickles until smooth. Pour over the salad and mix thoroughly. Transfer to a shallow dish and sprinkle with fennel to serve.

142 | Cauliflower in Stilton Sauce

Preparation time
5 minutes

Cooking time
16 minutes

Setting
Full power

Serves 4

Calories
285 per portion

You will need
450 g / 1 lb frozen cauliflower florets
6 tablespoons water
175 g / 6 oz Stilton cheese
250 ml / 8 fl oz milk
pinch of freshly grated nutmeg
1 tablespoon cornflour
1 tablespoon chopped chives
25 g / 1 oz potato crisps, crushed (see Cook's Tip)
tomato wedges to garnish

Place the cauliflower in a bowl, add the water, cover and cook on Full power for 8 minutes. Drain and transfer the florets to a shallow dish. Set aside.

Crumble the Stilton into a second bowl. Set 2 tablespoons of the milk aside in a cup. Add the remaining milk to the crumbled Stilton with the nutmeg. Stir well and cook for 4 minutes.

Mix the cornflour with the milk in the cup. Stir until smooth, then add to the Stilton mixture. Cook for 2 minutes until the sauce thickens. Add the chives and stir thoroughly.

Pour the sauce over the cauliflower and cook for 2 minutes to heat through. Top with the crushed crisps and garnish with tomato. Serve at once.

Cook's Tip

Swedish Potato Salad: Omit the hard-boiled eggs. Substitute with 100 g / 4 oz chopped cooked beetroot. To make the French dressing, place 3 tablespoons oil, 1 tablespoon white wine vinegar, ½–¾ teaspoon prepared mustard and salt and pepper to taste in a screwtop jar and shake well to combine.

Cook's Tip

Crushed crisps make an interesting topping for foods cooked in the microwave oven, adding texture as well as an attractive finish. Crushed peanuts may also be used. Add these toppings after cooking.

143 | Herby Potato Salad

Preparation time
15 minutes

Cooking time
8–9 minutes

Setting
Full power

Serves 4

Calories
200 per portion

You will need
450 g / 1 lb potatoes, diced
1 tablespoon water
1–2 teaspoons finely chopped
    fresh mint
3 tablespoons French dressing
1 tablespoon mayonnaise
1 tablespoon chopped chives
1 tablespoon finely chopped
    parsley
salt and pepper
sprig of mint to garnish

Place the diced potatoes in the water, in a medium-sized casserole. Cover and cook on Full power for 8–9 minutes until cooked.

Drain, and while still hot, add the mint and French dressing. Mix well. Allow to cool slightly, then add the mayonnaise, herbs and seasoning. Blend together thoroughly and serve garnished with a sprig of mint.

144 | Cauliflower à la Grecque

Preparation time
5 minutes

Cooking time
20–22 minutes

Setting
Full power

Serves 6

Calories
185 per portion

You will need
1 cauliflower, broken into florets

For the marinade
4 tablespoons concentrated
    tomato purée
4 tablespoons olive oil
120 ml / 4 fl oz dry white wine
1 medium onion, chopped
1 clove garlic, crushed
1-cm/½-inch piece fresh root
    ginger, grated
300 ml / ½ pint water
1 teaspoon sugar
salt and white pepper

Combine all the ingredients for the marinade in a large bowl. Stir thoroughly, cover and cook on Full power for 8 minutes.

Stir in the cauliflower and cook for 12–14 minutes more, until tender. Allow the mixture to cool, then chill overnight in the refrigerator. Serve with warmed pitta bread, if liked.

Cook's Tip

For the dressing, mix 1 tablespoon wine vinegar, 2 tablespoons oil, 1 teaspoon French mustard and a pinch of sugar in a screw-topped jar. Add salt and pepper to taste, replace lid and shake well before use.

Cook's Tip

To warm 6 pitta breads in the microwave oven, place on several sheets of absorbent kitchen paper and cook on Full power for 2 minutes, turning the pittas over halfway through cooking.

145 | Broad Beans with Ham and Cream

Preparation time
5 minutes

Cooking time
11–12 minutes

Setting
Full power

Serves 4

Calories
175 per portion

You will need
450 g / 1 lb frozen broad beans
3 tablespoons water
6 tablespoons single cream
50 g / 2 oz soft white breadcrumbs
100 g / 4 oz ham, chopped
salt and pepper

Place the beans in a bowl with the water. Cover and cook on Full power for 9–10 minutes. Drain.

Stir in the cream, breadcrumbs and chopped ham. Add salt and pepper to taste. Cook for 2 minutes more. Stir gently and serve at once with pasta shapes or rice.

146 | Harvest Marrow

Preparation time
15–20 minutes

Cooking time
30 minutes

Setting
Full power

Serves 4

Calories
235 per portion

You will need
4 (3.5-cm/1½-inch) thick slices marrow (about 675-g/1½-lb)
2 tablespoons water
1 large onion, chopped
25 g / 1 oz butter
175 g / 6 oz lean minced beef
salt and pepper
25 g / 1 oz Nutri-grain rye and oats with hazelnuts
2 tomatoes, chopped
1 stick celery, finely chopped
1 teaspoon chopped parsley

For the sauce
2 carrots, grated
1 medium onion, finely chopped
1 clove garlic, crushed
1 teaspoon basil
150 ml / ¼ pint beef or vegetable stock

Peel and core the marrow rings. Place in a shallow dish, add the water, cover and cook on Full power for 7–8 minutes. Cook the onion and the butter for 3 minutes. Add the beef, seasoning and cook for 3 minutes. Mix in the remaining ingredients, fill the marrow rings and arrange in a large shallow dish. Mix all the sauce ingredients in a large bowl and cook for 12 minutes, stirring every 4 minutes. Pour over marrow. Cover and cook for 5 minutes.

Cook's Tip

For topping a jacket potato, a single serving of this recipe makes an excellent luncheon dish. To serve one, use 100 g / 4 oz frozen broad beans, 2 tablespoons single cream, 2 tablespoons breadcrumbs and 50 g / 2 oz chopped ham. Cook the broad beans with 1 tablespoon water for 4 minutes, drain and add remaining ingredients. Cook for 1 minute more.

Cook's Tip

A whole marrow may be cooked remarkably easily in the microwave oven, provided it fits! Allow about 10 minutes for a stuffed 2 kg / 4½ lb marrow, cooking it in a roasting bag on Full power.

147 | Mangetout in Garlic Butter

Preparation time
15 minutes

Cooking time
10 minutes

Setting
Full power

Serves 4

Calories
125 per portion

You will need
675 g/1½ lb mangetout, topped and tailed
4 tablespoons water
25 g/1 oz butter
1 clove garlic, chopped
1 tablespoon chopped parsley to garnish

Place the mangetout in an ovenproof bowl or roasting bag with the water. Cover and cook on Full power for 8 minutes while preparing the garlic butter.

Place the butter and garlic in a small bowl or glass jug. Cook for 2 minutes.

Drain the mangetout thoroughly and return to a warmed serving dish. Pour over the hot garlic butter and garnish with parsley before serving.

Cook's Tip

To save on washing up, the mangetout can be cooked in an ovenproof serving dish as can the majority of vegetables cooked in a microwave oven.

148 | Baked Jacket Potatoes with Herb Butter

Preparation time
2 minutes

Cooking time
1 large potato, 8 minutes; 2 large potatoes, 15 minutes; 4 large potatoes, 27 minutes

Setting
Full power

Serves 4

Calories
445 per portion

You will need
1–4 large (350-g/12-oz) potatoes, scrubbed
75 g/3 oz soft butter
1 tablespoon chopped parsley
1 teaspoon lemon juice

Prick the potatoes with a fork (otherwise they burst), place well apart on a plate and cook on Full power for 27 minutes, rearranging them once or twice.

Meanwhile, beat the butter and gradually stir in the parsley and lemon juice. Place mixture on greaseproof paper and roll up into a 'sausage' shape. Chill. Remove from paper and cut into slices. Cut a cross on top of the potatoes and fill the openings with slices of herb butter.

Cook's Tip

If preferred the butter may be flavoured with 3 cloves garlic, crushed. Or cut butter into small cubes and toss them in paprika or grated nutmeg. Alternatively, scoop out the middle of the potato and mash with butter, then replace in the potato shells. Top with cubes of chopped ham and pork or slices of smoked cheese.

149 | Marrow in Dill Butter

Preparation time
10 minutes

Cooking time
17 minutes

Setting
Full power

Serves 4

Calories
155 per portion

You will need
65 g/2½ oz butter
2 onions, finely chopped
1 kg/2 lb marrow, peeled, cored
  and cubed
sprig of dill, chopped
salt and freshly ground black
  pepper

Place the butter and onion in a large ovenproof bowl and cook on Full power for 5 minutes. Add the cubed marrow, stir well and cook for a further 12 minutes. Stir twice during the cooking time. Season with the dill, salt and pepper to taste before serving hot.

150 | Courgettes with Lime and Mushrooms

Preparation time
10 minutes

Cooking time
9 minutes

Setting
Full power

Serves 4

Calories
40 per portion

You will need
1 onion, thinly sliced
grated rind and juice of 1 small
  lime
450 g/1 lb courgettes, trimmed
  and sliced
100 g/4 oz button mushrooms,
  sliced
pinch of salt
freshly ground black pepper
pared lime rind to garnish (optional)

Place the onion in a large ovenproof bowl or casserole with the rind and juice of the lime. Cook on Full power for 3 minutes, stirring once. Stir in the courgettes and cover. Cook for 3 minutes, stirring halfway through the cooking time. Stir in the mushrooms, reserving a few slices for a garnish, if liked, and season with salt and pepper. Cover as before and cook for a further 3 minutes, stirring halfway through the cooking time. Garnish with mushroom slices and a few strips of lime rind, if liked.

Cook's Tip

Lemon butter makes a fresh-tasting variation whose sharp flavour complements the marrow. Omit the dill and add the finely grated rind and juice of half a lemon. Serve with lemon twists.

Cook's Tip

Give the courgette slices a pretty scalloped edge by marking the whole courgettes with a cannelle knife before slicing. Use the knife to make parallel grooves the length of each courgette.

151 | *Ratatouille*

Preparation time
15 minutes, plus 30
minutes to degorge
aubergine

Cooking time
12 minutes

Setting
Full power

Serves 2–4

Calories
210–105 per portion

You will need
1 medium aubergine
salt and pepper
2 large onions, sliced
1 teaspoon freshly minced garlic
1 tablespoon oil
1 red pepper, cored, deseeded and
    sliced
1 green pepper, cored, deseeded
    and sliced
1 (397-g/14-oz) can tomatoes
4 courgettes, sliced

Trim the ends off the aubergine, then cut into chunks. Place in a colander, sprinkle generously with salt and set aside for 30 minutes. Rinse thoroughly and dry on absorbent kitchen paper.

Place the onions, garlic and oil in a large bowl with the peppers and aubergine. Cover and cook on Full power for 8 minutes, stirring halfway through cooking (see Cook's Tip).

Add the tomatoes and courgettes, replace the cover and cook for 4 minutes more. Serve hot or cold.

152 | *Braised Red Cabbage with Apple Cheese Dressing*

Preparation time
30 minutes

Cooking time
13 minutes

Setting
Full power

Serves 4

Calories
135 per portion

You will need
450 g / 1 lb red cabbage, shredded
100 g / 4 oz cooking apples, peeled,
    cored and sliced
100 g / 4 oz onion, sliced
25 g / 1 oz brown sugar
2 tablespoons vinegar
4 tablespoons water or stock

For the dressing
1 cooking apple, peeled, cored and
    diced
50 g / 2 oz soft cheese
salt and black pepper

Place the cabbage, apple, onion, sugar, vinegar and water or stock in a large casserole. Cover and cook on Full power for 10 minutes, until the cabbage is nearly soft.

Place the apple in a basin, cover and cook on Full power for about 3 minutes, until tender. Press the apple through a sieve or purée in a liquidiser. Blend the soft cheese and the apple purée together and stir into the cabbage. Season well.

Cook's Tip

Take care when removing the cover to stir the vegetables as scalding steam will be present.

Cook's Tip

Shred the cabbage in a food processor or by hand: cut the head in half vertically, remove the core from both halves, then place each cabbage half in turn flat side down on a board and slice thinly into shreds.

153 | Spiced Vegetable Medley

Preparation time
10 minutes

Cooking time
10½–12½ minutes

Setting
Full power

Serves 4

Calories
115 per portion

You will need
25 g/1 oz butter
2 tomatoes, peeled (see Cook's Tip) and chopped
1 tablespoon curry powder
¼ teaspoon chilli sauce
¼ teaspoon freshly grated nutmeg
¼ teaspoon wholegrain mustard
salt and pepper
2 carrots, chopped
1 cauliflower, divided into small florets
1 small onion, finely chopped
2 courgettes, sliced
40 g/1½ oz raisins

Place the butter in a large bowl. Melt on Full power for 30–45 seconds. Stir in the tomatoes, curry powder, chilli sauce, nutmeg, mustard and salt and pepper. Mix well. Cover loosely and cook for 2 minutes.

Add the carrots, cauliflower, onion, courgettes and raisins and stir lightly to coat with the sauce. Transfer to a shallow 2-litre/3½-pint dish, cover and cook for 8–9 minutes, stirring halfway through cooking. Allow the dish to stand for 2–3 minutes before serving.

154 | Summer Stir

Preparation time
10 minutes, plus 1 hour to marinate gammon

Cooking time
14 minutes

Setting
Full power

Serves 4

Calories
260 per portion

You will need
1 tablespoon soy sauce
1 tablespoon Worcestershire sauce
1 tablespoon dark soft brown sugar
¼ teaspoon five-spice powder (optional)
225 g/8 oz cooked gammon, diced
6 tablespoons oil
225 g/8 oz cauliflower florets
225 g/8 oz green beans, topped, tailed and thinly sliced
1 red pepper, cored, deseeded and diced
50 g/2 oz bean sprouts
pinch of mixed herbs
2 potatoes, grated

Combine the soy sauce, Worcestershire sauce and sugar in a shallow dish, with the five-spice powder, if using. Mix well. Add the gammon, stir to coat the chunks thoroughly and set aside for 1 hour.

Place 2 tablespoons oil in a bowl with the cauliflower, beans and pepper. Toss well, cook on Full power for 8 minutes, stirring once. Stir in the bean sprouts, herbs and gammon, with its marinade. Cook for 3 minutes. Meanwhile, heat the remaining oil in a frying pan on the hob. Cook the potato shreds until golden, keeping separate with two forks. Mix with the microwaved vegetables and serve at once.

Cook's Tip

To peel tomatoes, place around the rim of a plate lined with absorbent kitchen paper. Heat on Full power for 10–15 seconds. Allow to stand for 5 minutes. Use a sharp knife to slit the skins, which should slip off easily.

Cook's Tip

If you want to serve this dish with a colourful garnish, slice and reserve 2–3 rings from the red pepper after deseeding, and sprinkle over a few fresh herb sprigs – parsley would be a good choice.

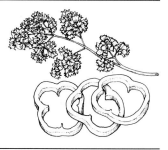

155 | *Creamed Savoy Cabbage*

Preparation time
10 minutes

Cooking time
14 minutes

Setting
Full power

Serves 4

Calories
170 per portion

You will need
1 kg/2 lb Savoy cabbage
1 onion, chopped
2 tablespoons oil
5 tablespoons hot stock
salt and freshly ground black
    pepper
pinch of freshly grated nutmeg
1 teaspoon caraway seeds
    (optional)
150 ml/¼ pint soured cream

Remove the thick stems and any damaged leaves from the cabbage and cut into wide strips. Place the cabbage in a sieve, rinse and drain thoroughly. Place the onion in a large ovenproof bowl with the oil and cook on Full power for 4 minutes. Add the cabbage, stock, salt and pepper to taste, nutmeg and caraway seeds, if using. Cover and cook for 10 minutes. Stir a couple of times during the cooking. Drain off any excess liquid.

Mix the soured cream with a little salt to taste. Stir into the cabbage mixture, mixing well. Serve immediately.

156 | *Brussels Sprouts au Gratin*

Preparation time
15 minutes

Cooking time
16 minutes, plus grilling
time

Setting
Full power

Serves 4

Calories
130 per portion

You will need
675 g/1½ lb Brussels sprouts
3 tablespoons water
25 g/1 oz butter
½ onion, chopped
100 g/4 oz cooked ham, cut into
    strips
salt
pinch of freshly grated nutmeg
3 tablespoons grated Parmesan
    cheese

Trim the sprouts and place in a roasting bag with the water and cook on Full power for 12 minutes. Place the butter and onion in a microwave-proof and heatproof serving dish and cook for 4 minutes. Add the ham and Brussels sprouts and season with salt and nutmeg. Mix together well, then sprinkle the Parmesan cheese over the top. Brown under a hot grill.

Cook's Tip

Creamed Savoy Cabbage is delicious served with roast pork or meat loaf.

Cook's Tip

When choosing Brussels sprouts for cooking in a microwave oven, try picking ones that are the same size. A mixture of large and small sprouts will cook unevenly. Avoid those that look yellowing or wilted.

157 | Pissaladière

Preparation time
15–20 minutes

Cooking time
25 minutes

Setting
Full power

Serves 4

Calories
430 per portion

You will need
175 g/6 oz self-raising flour
1 teaspoon baking powder
1 teaspoon dried thyme
75 g/3 oz margarine
6 tablespoons milk
1 (50-g/2-oz) can anchovy fillets,
    drained, halved lengthways
8 large black olives, halved and
    stoned

For the topping
2 tablespoons oil
2 onions, sliced
1 clove garlic, crushed
1 (397-g/14-oz) can tomatoes
1 bay leaf
salt and pepper

Make the topping by combining the oil, onions and garlic in a large jug. Cook on Full power for 6 minutes, then stir in the tomatoes and bay leaf. Add seasoning to taste and cook for 12 minutes, stirring every 3 minutes. Remove the bay leaf and set the topping aside.

Combine the flour, baking powder and thyme in a bowl. Rub in the margarine and mix to a dough with the milk. Lightly grease an oblong dish, about 25 × 18-cm/ 10 × 7-inch, or use a round pie plate and pat out the dough to fit. Cook on Full power for 2 minutes.

Spread the dough with the topping. Arrange the anchovies in a lattice design over the topping, placing a half olive in each square. Cook on Full power for 5 minutes, then allow to stand for 3 minutes.

Cook's Tip

Use 2 tablespoons of the oil from the can of anchovies when making the topping for a more robust flavour. Taste before seasoning as additional salt may not be required.

158 | Continental Stuffed Aubergines

Preparation time
10 minutes, plus 30
minutes to degorge
aubergines

Cooking time
15 minutes, plus 2
minutes to grill

Setting
Full power

Serves 4

Calories
165 per portion

You will need
2 (350-g/12-oz) aubergines
salt and pepper
1 (283-g/10-oz) pack frozen
    Continental stir-fry vegetables
100 g/4 oz cooked chicken, diced
150 ml/¼ pint soured cream
watercress to garnish

Halve the aubergines and scoop out the centres. Sprinkle the flesh generously with salt. Set aside for 30 minutes. Trim the shells neatly, place them in a roasting bag and secure loosely. Cook on Full power for 5 minutes. Set aside.

Cook the vegetables in a dish for 5 minutes, stirring once. Stir in the chicken and mix well. Add the rinsed and dried aubergine to the vegetable mixture. Season to taste, cover and cook for 5 minutes.

Fill the shells with the vegetable mixture. Top with soured cream and warm under a hot grill for 2 minutes. Serve immediately garnished with watercress.

Cook's Tip

If you do not have any commercially soured cream, use single cream to which 1 tablespoon lemon juice has been added. Stir and set aside for at least 15 minutes.

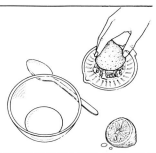

159 | *Stuffed Onions*

Preparation time
30 minutes

Cooking time
*12–15 minutes, plus
3–4 minutes to grill*

Setting
Full power

Serves 4

Calories
275 per portion

You will need
*4 large onions
2 tablespoons water
100 g/4 oz mushrooms, finely
  chopped
50 g/2 oz fresh breadcrumbs
1 teaspoon rubbed sage
50 g/2 oz sunflower seeds, ground
salt and pepper
2 tablespoons chopped parsley
100 g/4 oz cheese, grated
watercress to garnish*

Stand the onions as far apart as possible in a shallow dish, add the water and cover. Cook on Full power for 9–10 minutes, or until the onions are tender. Leave until cool enough to handle, then scoop out the middle of the onions, leaving an outer shell about two layers thick. Chop the scooped out onion and mix with all the remaining ingredients apart from the cheese. Use a teaspoon to stuff the mixture into the onion shells, place them in the dish and cook for 3–5 minutes. Sprinkle with the grated cheese and brown lightly under a hot grill for 3–4 minutes before serving garnished with watercress.

160 | *Savoury Stuffed Mushrooms*

Preparation time
15–20 minutes

Cooking time
$4\frac{1}{2}$–$6\frac{1}{2}$ minutes

Setting
Full power, Medium

Serves 6

Calories
200 per portion

You will need
*12 large flat mushrooms, wiped
parsley sprigs to garnish*

For the stuffing
*75 g/3 oz butter
100 g/4 oz button mushrooms,
  wiped and very finely chopped
75 g/3 oz brown breadcrumbs
2 tablespoons chopped parsley
$\frac{1}{4}$ teaspoon dried rosemary
1 clove garlic, crushed
100 g/4 oz ham, very finely
  chopped
50 g/2 oz Cheddar cheese, grated
1 egg, beaten
salt and pepper*

Make the stuffing: place the butter in a bowl and melt on Full power for 30–45 seconds. Stir in the remaining stuffing ingredients.

Arrange the mushrooms, cups uppermost around the rim of two plates. Fill the cups with the stuffing mixture piling it up in the centre. Cover and cook each plate on Medium for 4–6 minutes. Garnish with parsley sprigs to serve.

Cook's Tip

Use a grapefruit spoon to scoop out the middle of the onion. These elongated teaspoons have a serrated side to ease the removal of grapefruit segments.

Cook's Tip

For an equally tasty but creamier fiilling, reduce the quantity of ham to 50 g/2 oz, and add 50 g/2 oz cream cheese to the basic stuffing mixture. Add only enough of the egg to bind the stuffing – it should be stiff enough to hold **its shape. Fill the mushrooms and proceed as in the recipe.**

161 | Special Stuffed Peppers

Preparation time
10 minutes

Cooking time
10 minutes

Setting
Full power

Serves 4

Calories
290 per portion

You will need
4 even-sized green, red or yellow
    peppers
225 g/8 oz cooked long-grain rice
1 (185-g/6½-oz) can prawns in
    brine, drained
1 (285-g/10-oz) can pear quarters in
    fruit juice
salt and pepper

Cut the stalk ends off the peppers to form lids, if liked. Scoop out the cores and seeds, keeping the pepper shells whole (see Cook's Tip).

Combine the rice and prawns in a bowl. Drain the pears, reserving the juice. Chop the fruit roughly and add to the bowl with enough pear juice to moisten. Season to taste.

Spoon the rice filling into the prepared peppers. Stand them in a straight-sided dish just large enough to hold them firmly without cramping. Replace the reserved pepper lids, if using, cover and cook on Full power for 10 minutes. Allow to stand for 2 minutes before serving.

Cook's Tip

Be very careful when coring and deseeding the peppers to avoid piercing the flesh of the shells. If the knife does slip, pare a little flesh from the inside of one of the lids to stop the gap.

162 | Smoked Chicory Au Gratin

Preparation time
15 minutes

Cooking time
14–16 minutes

Setting
Full power

Serves 4

Calories
350 per portion

You will need
8 heads chicory
4 tablespoons boiling water
few drops of lemon juice
8 slices smoked ham
50 g/2 oz butter
25 g/1 oz plain flour
450 ml/¾ pint milk
salt and pepper
pinch of paprika
few sprigs of fresh thyme,
    chopped
100 g/4 oz cheese, grated
2 tablespoons browned
    breadcrumbs
parsley sprig to garnish

Put the chicory in a bowl with the boiling water and lemon juice. Cover and cook on Full power for 2 minutes. Drain. Cool and wrap each piece of chicory in a slice of ham. Lay the chicory side by side in a greased shallow dish.

Melt the butter in a bowl for 40–60 seconds, then stir in the flour. When smooth, gradually whisk in the milk, then cook for 3–5 minutes until the sauce boils and thickens. Stir in the seasoning, paprika, thyme and cheese. Pour the sauce over the chicory and sprinkle with breadcrumbs. Cook for 8 minutes on Full power. Serve hot, garnished with parsley.

Cook's Tip

Chicory needs little preparation. Simply trim off the end, rinse under cold running water, then shake off excess moisture.

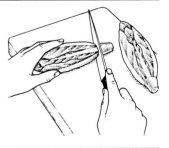

163 | *Colourful Beetroot Salad*

Preparation time
15–20 minutes

Cooking time
13 minutes, plus 5 minutes standing time

Setting
Full power

Serves 4

Calories
195 per portion

You will need
575–675 g/1¼–1½ lb beetroot
1 bulb fennel, cut into julienne strips
1 apple, cored and chopped
1 small bunch spring onions, chopped
1 (150-g/5.2-oz) carton natural yogurt
4 tablespoons double cream
1 teaspoon creamed horseradish
pinch of sugar
1 tablespoon chopped hazelnuts
salt and freshly ground pepper
1–2 hard-boiled eggs
fennel sprigs to garnish (optional)

Scrub the beetroot under running water. Place the beetroot in a large ovenproof bowl and cover. Cook on Full power for 8 minutes, then turn the beetroots over and cook for a further 5 minutes. Allow to stand for 5 minutes before rubbing the skins off or peeling. Slice the beetroot thinly and place in a large serving bowl. Add the fennel, apple and onion and toss well to mix.

To make the dressing, beat the yogurt with the cream, horseradish, sugar and hazelnuts. Season to taste with salt and pepper. Pour over the beetroot salad and toss well to mix. Cut the hard-boiled egg into quarters and arrange on top of the salad. Garnish with fennel sprigs, if liked.

Cook's Tip

This unusual and tasty salad makes a delicious accompaniment to cold ham or roast beef.

164 | *Vegetable Tongue Aspic*

Preparation time
20 minutes

Cooking time
7–9 minutes

Setting
Full power

Serves 4–6

Calories
205–135 per portion

You will need
350 g/12 oz frozen mixed vegetables or a selection of summer vegetables
2 tablespoons water
1 (15-g/½-oz) packet beef or chicken aspic powder
450 ml/¾ pint water
1 hard-boiled egg, thinly sliced
350 g/12 oz cooked tongue, sliced
watercress to garnish

Place the vegetables with the water in a dish, cover and cook on Full power for 6–8 minutes, stirring once. Stand for 2–3 minutes. Drain and cool. Place the aspic powder in a basin with 150 ml/¼ pint of the water. Heat for 1 minute. Stir well until dissolved. Stir in the remaining water and leave until syrupy. Pour a little into an 18-cm/7-inch soufflé dish. Chill until set. Arrange the sliced egg on the jelly. Pour in just enough aspic to cover the slices. Set again. Arrange half the tongue in the dish, cover with aspic. Set again. Top with half the vegetables, set in aspic. Repeat tongue and aspic layer, and vegetable and aspic layer. Chill until firm. Turn out aspic and cut into wedges to serve garnished with watercress.

Cook's Tip

Never attempt to hard-boil eggs in the microwave oven. Pressure inside the shells will cause them to explode.

Vegetarian Dishes

More and more people are finding that they feel healthier if they eat vegetarian dishes once or twice a week, but it is important to ensure that their diet includes plenty of protein on these meatless days. The recipes in this chapter are for delicious and nutritious meals and snacks using pulses, pasta, cheese and eggs.

165 | Leek and Bean Gratin

(Illustrated on front jacket)

Preparation time
10 minutes

Cooking time
9 minutes, plus 1 minute grilling time

Setting
Full power

Serves 4

Calories
305 per portion

You will need
675 g/1½ lb leeks, washed, trimmed and sliced
150 ml/¼ pint dry white wine
1 (425-g/15-oz) can red kidney beans, drained
150 ml/¼ pint vegetable stock
3 teaspoons cornflour
3 tablespoons double cream
salt and freshly ground black pepper
50 g/2 oz wholemeal breadcrumbs
50 g/2 oz Gruyère cheese, grated

Place the leeks and wine in a roasting bag and seal loosely with an elastic band. Cook on Full power for 6 minutes.

Strain the leeks, reserving the cooking liquid, and place in an ovenproof serving dish with the kidney beans. Pour the cooking liquid into a 300-ml/½-pint glass measuring jug, together with the stock. Blend the cornflour with the cream and stir this mixture into the stock, together with the seasoning.

Cook on Full power for 3 minutes, stirring twice during cooking. Pour this sauce over the leeks. Top with breadcrumbs and Gruyère cheese and brown under a conventional grill for 1 minute. Serve at once.

166 | Chick Peas in Soy Sauce

Preparation time
10 minutes

Cooking time
9 minutes

Setting
Full power

Serves 4

Calories
240 per portion

You will need
2 tablespoons oil
50 g/2 oz onions, chopped
2 cloves garlic, crushed
2 (415-g/14-oz) cans chick peas, drained
2 tablespoons soy sauce
4 chopped spring onions to garnish

Place the oil in a medium bowl, add the onions and garlic and cook on Full power for 3 minutes until soft. Add the chick peas and cook for another 4 minutes. Add the soy sauce and cook for another 2 minutes or until all the liquid is absorbed.

Stir in the spring onions and serve with pitta bread or rice and a good mixed salad.

Cook's Tip

Other vegetables, such as broccoli or courgettes, can be used instead of leeks in this dish.

Cook's Tip

These chick peas make a good filling for baked potatoes, topped with a spoonful of soured cream, fromage frais or mayonnaise.

167 | Whole Wheat Salad

Preparation time
15–20 minutes

Cooking time
50 minutes, plus 10 minutes standing time

Setting
Full power

Serves 4

Calories
320 per portion

You will need
50 g/2 oz dried apricots, chopped
50 g/2 oz sultanas or raisins
2 tablespoons lemon juice
2 tablespoons orange juice
175 g/6 oz whole wheat
900 ml/1½ pints hot water
pinch of salt
4 tablespoons grapeseed or sunflower oil
freshly ground black pepper
3 spring onions, finely chopped
3 small tomatoes, cut into wedges
2 tablespoons chopped parsley
1 tablespoon chopped mint

Place the apricots and sultanas or raisins in a bowl. Add the lemon and orange juice and leave to soak while cooking the wheat.

Put the wheat in a large ovenproof bowl with the hot water and salt. Cover and cook on Full power for 50 minutes, stirring several times during cooking. Allow to stand, covered, for 10 minutes.

Drain the excess liquid from the wheat. Stir in the apricots and sultanas with their soaking liquid and add the oil. Cover again and set aside until completely cool, stirring several times. Just before serving season with pepper and stir in the remaining ingredients, mixing well.

168 | Cauliflower and Chick Peas Provençal

Preparation time
10 minutes

Cooking time
20 minutes

Setting
Full power

Serves 4

Calories
230 per portion

You will need
1 cauliflower, divided into small florets
600 ml/1 pint boiling water
1 tablespoon oil
1 clove garlic, crushed
1 small onion, finely chopped
1 (397-g/14-oz) can tomatoes
1 (425-g/15-oz) can chick peas, drained
salt and pepper
few drops mushroom ketchup
1 teaspoon chopped fresh marjoram
75 g/3 oz Cheddar cheese, grated
chopped parsley to garnish

Place the cauliflower in a 1.5-litre/2½-pint round oven-proof dish. Pour in the boiling water and cook on Full power for 5 minutes. Drain well and set to one side.

Add the oil, garlic and onion to the same dish and cook for 3 minutes. Stir in the tomatoes, chick peas, seasoning, Worcestershire sauce, herbs and drained cauliflower. Cover and cook on Full power for 10 minutes, stirring once during cooking.

Remove and sprinkle over the cheese. Cook for 2 minutes, until the cheese has melted. Garnish with chopped parsley and serve at once.

Cook's Tip

Using whole wheat grain, or berry, is the most nutritious way to eat wheat, as the vitamin rich germ and fibrous outer layers have not been removed. When cooked, the wheat should remain slightly chewy. However, if a softer texture is preferred, cook the wheat on Full power for an extra 5–10 minutes, and increase the water to 1 litre/1¾ pints.

Cook's Tip

If you are lucky enough to have access to fresh herbs – and parsley is as happy in a pot on the windowsill as it is in a garden plot – invest in a curved herb chopper.

169 | Pilaf with Almonds

Preparation time
5 minutes

Cooking time
16–18 minutes, plus
5–10 minutes standing
time

Setting
Full power

Serves 4

Calories
465 per portion

You will need
25 g/1 oz butter
1 small onion, finely chopped
225 g/8 oz long-grain rice
600 ml/1 pint boiling chicken stock
350 g/12 oz frozen peas
salt and pepper
1 (415-g/14-oz) can chick peas
50 g/2 oz flaked almonds,
  browned

Place the butter and onion in a basin and cook for 3 minutes. Add the rice, stock, peas and a little salt and pepper, cover and cook on Full power for 12–14 minutes. Stir in the chick peas and cook for a further 1 minute. Stand for 5–10 minutes or until the stock has been absorbed. Add the almonds, stir in lightly, and cook for another minute to reheat.

170 | Tomato Fondue

Preparation time
15–20 minutes

Cooking time
23 minutes

Setting
Full power

Serves 4

Calories
365 per portion

You will need
100 g/4 oz frozen whole green
  beans
2 tablespoons water
8 button mushrooms, wiped
8 radishes, trimmed
2 courgettes, trimmed and
  quartered lengthways
1 small cauliflower, separated into
  florets

For the fondue sauce
50 g/2 oz butter
1 clove garlic, crushed
1 small onion, finely chopped
2 (397-g/14-oz) cans tomatoes
250 ml/8 fl oz dry cider
1 teaspoon oregano
2 tablespoons tomato ketchup
1 tablespoon cornflour
150 ml/¼ pint double cream
salt

Cook the beans with the water, covered, on Full power for 3 minutes. Drain, refresh and drain. Serve with the other vegetables to dip in the fondue.

Cook the butter, garlic and onion in a large bowl for 4 minutes, then add the tomatoes, cider, oregano and ketchup. Cook for 12 minutes, stirring twice. Mix the cornflour with the cream. Stir in a little of the tomato mixture, then add to the fondue, stirring. Cook for 4 minutes, stirring every minute. Season and serve in the cooking bowl. Alternatively transfer it to a special fondue pot (as shown).

Cook's Tip

Use pine nuts in place of almonds, if preferred. Nuts are useful in vegetarian dishes as a cholesterol free source of protein and fibre.

Cook's Tip

Thanks to microwave cooking, the sauce will stay hot for quite some time in the dish in which it is cooked. So it is not essential to use a fondue pot. Do remember that metal fondue pots must not be used in the microwave. By cooking the fondue in the microwave first, then transferring it to a pan the sauce is less likely to burn on the base.

171 | Bombay Vegetables

Preparation time
10–15 minutes

Cooking time
18 minutes

Setting
Full power

Serves 2–4

Calories
365–185 per portion

You will need
2 cloves garlic, crushed
1–2 teaspoons curry powder
½ teaspoon cumin
juice of ½ lemon
150 ml/¼ pint vegetable or
    chicken stock
1 onion, chopped
40 g/1½ oz butter or margarine
1 small red pepper, cored,
    deseeded and thinly sliced
1 large courgette, diced
1 (230-g/8¼-oz) can tomatoes
350 g/12 oz potatoes, diced
salt and pepper

In a small bowl, mix together the garlic, curry powder, cumin, lemon juice and stock. Place the onion and butter in a medium-sized casserole and cook on Full power for 3 minutes. Add the red pepper and courgette, cover and cook for a further 4 minutes. Add the tomatoes, potatoes and seasoning with the stock. Cover and cook for 8 minutes. Stir the mixture, cover and cook for a further 3 minutes.

Serve with a selection of side dishes. For example, cucumber in yogurt, diced cucumber, sliced bananas, chutney, desiccated coconut and pappadums.

172 | Vegetable Terrine

Preparation time
15–20 minutes

Cooking time
23 minutes

Setting
Full power

Serves 4

Calories
120 per portion

You will need
6–8 large spinach leaves, trimmed
    and blanched
350 g/12 oz carrots, scraped and
    sliced
1 onion, finely chopped
1 clove garlic, crushed
2 potatoes, cubed
6 tablespoons skimmed milk
salt and pepper
1 egg, lightly beaten
2 small egg whites
2 courgettes, cut into sticks and
    blanched
225 g/8 oz green beans, blanched

Lightly oil a 1.5-litre/2½-pint loaf dish and line with 4–5 of the spinach leaves.

Place the carrots, onion, garlic, potatoes and skimmed milk in a large bowl, cover and cook on Full power for 12 minutes, or until tender, stirring two or three times. Purée and transfer to a bowl, then season and stir in the egg.

Whisk the egg whites to soft peaks and fold in the vegetable purée. Add alternate layers of the purée and blanched vegetables to the spinach-lined loaf dish; starting with and ending with a layer of purée. Fold over the overlapping spinach and cover with the remaining leaves. Cover with greaseproof paper and cook for 11 minutes, repositioning once. Cool, chill and turn out, then slice to serve with chilled tomato sauce, if liked.

Cook's Tip

When buying lemons, always choose shiny bright lemon-yellow fruits; duller yellow specimens may be over-ripe and not so juicy.

Cook's Tip

When fresh spinach is not available, the terrine can also be made without. This terrine can also be eaten warm. After cooking, allow to stand, covered, for 10–15 minutes before unmoulding.

173 | Bamboo Shoots with Broccoli

Preparation time
10 minutes

Cooking time
6 minutes

Setting
Full power

Serves 4

Calories
190 per portion

You will need
375 g/12 oz broccoli
½ (227-g/8-oz) can bamboo shoots, drained with juice reserved
3–4 tablespoons oil
1 onion, chopped
pinch of ground cinnamon
salt
cayenne
2 egg yolks
2 tablespoons cream
dash of Tabasco sauce

Divide the broccoli into tiny florets. Cut the bamboo shoots into thin strips. Place the oil in a large ovenproof bowl. Add the broccoli, onion, and bamboo shoots and cook on Full power for 4 minutes. Add a little of the bamboo shoot juice, the cinnamon, salt and cayenne pepper to taste, blending well. Cover and cook for a further 2 minutes. Beat the egg yolks with a little salt, the cream and the Tabasco sauce. Stir the egg mixture into the bamboo shoots and broccoli, coating the vegetables well. Transfer to a serving dish and serve immediately.

174 | Celery Cheese

Preparation time
10 minutes

Cooking time
25½ minutes, plus 10 minutes standing time

Setting
Full power

Serves 4

Calories
235 per portion

You will need
1 head celery
4 tablespoons water
40 g/1½ oz margarine
40 g/1½ oz plain flour
½ teaspoon dried mixed herbs
½ stock cube made up to 300 ml/ ½ pint with celery juices and water
75 g/3 oz Cheddar cheese, grated
75 g/3 oz browned breadcrumbs

Trim the celery, wash and drain. Cut into 7.5-cm/3-inch lengths and place in a large casserole with the water. Cover and cook on Full power for about 14 minutes or until tender. Stir halfway through cooking time. Stand, covered, for 5 minutes.

Place margarine in a glass measuring jug and cook for 30 seconds to melt. Blend in the flour, herbs and stock. Cook for about 2 minutes, stirring after 1 minute, or until sauce is thick and smooth. Stir again. Place a layer of celery in a serving dish, cover with about half the sauce, cheese and breadcrumbs. Repeat layers. Cook for about 9 minutes. Stand for 5 minutes. Serve hot.

Cook's Tip

Bamboo Shoots with Broccoli is an excellent vegetable dish to serve with fried fish, chops, or minced meat and cooked long-grain rice.

Cook's Tip

To keep celery crisp, prepare it as soon as possible after purchase. Trim and wash the sticks, then store in the refrigerator in a jug of iced water.

175 | Broccoli with Duxelles Sauce

Preparation time
5 minutes

Cooking time
20–21 minutes

Setting
Full power

Serves 4

Calories
390 per portion

You will need
50 g/2 oz butter
450 g/1 lb open or cup
  mushrooms, very finely
  chopped
50 g/2 oz shallots, finely chopped
salt and pepper
450 g/1 lb broccoli
2 tablespoons water
50 g/2 oz margarine
50 g/2 oz plain flour
600 ml/1 pint milk

Place the butter in a basin and cook on Full power for 30 seconds. Stir in the mushrooms and shallots. Cover and cook for 4 minutes, stirring halfway through the cooking time. Season to taste.

Place the broccoli in a roasting bag with the water, secure the end loosely with an elastic band and cook for about 8 minutes. Close bag tightly and set aside while you make the sauce.

Place margarine in a basin, cook for 30 seconds to melt, stir in flour and whisk in milk. Cook for 5 minutes, whisking three times during cooking. Season lightly. Arrange the broccoli in a serving dish, stir the duxelles mixture into the sauce and pour over. Cook for 2–3 minutes to heat through.

176 | Stuffed Cabbage Rolls

Preparation time
30 minutes

Cooking time
18 minutes

Setting
Full power, Medium

Serves 4

Calories
180 per portion

You will need
8 large cabbage leaves
4 tablespoons water
1 (397-g/14-oz) can chopped
  tomatoes
1 tablespoon chopped parsley, to
  garnish

For the filling
50 g/2 oz brown rice, cooked
50 g/2 oz onion, chopped
100 g/4 oz cheese, cubed
salt and black pepper

Place the cabbage in a bowl with the water. Cover and cook on Full power for 8 minutes. Drain and cool.

Mix the filling ingredients together and season well. Roll up a spoonful of the filling in each leaf. Spoon the tomatoes into a shallow dish. Pack the cabbage rolls tightly on top, cover and cook on Medium for 10 minutes. Garnish with chopped parsley.

Cook's Tip

Vegetables cooked in roasting bags retain moisture during cooking and can easily be shaken or stirred during the cooking time. Always use rubber bands or string to tie, or cut a piece of plastic from the top of the bag.

Cook's Tip

Trim any woody sections of cabbage leaf with a sharp knife and form the leaf into a rough rectangle before filling and folding.

177 | Jerusalem Artichokes in Egg Sauce

Preparation time
20 minutes

Cooking time
17 minutes

Setting
Full power

Serves 6

Calories
135 per portion

You will need
750 g–1 kg/1½–2 lb Jerusalem artichokes, peeled and halved
3 tablespoons water
1 tablespoon lemon juice

For the sauce
25 g/1 oz butter
25 g/1 oz flour
300 ml/½ pint milk
salt and freshly ground white pepper
2 hard-boiled eggs, chopped
pinch of freshly grated nutmeg
chopped parsley to garnish

Place the artichokes in a roasting bag with the water and lemon juice. Secure the end loosely with a rubber band. Cook on Full power for 12 minutes. Keep hot while making the sauce by draining and reserving the liquid then closing the roasting bag tightly.

To make the sauce, melt the butter in a glass jug or bowl by cooking on Full power for 1 minute. Stir in the flour, then the milk and reserved cooking liquid. Cook for 4 minutes, stirring or whisking two or three times during cooking. Season to taste with salt and pepper. Add the egg to the sauce with a pinch of nutmeg.

To serve arrange the Jerusalem artichokes in a warmed serving dish, cover with the sauce and sprinkle with chopped parsley to garnish.

Cook's Tip

The delicate and delicious flavour of Jerusalem artichokes is fully retained when they are cooked in a microwave. As they discolour quite rapidly remember to add lemon or vinegar to the water in which they are to cook.

178 | Macaroni Nut Curry

Preparation time
10 minutes

Cooking time
16½ minutes, plus 5 minutes standing time

Setting
Full power

Serves 4

Calories
650 per portion

You will need
175 g/6 oz short-cut macaroni
600 ml/1 pint boiling water
1 teaspoon salt
25 g/1 oz butter
1 large onion, chopped
1 tablespoon curry powder
1 tablespoon flour
2 tablespoons concentrated tomato purée
1 (397-g/14-oz) can tomatoes
100 g/4 oz mushrooms, sliced
50 g/2 oz sultanas
225 g/8 oz salted cashew nuts

Place the macaroni in a mixing bowl, pour over the boiling water and add the salt. Cook on Full power for 10 minutes, then allow to stand for 5 minutes. Drain and reserve.

Place the butter in the same bowl and cook on Full power for 30 seconds. Add the onion and curry powder and cook for 3 minutes. Stir in the flour well, then add the tomato purée, tomatoes, mushrooms, sultanas and cashew nuts. Cook for 3 minutes, stirring every minute. Stir in the drained macaroni and cook for 3 minutes, stirring three times. Serve piping hot.

Cook's Tip

Fresh coriander leaves, chopped and sprinkled over the curry, lends a particularly exotic flavour to this dish. You may like to offer a variety of side dishes as accompaniments: natural yogurt with peeled, chopped cucumber, diced apple, mango chutney, orange segments with chopped celery and quartered hard-boiled eggs with tomato slices, for example.

179 | Spinach au Gratin

Preparation time
10 minutes

Cooking time
11 minutes

Setting
Full power

Serves 4

Calories
245 per portion

You will need
450 g/1 lb spinach, washed, dried
 and shredded
1 small onion, grated
2 tablespoons butter
salt and pepper
pinch of freshly grated nutmeg
3 tomatoes, peeled and sliced
150 ml/¼ pint double cream

For the garnish
grated Parmesan cheese
chopped parsley

Place the spinach in a roasting bag, secure loosely with an elastic band and make several snips to allow steam to escape. Cook on Full power for 4 minutes.

Place the onion and 1 tablespoon butter in a 1-litre/1¾-pint oval ovenproof dish and cook on Full power for 4 minutes. Add the spinach, remaining butter and seasoning, top with the tomatoes and pour over the cream. Cook for a further 3 minutes.

Garnish with Parmesan cheese and parsley. Allow to stand for a few minutes before serving.

180 | Broccoli Platter

Preparation time
5 minutes

Cooking time
7 minutes

Setting
Full power

Serves 4

Calories
125 per portion

You will need
225 g/8 oz broccoli
3 tablespoons water
175 g/6 oz low-fat cheese spread
1 (213-g/7½-oz) can butter beans
paprika to garnish (optional)

Slit down the stems of broccoli for faster cooking. Arrange head towards the centre of a medium bowl and add the water, cover and cook on Full power for 4 minutes. Rearrange the broccoli and cook for a further 1 minute, drain and keep warm. Blend the cheese in a liquidiser with the beans including the juice, until smooth. Pour into a jug and heat on Full power for 2 minutes, stirring after 1 minute. Pour over the broccoli and garnish with paprika, if liked.

Cook's Tip

Try to buy young, small leaves of spinach for the most delicious flavour.

Cook's Tip

Serve this tasty dish with jacket potatoes, pasta or brown rice.

Rice Recipes

Although rice takes about the same length of time to cook in the microwave oven as it does by conventional methods, it cooks much more efficiently. A good flavour and firm texture is guaranteed, there are no sticky saucepans to clean and it can be cooked and served in the same dish. Rice reheats either from cold or frozen superbly well in a microwave, without drying out.

181 | Paella

(Illustrated on back jacket)

Preparation time
15 minutes

Cooking time
30 minutes

Setting
Full power

Serves 4

Calories
540 per portion

You will need
1 red pepper, cored, deseeded and cut into strips
225 g/8 oz carrots, sliced
1 large onion, chopped
4 tablespoons olive oil
2 large cloves garlic, crushed
½ teaspoon saffron strands
450 ml/¾ pint, plus 2 tablespoons, boiling water
1 chicken stock cube
225 g/8 oz long-grain rice
2 chicken thighs
salt and pepper
225 g/8 oz peeled cooked prawns
100 g/4 oz frozen peas
225 g/8 oz frozen mussels
a few whole cooked prawns to garnish

Mix the pepper, carrots, onion, oil and garlic together in a large bowl. Cook on Full power for 5 minutes. Pound the saffron strands in a pestle and mortar until crushed. Mix in the 2 tablespoons boiling water. Dissolve the stock cube in the remaining water. Stir the rice into the vegetables and add the chicken. Add salt and pepper, the saffron mixture and the stock. Cover and cook for 10 minutes. Remove the chicken and cut all the meat off the bones. Roughly chop it and return to the bowl. Add the prawns, peas and frozen mussels and stir well to mix thoroughly. Cook, covered, for a further 15 minutes. Stand for 3–4 minutes before serving. Garnish.

Cook's Tip

Saffron comes from the stigmas of a mauve crocus. It is almost as expensive as the gold thread it resembles. The colour it imparts may be imitated by turmeric but the flavour is unique.

182 | Kedgeree

Preparation time
15 minutes

Cooking time
23 minutes, plus 5 minutes standing time

Setting
Full power

Serves 4

Calories
390 per portion

You will need
1 medium onion, chopped
50 g/2 oz butter
grated rind of 1 lemon
175 g/6 oz long-grain rice
450 ml/¾ pint water
450 g/1 lb smoked haddock fillet, skinned and cut into large chunks
3 tablespoons chopped parsley
black pepper
2 hard-boiled eggs, chopped
1 hard-boiled egg, sliced, to garnish (optional)

Place the onion in a large bowl with the butter and lemon rind. Cook on Full power for 3 minutes, then stir in the rice. Pour in the water, cover and cook on Full power for 20 minutes. Add the fish chunks 5 minutes before end of cooking time, placing them apart on top of the rice. Cover again and continue cooking. Stand for 5 minutes.

Stir in most of the parsley, black pepper to taste and the chopped eggs. Transfer to a serving dish and sprinkle over the remaining parsley and garnish with sliced hard-boiled egg, if liked.

Cook's Tip

Try kedgeree based on brown rice. For 100 g/4 oz you need 350 ml/12 fl oz water and to cook it as above but for slightly longer: 25 minutes plus standing time.

183 | Eggs Mornay

Preparation time
15 minutes

Cooking time
8–10 minutes, plus 3–5
minutes to grill

Setting
Full power

Serves 4

Calories
245 per portion

You will need
8 hard-boiled eggs
40 g / 1½ oz plain flour
salt and pepper
25 g / 1 oz butter
600 ml / 1 pint milk
175 g / 6 oz cheese, grated
25 g / 1 oz fresh breadcrumbs
cooked rice to serve (optional)
chopped parsley to garnish

The eggs have to be cooked conventionally. While they are boiling, whisk the flour with the seasoning, butter and a little milk in a large basin. Gradually whisk in the rest of the milk. Cook on Full power for 8–10 minutes, until boiling. Whisk the sauce once or twice during cooking to make sure that it is smooth. Whisk in most of the cheese.

Shell and halve the eggs, arrange in a serving dish or on a bed of rice. Pour the sauce over and sprinkle with the breadcrumbs and reserved cheese. Brown under a hot grill for 3–5 minutes and serve at once garnished with parsley.

Cook's Tip

The secret of successful sauce making in the microwave is to have a good strong whisk to make sure that there are no lumps in the mixture. A good strong metal whisk is best.

184 | Tuna and Pepper Rice Salad

Preparation time
10 minutes, plus about
1 hour to chill

Cooking time
18 minutes

Setting
Full power

Serves 4–6

Calories
340–230 per portion

You will need
225 g / 8 oz long-grain rice
600 ml / 1 pint water
1 teaspoon salt
25 g / 1 oz butter
1 small onion, finely chopped
1 clove garlic, crushed
25 g / 1 oz All-bran breakfast cereal, crushed
1 (198-g / 7-oz) can tuna in brine, drained and flaked
100 g / 4 oz green, red or yellow pepper, cored, deseeded and chopped
100 g / 4 oz canned sweetcorn kernels
1 tablespoon lemon juice

Place the rice in a large bowl. Stir in the water and ½ teaspoon salt. Cover and cook on Full power for 15 minutes. Allow to stand until cool.

Combine the butter, onion and garlic in a bowl and cook for 3 minutes. Stir in the remaining salt and the crushed cereal. Set aside to cool.

Add the flaked tuna, pepper, sweetcorn and lemon juice to the cool rice, mixing thoroughly but gently. Cover the bowl and chill lightly.

Just before serving, sprinkle the onion and cereal mixture over the salad.

Cook's Tip

Brown rice may be used, if preferred. Increase the quantity of water to 750 ml / 1¼ pints and use 1 teaspoon salt. Increase the cooking time to 25 minutes. For a particularly colourful salad, use a combination of brown and white rice and a mixture of red, green and yellow peppers.

185 | Chicken Liver Risotto

Preparation time
15 minutes

Cooking time
32 minutes

Setting
Full power

Serves 4

Calories
530 per portion

You will need
2 tablespoons oil
1 large onion, chopped
1 medium carrot, chopped
2 cloves garlic, crushed
225 g/8 oz chicken livers, chopped
100 g/4 oz rindless bacon, chopped
1 tablespoon concentrated tomato purée
225 g/8 oz long-grain rice
1 teaspoon dried thyme
dash of Tabasco sauce
2 teaspoons Worcestershire sauce
1 (397-g/14-oz) can chopped tomatoes
600 ml/1 pint boiling stock
300 ml/½ pint dry cider
100 g/4 oz frozen peas
grated cheese to garnish

Place oil, onion, carrot and garlic in a large bowl. Cover and cook on Full power for 2 minutes. Add the chicken livers and bacon and cook for 5 minutes. Remove most of the liver and bacon and reserve. Stir in all remaining ingredients apart from the peas. Cover and cook for 15 minutes. Stir in the reserved liver mixture and peas. Cover and cook for a further 10 minutes. Garnish with cheese.

Cook's Tip

Give the chicken livers extra flavour by marinating them in a little red wine for about an hour before adding them to the dish.

186 | Spinach Risotto

Preparation time
15 minutes

Cooking time
34 minutes

Setting
Full power

Serves 4—6

Calories
760–505 per portion

You will need
450 g/1 lb spinach
100 g/4 oz butter
1 small onion, finely chopped
1 clove garlic, crushed
450 g/1 lb short-grain Italian rice
1.6 litres/2¾ pints hot chicken stock
½ teaspoon oregano
salt and pepper
75 g/3 oz Parmesan cheese, grated

Wash the spinach thoroughly and shake off excess water. Trim off the stalks, then place the leaves in a roasting bag and loosely secure the end with an elastic band. Cook for 5 minutes on Full power. Place the butter, onion, and garlic in a large ovenproof bowl and cook for 4 minutes. Stir in the rice, stock, oregano and seasoning to taste. Cover and cook for 20 minutes. Add the spinach and all but 1 tablespoon of the Parmesan cheese. Stir well and re-cover as before, then cook for a further 5 minutes.

Pile on to a heated serving dish and sprinkle with the remaining cheese.

Cook's Tip

Some tasks are best performed conventionally, leaving the microwave free for what it does best: while the onions are cooking, therefore, boil the stock in a saucepan on the hob.

187 | *Spiced Risotto*

Preparation time
20 minutes

Cooking time
18–23 minutes

Setting
Full power

Serves 4

Calories
670 per portion

You will need
675 g/1½ lb chicken livers
salt and black pepper
1 teaspoon paprika
1 teaspoon ground cumin
1 onion, sliced
2 tablespoons oil
225 g/8 oz brown rice
½ teaspoon turmeric
600 ml/1 pint well-flavoured
   chicken stock
25–50 g/1–2 oz whole blanched
   almonds
50 g/2 oz raisins
1 tablespoon lemon juice
175 g/6 oz low-fat soft cheese
3 tablespoons milk
8 fresh or canned apricot halves,
   roughly chopped
coriander sprig to garnish

Season the chicken livers with salt, pepper, paprika and cumin. Cook the onion in the oil in a casserole on Full power for 3 minutes until soft. Add the chicken livers, rice and turmeric. Stir in the stock. Re-cover and cook for 15–20 minutes, until the rice is tender, stirring once during cooking.

Stir in the almonds, raisins and lemon juice. Blend the low-fat cheese and milk together and stir into the rice. Adjust the seasoning and add the apricots. Garnish with coriander.

188 | *Plain Cooked Rice*

Preparation time
2 minutes

Cooking time
15–20 minutes, plus 5
minutes standing time

Setting
Full power

Serves 4

Calories
205 per portion

You will need
225 g/8 oz long-grain rice (white)
600 ml/1 pint water
½ teaspoon salt

Place the rice in a bowl or casserole. Pour in the water and stir in the salt. Cover and cook on Full power for 15–20 minutes. Stand for 5 minutes. Fluff up grains with a fork before serving.

Variations
Citrus rice: add the grated rind of 1 lemon or orange to the rice. Cook as above. Serve the lemon-flavoured rice with fish dishes, the orange with pork.

Herb rice: add chopped fresh herbs to the cooked rice using parsley or dill with fish dishes, sage and rosemary with pork, and mint or rosemary with lamb.

Cook's Tip

To blanch almonds, heat 250 ml/8 fl oz water in a measuring jug on Full power for 2½ minutes. Add almonds, cook for 30 seconds, then strain and remove the skins.

Cook's Tip

Dried lemon rind may be used to flavour citrus rice. Grate the rind in the usual way, then dry in the microwave oven, following the instructions given under Cook's Tip 258.

189 | New Iberia Chicken

Preparation time
10 minutes

Cooking time
32–35 minutes, plus browning chicken

Setting
Full power

Serves 6

Calories
570 per portion

You will need
1 (1.5-kg/3-lb) chicken, cut into 6
1 clove garlic, crushed
2 teaspoons vinegar
3 tablespoons oil
salt and pepper
50 g/2 oz stuffed green olives
 (optional)

For the savoury rice
2 medium onions, sliced
2 teaspoons oil
350 g/12 oz long-grain rice
1 (397-g/14-oz) can tomatoes
25 g/1 oz raisins
½ teaspoon Tabasco sauce
1 small bunch of chives, chopped
1 tablespoon chopped thyme
600 ml/1 pint boiling water

Place the chicken in a single layer in a dish. Combine the garlic, vinegar and 2 tablespoons of the oil in a jug. Season, stir and pour over the chicken.

Place the onions and oil in a casserole and cook on Full power for 2 minutes. Stir in the remaining ingredients. Cover and cook for 15 minutes, stirring once.

Drain the chicken and discard the marinade. Heat a browning dish according to the manufacturer's instructions. Add the remaining oil and brown the chicken on all sides. Cover and cook for 13–15 minutes, turning and rearranging the chicken once. Stir the chicken and olives, if liked, into the rice. Reheat for 2–3 minutes.

Cook's Tip

It is not essential to brown the chicken portions for this dish, however if you do not brown them they taste best with the skin removed. If you do not have a browning dish and really want to brown the portions, then do this in a large **frying pan over high heat before cooking in the microwave.**

190 | Rice Castles

Preparation time
15 minutes, plus 30 minutes to chill

Cooking time
18–19 minutes

Setting
Full power

Serves 6

Calories
310 per portion

You will need
175 g/6 oz long-grain rice
550 ml/18 fl oz water
salt and pepper
1 red apple, cored and diced
2 tablespoons orange juice
½ red pepper, cored, deseeded and
 sliced
4 no-need-to-soak dried apricots,
 chopped
25 g/1 oz sultanas
1 tablespoon chopped parsley
50 g/2 oz unsalted cashew nuts or
 peanuts
100 g/4 oz Mycella cheese,
 crumbled
50 g/2 oz butter

For the garnish
curly endive
parsley sprigs

Place the rice, water and ½ teaspoon salt in a large bowl. Cover and cook on Full power for 15 minutes; cool.

Toss the apple in the orange juice. Drain and add to the rice with all the remaining ingredients except the butter. Mix well and season to taste. Place the butter in a bowl and cook for 3–4 minutes until melted. Stir into the rice mixture.

Gently grease six (150-ml/¼-pint) individual pudding moulds (see Cook's Tip). Divide the rice mixture between them, pressing it down well. Chill the moulds for 30 minutes, then invert on individual plates. Garnish with curly endive and parsley and serve.

Cook's Tip

Do not worry if you do not have individual moulds – clean, empty yogurt or cream pots will do just as well. Alternatively, make the salad in a 1-litre/1¾-pint ring mould.

191 | Golden Rice Cakes

Preparation time
10 minutes, plus 2–3 hours to chill

Cooking time
29–30 minutes, plus about 8 minutes to fry cakes

Setting
Full power

Serves 4

Calories
515 per portion

You will need
175 g/6 oz long-grain rice
550 ml/18 fl oz water
salt and pepper
4 rashers rindless streaky bacon
1 teaspoon oil
1 leek, very finely chopped
3 tablespoons wholemeal flour
150 ml/¼ pint milk
2 tomatoes, finely chopped
3 tablespoons peanut butter
dash of Tabasco sauce
1 egg, beaten
100 g/4 oz breadcrumbs
oil for shallow frying

Place the rice, water and salt in a large bowl. Cover and cook on Full power for 15 minutes; cool. Place the bacon on a plate, cover with absorbent kitchen paper and cook for 4–5 minutes. Cook the oil and leek for 3 minutes. Stir in the flour and milk. Cook for 5 minutes, stirring once. Add tomatoes, peanut butter, Tabasco and seasoning. Cook for 2 minutes. Stir the tomato mixture into the rice. Cool, crumble the bacon and stir it into the mixture. Shape into eight cakes. Coat in egg and breadcrumbs, chill well, then shallow fry conventionally until golden. Serve with a salad garnish.

Cook's Tip

A mere dash of Tabasco sauce is sufficient to impart a distinctive, hot tang to a dish. The sauce is named after the area in Mexico where the peppers used in its composition originated.

192 | Curried Rice Salad

Preparation time
10–15 minutes

Cooking time
16 minutes

Setting
Full power

Serves 4

Calories
330 per portion

You will need
1 tablespoon corn oil
1 small onion, chopped
225 g/8 oz long-grain rice
2 teaspoons curry powder
1 chicken stock cube
600 ml/1 pint boiling water
4 tablespoons natural yogurt
1 red apple
1 green apple
4 tablespoons lemon juice
50 g/2 oz raisins
4 canned pineapple rings, chopped
shredded lettuce to serve

Place the oil in a large bowl with the onion. Cook on Full power for 3 minutes. Stir in the rice and curry powder and cook for 1 minute. Crumble in the stock cube, add the water, cover and cook for 12 minutes.

Allow the rice to stand for 3 minutes, then add the yogurt, stirring to coat all the rice grains thoroughly. Set aside to cool.

Core the apples, dice them and toss in the lemon juice (see Cook's Tip). Drain and add to the rice mixture with the raisins and pineapple. Chill until required. Serve on a bed of shredded lettuce.

Cook's Tip

Do not be tempted to prepare the apples in advance of cooking the rice. Core and dice them just before use, and prevent discoloration of the cut portions by tossing them in lemon juice.

Suppers and Snacks

A microwave oven is marvellous as it makes quick meals even quicker; a jacket potato with a filling can be cooked in a fraction of the time it would take in a conventional oven, and the dishes the egg and cheese recipes are cooked in are so much easier to wash up. Many of these recipes can be prepared in advance and each member of the family can heat and eat their meal just when they like.

193 | Spaghetti with Chicken and Ham Sauce

(Illustrated on title page)

Preparation time
10–15 minutes

Cooking time
8 minutes, plus 15–20 minutes to cook pasta

Setting
Full power

Serves 4

Calories
445 per portion

You will need
1 small onion, finely chopped
1 clove garlic, crushed
2 teaspoons oil
1 (397-g/14-oz) can chopped tomatoes
1 teaspoon clear honey
350 g/12 oz cooked chicken, skinned and chopped
100 g/4 oz cooked lean ham, chopped
salt and freshly ground black pepper
350 g/12 oz wholewheat spaghetti
chopped parsley to garnish

Place the onion and garlic with the oil in a large oven-proof bowl. Cook on Full power for 4 minutes. Add the tomatoes, honey, chicken and ham and season to taste with salt and pepper. Cover and cook for a further 4 minutes. Meanwhile, cook the spaghetti in plenty of boiling salted water in a large saucepan on the hob for 15–20 minutes, until tender but not soft. Drain the spaghetti, spoon over the sauce and serve topped with parsley.

194 | Suffolk Bakes

Preparation time
15 minutes

Cooking time
20 minutes

Setting
Full power

Serves 4

Calories
430 per portion

You will need
4 (225-g/8-oz) potatoes, scrubbed
175 g/6 oz rindless back bacon, chopped
50 g/2 oz mushrooms, sliced
25 g/1 oz butter
2 tablespoons curried chutney
salt and pepper
chopped parsley to garnish

Place the potatoes on absorbent kitchen paper in a casserole dish and cook on Full power for 16 minutes, turning once.

Meanwhile, place all the remaining ingredients in a small glass bowl and mix together well.

Put the bowl in the microwave with the potatoes and cook for 2 minutes. Stir well and cook for a further 2 minutes until the potatoes and bacon mixture are cooked.

Make a crosswise incision in the top of each potato and divide the filling between the potatoes, adding extra butter to the potato if needed. Garnish with the chopped parsley and serve hot.

Cook's Tip

It is not really worth cooking large quantities of pasta in a microwave oven as it does have to be cooked in plenty of liquid and this takes a long time to heat up in the microwave. It is far better to cook the pasta conventionally and use the microwave for making a quick, easy sauce.

Cook's Tip

Keep a small scrubbing brush especially for potatoes. Wash and dry after use and keep clean by storing in a plastic bag.

195 | *Chilled Ham Rolls*

Preparation time
20 minutes

Cooking time
5½ minutes

Setting
Full power

Serves 4–6

Calories
650–435 per portion

You will need
4 sticks celery, chopped
1 small onion, chopped
2 tablespoons oil
2 teaspoons gelatine
3 tablespoons water
2 tablespoons mayonnaise
150 ml/¼ pint soured cream
salt and pepper
175 g/6 oz Double Gloucester
  cheese, grated
25 g/1 oz pine kernels, chopped
8–10 slices cooked ham

For the dressing
6 tablespoons salad oil
1–2 tablespoons wine vinegar
salt, pepper and mustard
3–4 large tomatoes, quartered
1 tablespoon chopped parsley
1 teaspoon each mint and chives

Mix the celery, onion and oil in a basin. Cover and cook on Full power for 5 minutes. Soak the gelatine in the water in a very small bowl or mug, leave to stand for 2–3 minutes and then melt by heating on Full power for 30 seconds. When melted, add to the mayonnaise and soured cream and season. When beginning to set, stir in the cheese and pine kernels. Divide the filling between the slices of ham, roll up like a cigar and place in a shallow serving dish. Cover and chill. Whisk the oil, vinegar and seasonings. Add the tomatoes and herbs and spoon over the rolls just before serving.

Cook's Tip

Use basil vinegar in the dressing. It goes particularly well with tomatoes. Prepare the vinegar by immersing a sprig of basil in a bottle of white wine vinegar for 1 month.

196 | *Lancashire Cheese Hot Pot*

Preparation time
15 minutes

Cooking time
25–28 minutes, plus 3 minutes to grill

Setting
Full power

Serves 4–6

Calories
430–288 per portion

You will need
675 g/1½ lb potatoes
450 g/1 lb cod fillet
40 g/1½ oz flour
1–2 tablespoons lemon juice
salt and pepper
1 medium onion, thinly sliced
100 g/4 oz mushrooms, sliced
15 g/½ oz butter
150 ml/¼ pint milk
100 g/4 oz Lancashire cheese

Put the potatoes in a dish, cover and cook on Full power for 10 minutes. Cool and cut into thin slices.

Skin cod, cut into 1-cm/½-inch cubes and toss in 25 g/1 oz of the flour. Arrange one-third of potatoes on bottom of a buttered casserole. Cover with half the cod, sprinkle with lemon juice and season. Combine the onion and mushroom, arrange half over the fish. Cover with remaining cod, lemon juice, half the remaining potatoes, the remaining onions and mushrooms.

Put the butter in a jug, melt on Full power for 40–60 seconds, then stir in the remaining flour. When smooth, gradually whisk in the milk then cook, uncovered, for 3–4 minutes until it boils and thickens. Add half the cheese and season. Pour sauce over casserole, top with remaining potatoes and cheese. Cover and cook for 10 minutes. Brown under a hot grill for 3 minutes.

Cook's Tip

The easiest way to coat the fish cubes is to place them in a plastic bag with the flour. Close the bag and shake gently, to coat the cubes without breaking them.

197 | Double Gloucester and Potato Pie

Preparation time
15 minutes

Cooking time
34 minutes

Setting
Medium, Full power

Serves 4

Calories
740 per portion

You will need
275 g/10 oz Double Gloucester cheese
1 large cooking apple, peeled, cored and chopped
225 g/8 oz rindless streaky bacon, chopped
2 tablespoons butter
675 g/1½ lb cooked potatoes, sliced

For the garnish
parsley sprig
3 rindless bacon rolls, halved (optional)

Grate 50 g/2 oz of the cheese and set it aside. Cut the remaining cheese into 5-mm/¼-inch cubes and place it in a bowl with the apple and bacon.

Line a generously buttered 1.2-litre/2-pint casserole with two-thirds of the sliced potato. Spoon the cheese mixture into the centre of the casserole, taking care not to disturb the potato slices. Top with the remaining potato.

Cook on Medium for 30 minutes. Sprinkle the reserved grated cheese over the top, return the casserole to the microwave oven and increase the power to Full. Cook for 4 minutes more. Allow to stand for 4 minutes before serving with a garnish of parsley and bacon rolls, if liked.

Cook's Tip

To cook the bacon, roll up and secure with wooden cocktail sticks. Put on a dish or plate and cover with absorbent kitchen paper. Cook on Full power for 5–7 minutes.

198 | Gloucester Apples

Preparation time
20 minutes

Cooking time
10–12 minutes, plus grilling time

Setting
Full power

Serves 4

Calories
355 per portion

You will need
4 large cooking apples
3 tablespoons dry cider
1 large onion, chopped
4 rashers rindless streaky bacon, chopped
2 sausages, well grilled and chopped
175 g/6 oz Double Gloucester cheese, grated
¼ teaspoon chopped sage
salt and black pepper

Core the apples, score around centre and place on a shallow ovenproof dish, pour in the cider and cover. Cook on Full power for 5–7 minutes.

Cook the onion and bacon together in a basin on Full power for 5 minutes. Add the sausages, 100 g/4 oz of the cheese, the chopped sage and seasoning. Remove the upper skin from the apples and stuff the centre with the filling. Baste with the cooking juices, scatter the remaining cheese over the apples and brown under a hot grill. Serve piping hot.

Cook's Tip

Any food surrounded by a membrane must be pierced before microwave cooking or pressure build-up will cause the membrane or skin to burst unattractively. This is why each apple is scored around its equator.

199 | Mushrooms on Toast

Preparation time
10 minutes

Cooking time
12 minutes

Setting
Full power

Serves 4

Calories
240 per portion

You will need
2 tablespoons oil
1 onion, finely chopped
1 small red pepper, cored,
   deseeded and sliced
3 tablespoons plain flour
350 ml/12 fl oz milk
350 g/12 oz cup mushrooms,
   sliced
salt and pepper
4 slices wholemeal bread

Place the oil, onion and red pepper in a bowl. Cover and cook on Full power for 4 minutes.

Stir in the flour and gradually add the milk. Cook for 6 minutes, whisking thoroughly once during cooking, and making sure that all the flour is incorporated into the sauce.

Stir in the mushrooms and seasoning. Cook for 2 minutes more.

Meanwhile toast the bread and place a slice on each of four individual plates. Spoon the mushroom mixture on top and serve immediately.

200 | Nut Scramble

Preparation time
5 minutes

Cooking time
4 minutes

Setting
Full power

Serves 4

Calories
255 per portion

You will need
4 eggs
4 tablespoons milk
2 tablespoons peanut butter
2 teaspoons chopped chives
salt and pepper
3 tomatoes, peeled, deseeded and
   chopped
4 waffles, toasted
parsley to garnish

In a large bowl or jug, whisk the eggs thoroughly with the milk and peanut butter. Stir in the chives with salt and pepper to taste.

Cook on Full power for 2 minutes, then whisk the mixture thoroughly. Stir in the tomatoes and cook for 1 minute more. Stir the mixture thoroughly, then cook for a further minute, or until the eggs are just beginning to set. Stir thoroughly.

Spoon the mixture on to toasted waffles and garnish with parsley. Serve immediately on four individual plates.

Cook's Tip

Crumbled bacon would make a delicious and contrasting topping to the mushroom mixture. Use 2 rashers bacon and follow the instructions given under Pasta with Tuna and Avocado, allowing 2–3 minutes to cook the bacon.

Cook's Tip

When scrambling eggs in the microwave oven, it is vital to beat or stir the mixture frequently. Do not overcook. The eggs should be very moist when removed from the oven as they will continue to cook for 2–3 minutes.

201 | Cheese and Bread Pudding

Preparation time
5 minutes, plus 10 minutes standing time

Cooking time
12 minutes, plus grilling time

Setting
Full power

Serves 4

Calories
565 per portion

You will need
50 g/2 oz soft butter
6 large slices white bread
3 slices cooked ham
175 g/6 oz Havarti or Samsoe cheese
mild mustard (optional)
2 eggs, beaten
300 ml/½ pint milk
salt and pepper

Butter the bread and make three sandwiches, using the ham and 100 g/4 oz of the cheese as filling. Add the mustard, if using. Cut each sandwich into four triangles.

Arrange the sandwiches, points uppermost, in a lightly greased rectangular dish.

In a bowl, beat the eggs with the milk and the seasoning. Carefully pour over the bread and cook on Full power for 5 minutes. Allow to stand for 5 minutes, pressing the sandwiches down into the milk mixture if necessary, then cook for 5 minutes more. Allow to stand for 5 minutes. Finally cook for a further 2 minutes. Grate the remaining cheese, sprinkle over the top and brown under a hot grill before serving.

Cook's Tip

You may like to try cooking this delicious savoury bread and butter pudding in four individual dishes instead of one large dish. Cook the puddings two at a time and reduce the cooking time to 6–9 minutes for each batch.

202 | Broccoli in Ham and Cheese Sauce

Preparation time
10 minutes

Cooking time
17–19 minutes

Setting
Full power

Serves 4

Calories
240 per portion

You will need
450 g/1 lb frozen broccoli spears
4 tablespoons water

For the sauce
300 ml/½ pint milk
25 g/1 oz plain flour
25 g/1 oz butter
50 g/2 oz ham, finely chopped
1 teaspoon wholegrain mustard
75 g/3 oz Cheddar cheese, grated
salt and pepper

Place the broccoli in a large shallow quiche dish with the water. Cover loosely and cook on Full power for 7–8 minutes, separating the spears as soon as they have thawed sufficiently and rearranging them like the spokes of a wheel, with the stalks to the outside of the dish. When cooked, drain the broccoli and place in a shallow dish.

Make the sauce: place the milk in a large jug. Whisk in the flour gradually, then add the butter. Cook for 3–4 minutes until the sauce thickens, stirring every minute and making certain that any flour on the base of the jug is thoroughly incorporated in the sauce.

Stir in the ham, mustard and 50 g/2 oz of the cheese. Season to taste, pour over the broccoli and sprinkle with the remaining cheese. Cook for 7 minutes. Serve immediately.

Cook's Tip

Fresh broccoli may be used instead of frozen. Allow 8–10 minutes for the initial cooking, then proceed as in the recipe. Use Red Leicester cheese instead of Cheddar if preferred.

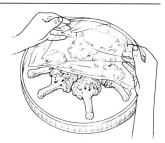

203 | *Haricot Beans Burgundy-Style*

Preparation time
15 minutes

Cooking time
12 minutes

Setting
Full power

Serves 4–6

Calories
275–185 per portion

You will need
1 tablespoon oil
2 shallots, finely sliced
sprig of rosemary
100 g/4 oz rindless bacon, chopped
1 bay leaf
1 (64-g/2¼-oz) can concentrated tomato purée
1 (425-g/15-oz) can haricot beans, drained
150 ml/¼ pint dry red wine
salt and freshly ground black pepper
1 tablespoon chopped mixed herbs

Place the oil, shallots and sprig of rosemary in a large ovenproof dish and cook on Full power for 4 minutes. Add the bacon, bay leaf and tomato purée and stir well. Cook for a further 3 minutes. Add the drained beans, red wine and seasoning to taste, then cover and cook for 5 minutes. Discard the rosemary sprig and bay leaf before serving sprinkled with the herbs.

Cook's Tip

Haricot describes a variety of white beans that are usually meant to mean small oval beans. However, cannelini, flageolet and white kidney beans are all part of the haricot family.

204 | *Ratatouille with Cannellini Beans and Sausage*

Preparation time
20 minutes, plus 30 minutes to degorge aubergines

Cooking time
18 minutes

Setting
Full power

Serves 4

Calories
405 per portion

You will need
2 aubergines
salt
2 tablespoons olive oil
50 g/2 oz rindless smoked bacon, chopped
1–2 onions, sliced into rings
2–3 courgettes, sliced
4 tomatoes, cut into wedges
freshly ground black pepper
1 tablespoon dried Herbes-de-Provence
1 (397-g/14-oz) can cannellini beans, drained
275 g/9 oz garlic sausage, sliced
50 g/2 oz ham, finely chopped

Chop the aubergines into bite-sized pieces. Place in a sieve, sprinkle with salt and leave for 30 minutes. Rinse, drain and pat dry with absorbent kitchen paper.

Place the oil, bacon, onions and aubergines in a large bowl and cover. Cook on Full power for 8 minutes.

Add the courgettes and tomatoes to the bowl and season with pepper and Herbes de Provence. Mix together well, then re-cover the bowl and cook for a further 5 minutes.

Add the canellini beans, garlic sausage and ham and cook for a final 5 minutes to heat through.

Cook's Tip

Sprinkling the aubergine cubes with salt draws out any bitter juices and also prevents the aubergine absorbing too much oil. Rinse thoroughly, though, or the cubes will taste salty.

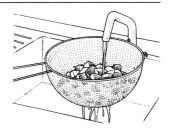

205 | Beansprouts with Mushrooms

Preparation time
15 minutes

Cooking time
7 minutes

Setting
Full power

Serves 4

Calories
125 per portion

You will need
1 small onion, chopped
150 g/5 oz mushrooms, sliced
25 g/1 oz lard
1 (275-g/10-oz) can beansprouts, drained
1 tablespoon sherry (optional)
about 300 ml/½ pint water
salt
100 g/4 oz cooked ham, chopped
2 tablespoons cornflour
1 tablespoon soy sauce

Place the onion, mushrooms and lard in a large bowl. Cover and cook on Full power for 3 minutes.

Add the remaining ingredients, mixing well. Re-cover and cook for about 4 minutes, or until thoroughly heated. Stir after 2 minutes. Leave to stand for 2–3 minutes before serving.

206 | Eggs Benedict

Preparation time
10 minutes

Cooking time
about 7 minutes

Setting
Full power

Calories
440 per portion

You will need
4 eggs
4 slices toast, crusts removed and buttered
4 slices lean ham, cut about same size as toast
dill sprigs to garnish (optional)

For the hollandaise sauce
4 tablespoons white wine vinegar
100 g/4 oz butter, cut into pieces
4 egg yolks, beaten
salt and pepper

Place 1 teaspoon of hot water into four ramekins and cook on Full power until the water boils. Break an egg into each dish and prick each yolk with a cocktail stick, cook for 2¼ minutes. Stand for 1½ minutes. Drain carefully. Place the eggs on the pieces of toast and cover with the ham.

To make the sauce, place the vinegar in a basin and boil until reduced by half (or use 2 tablespoons lemon juice instead). Add the butter and cook for 1–1½ minutes until hot. Slowly whisk the egg yolks into the butter, then whisk until the sauce has thickened. Season to taste and pour over the eggs. Reheat for 1 minute, if necessary. Garnish with the dill, if using.

Cook's Tip

To grow beansprouts, place alfalfa seeds, soya beans or mung beans in a glass jar (to fill less than one-quarter of jar). Close top with muslin held by rubber band. Fill jar with water, drain and leave in a dark place until next day.

Repeat daily rinsing and draining until sprouts are about 2.5 cm/1 in long. Drain. Store in the refrigerator.

Cook's Tip

Pricking an egg yolk punctures the membrane and prevents the egg bursting during cooking.

207 | Chicken Peanut Pies

Preparation time
20 minutes

Cooking time
7–9 minutes, plus 25 minutes in a conventional oven

Setting
Full power

Oven temperature
200C, 400F, gas 6

Makes 12

Calories
120 per pie

You will need
1 boneless chicken breast, skinned
2 spring onions, chopped
1 teaspoon ground cumin
½ teaspoon chopped thyme
1 tablespoon chopped parsley
2 teaspoons lemon juice
2 tablespoons natural yogurt
salt and pepper

For the peanut pastry
175 g/6 oz wholemeal flour
50 g/2 oz plain flour
6 tablespoons water
50 g/2 oz margarine
2 tablespoons smooth peanut butter
milk for glazing
sesame seeds (optional)

Cook the chicken on Full power for 5–6 minutes. Cool and chop, then mix with the remaining filling ingredients. Mix the flours. Place the water, margarine and peanut butter in a basin and cook for 2–3 minutes. Stir this into the flours to make a soft dough. Knead briefly. Roll out two-thirds of the dough and line 12 bun tins, then spoon in the filling. Roll out the remaining dough to make lids. Dampen the edges and press on lids to seal. Brush with milk and sprinkle over the sesame seeds, if using. Bake in a conventional oven for 25 minutes or until the pastry is crisp and golden. Serve with a crisp salad.

Cook's Tip

Alternatively cook the pies in a special bun tray and place in a combination microwave oven at 200C using a Medium setting for 8 minutes.

208 | Tuna Noodles

Preparation time
10 minutes

Cooking time
14 minutes, plus 12–15 minutes to cook pasta

Setting
Full power

Serves 4

Calories
470 per portion

You will need
350 g/12 oz ribbon noodles
salt and pepper

For the sauce
2 tablespoons oil
1 small onion, finely chopped
2 sticks celery, finely sliced
1 clove garlic, crushed
1 (397-g/14-oz) can tomatoes
1 (200-g/7-oz) can tuna in brine, drained
175 g/6 oz button mushrooms, sliced
½ teaspoon dried basil

Cook the pasta conventionally on the hob, adding to a large saucepan of boiling salted water. Cook for 12–15 minutes until the noodles are tender but not soft.

Meanwhile make the sauce in the microwave oven. Place the oil in a large bowl, add the onion, celery and garlic and cook on Full power for 4 minutes. Stir in the tomatoes and cook for 6 minutes more, stirring occasionally to break up and rearrange the tomatoes.

Add the tuna and mushrooms, with the basil. Stir thoroughly. Cook for 4 minutes, stirring once. When the pasta is cooked, drain it thoroughly and pile on to a large serving platter. Top with the tuna sauce (see Cook's Tip).

Cook's Tip

When topping pasta with a sauce, begin by adding about a quarter of the sauce, forking it through the pasta to coat the strands or shapes. Top with the remaining sauce.

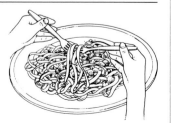

209 | Spaghetti Carbonara

Preparation time
10 minutes

Cooking time
8 minutes, plus 12–15 minutes to cook pasta

Setting
Full power

Serves 4

Calories
770 per portion

You will need
450 g/1 lb spaghetti
salt and pepper
50 g/2 oz Cheddar cheese, grated
50 g/2 oz Parmesan cheese, grated
8 rashers rindless bacon, chopped
2 eggs
2 egg yolks
4 tablespoons single cream
1 (185-g/6½-oz) can prawns, drained
2 tablespoons chopped parsley

Cook the spaghetti conventionally on the hob. Cook for 12–15 minutes until tender but not soft. Combine the grated cheeses in a bowl and mix well.

Meanwhile place the bacon in a large mixing bowl, cover with absorbent kitchen paper and cook on Full power for 4 minutes.

Place the eggs, egg yolks, cream, seasoning and half the cheese in a bowl and beat well. Add the egg mixture to the bacon and cook for 4 minutes, stirring once while cooking. The eggs should be creamy and on the point of setting (see Cook's Tip).

Drain the pasta and add it to the eggs with the prawns and parsley. Toss and serve immediately, offering the remaining grated cheese to be sprinkled on the pasta as required.

Cook's Tip

The egg mixture should be on the sloppy side since it will continue to cook after being removed from the microwave oven. The hot spaghetti will speed this process.

210 | Pasta with Tuna and Avocado

Preparation time
10–15 minutes

Cooking time
14–15 minutes, plus 12–15 minutes to cook pasta

Setting
Full power

Serves 4

Calories
640 per portion

You will need
6 rashers rindless back bacon
1 ripe avocado
2 teaspoons lemon juice
1 (198-g/7-oz) can tuna, drained
225 g/8 oz tri-coloured pasta spirals
salt and pepper
1 teaspoon oil
basil leaves to garnish (optional)

For the sauce
25 g/1 oz plain flour
600 ml/1 pint milk
20 g/¾ oz concentrated butter
salt and pepper
75 g/3 oz mature Cheddar cheese, grated
1 tablespoon chopped fresh basil or 1 teaspoon dried basil

Place the bacon on a rack or shallow dish, cover with absorbent kitchen paper and cook for 4–5 minutes. Peel and stone the avocado, then dice the flesh. Mix with the lemon juice and flaked tuna. Cook the pasta conventionally in boiling salted water for 12–15 minutes.

Make the sauce: whisk the flour and milk together, add the butter, season and cook for 9 minutes, whisking twice. Whisk in the cheese, cook for 1 minute more, then stir in the basil and tuna mixture. Toss with the drained pasta and top with crumbled bacon. Garnish with basil, if using.

Cook's Tip

Pasta can be cooked in the microwave oven, although it is generally more convenient to use a saucepan on the hob and save the microwave for making accompanying sauces. Place the dry pasta in a 3-litre/5-pint bowl and add

1.75 litres/3 pints boiling water. Stir in 1 teaspoon salt and 1 tablespoon oil. Cover and cook on Full power for 9 minutes, stand for 8 minutes, then drain.

211 | Savoury Charlotte

Preparation time
40 minutes

Cooking time
22–23 minutes, plus
frying time

Setting
Full power

Serves 4–6

Calories
690–460 per portion

You will need
100 g/4 oz butter
1 onion, chopped
salt and pepper
1 chicken stock cube
300 ml/½ pint boiling water
300 ml/½ pint milk
225 g/8 oz frozen mixed
    vegetables
225 g/8 oz cooked chicken, diced
100 g/4 oz mushrooms, sliced
2 tablespoons oil
450 g/1 lb fresh breadcrumbs
4 tablespoons chopped mixed
    fresh herbs

Garnish
1 tomato, sliced
parsley sprigs

Put one-third of the butter in a bowl with the onion and cook on Full power for 3 minutes. Stir in seasoning to taste and the flour. Add the stock cube, water and milk. Cook for 8 minutes, whisking once. Stir in the vegetables, chicken and mushrooms and cook for a further 10 minutes.

Heat the oil with the remaining butter in a frying pan on the hob. Add the breadcrumbs and cook until lightly browned, stirring all the time. Stir in the herbs. Layer the sauce and breadcrumbs in a dish, cook for 1–2 minutes, garnish and serve.

212 | Salmon Savoury

Preparation time
20 minutes

Cooking time
13–15 minutes, plus 15
minutes to cook pasta

Setting
Full power

Serves 4

Calories
670 per portion

You will need
225 g/8 oz pasta shells
salt and pepper
1 onion, chopped
50 g/2 oz butter
40 g/1½ oz plain flour
600 ml/1 pint milk
1 (439-g/15½-oz) can salmon
100 g/4 oz mushrooms, sliced
50 g/2 oz cheese, grated

Cook the pasta conventionally in plenty of boiling salted water for 15 minutes. Meanwhile, place the onion in a large bowl with the butter and cook on Full power for 3 minutes. Stir in the flour and milk, then continue to cook for 8–10 minutes, until boiling. Whisk once during cooking and again at the end. Add the liquid from the salmon, flake the fish and add to the sauce. Stir in the mushrooms, cheese and the drained pasta. Season to taste. Heat for 2 minutes, then serve.

Cook's Tip

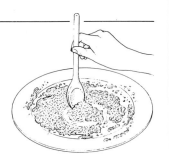

Instead of browning the breadcrumbs as above, use dried breadcrumbs and toss them in butter in a large dish, then cook on Full power for 2–3 minutes to heat through before layering.

Cook's Tip

If you like, the pasta mixture can be turned into an ovenproof dish and browned under the grill before serving.

213 | Pasta Beanfeast

Preparation time
15 minutes

Cooking time
9 minutes, plus 10–12 minutes to cook pasta

Setting
Full power

Serves 4

Calories
355 per portion

You will need
225 g/8 oz pasta shapes
salt and pepper
8 rashers rindless bacon
1 medium onion, chopped
1 tablespoon oil
1 small red pepper, cored, deseeded and sliced
1 small green pepper, cored, deseeded and sliced
1 teaspoon dried basil (see Cook's Tip)
1 (397-g/14-oz) can chopped tomatoes
1 (415-g/14½-oz) can flageolet beans, drained
chopped parsley to garnish

Cook the pasta shapes conventionally on the hob, adding them to a saucepan of salted boiling water. Cook for 10–12 minutes, until tender but not soft.

Meanwhile place the bacon on a rack or shallow dish, cover with absorbent kitchen paper and cook on Full power for 4 minutes. Set aside.

Combine the onion, oil, peppers, basil, tomatoes and flageolet beans in a large bowl, cover and cook for 5 minutes. Crumble the bacon and add it to the bowl. Season to taste and set aside for 2 minutes.

Drain the pasta and add it to the vegetable mixture. Toss and serve immediately sprinkled with chopped parsley.

214 | Chicken and Broccoli Layer

Preparation time
15   20 minutes

Cooking time
30 minutes

Setting
Full power

Serves 4

Calories
635 per portion

You will need
450 g/1 lb broccoli
150 ml/¼ pint water
1 (295-g/10.4-oz) can condensed chicken soup
6 tablespoons mayonnaise
150 ml/¼ pint milk
salt and pepper
225 g/8 oz chicken, cooked and diced
450 g/1 lb potatotes, medium sliced
175 g/6 oz Red Leicester cheese, grated
chopped parsley to garnish

Place the broccoli spears in a large bowl with the water. Cover and cook on Full power for 12 minutes. Drain and chop finely.

Mix the soup, mayonnaise and milk together in a small bowl and season. Pour half of the soup mixture into a shallow casserole dish. Arrange the broccoli evenly over the top, then the cooked chicken and finish with a layer of sliced potatoes. Pour the remaining sauce over the potatoes, cover and cook for 14 minutes.

Sprinkle the cheese on top and cook, uncovered, for 4 minutes, then leave to stand for a further 2–3 minutes. Garnish with the parsley and serve.

Cook's Tip

Basil may be successfully dried in the microwave oven. Rinse about 25 g/1 oz fresh basil leaves under cold water, drain and dry. Spread between two sheets of absorbent kitchen paper and cook on Full power for 2 minutes. Remove the top sheet of paper and cook for 1 or 2 minutes more until all the moisture has been extracted from the leaves.

Cook's Tip

Serve with garlic squares. Cut 4 slices of granary bread into quarters, place on a microwave roasting rack and brush with garlic butter. Cook on Full power until dry and firm – the squares will become crisp as they cool.

215 | Scrambled Eggs

Preparation time
2 minutes

Cooking time
3½–4 minutes

Serves 4

Setting
Full power

Calories
180 per portion

You will need
6 eggs
6 tablespoons milk
salt and pepper
25 g / 1 oz butter

Whisk together the eggs and milk and add salt and pepper to taste. Cut the butter into small pieces or flakes and stir in. Cook on Full power for 1 minute. Stir the eggs thoroughly, cook for a further 1 minute and stir again. Cook for a final 1½–2 minutes and stir again until creamy. Serve immediately.

216 | Spaghetti Prosciutto

Preparation time
10 minutes

Cooking time
13–14 minutes, plus 15–20 minutes to cook pasta

Setting
Full power, Medium

Serves 4

Calories
320 per portion

You will need
275 g / 10 oz wholewheat, green or plain spaghetti
1 large onion, chopped
2 cloves garlic, chopped
1 bay leaf
1 tablespoon oil
1 tablespoon chopped fresh basil or 2 teaspoons dried
1 (397-g/14-oz) can chopped tomatoes
1 tablespoon dry white wine
150 ml / ¼ pint water
½ chicken stock cube
freshly ground black pepper
100 g / 4 oz low-fat soft cheese, such as Shape
100 g / 4 oz prosciutto, chopped
watercress to garnish

Cook the spaghetti conventionally in plenty of boiling salted water on the hob for 15–20 minutes.

While the spaghetti is cooking, put the onion, garlic, bay leaf and oil in a bowl and cook on Full power for 4–5 minutes. Add the basil, tomatoes, wine, water and stock cube. Cook on Full power for 4 minutes and then on Medium for 5 minutes. Season and stir in the soft cheese until it melts. Add the prosciutto.

Drain the spaghetti and serve immediately with the hot sauce poured over and garnished with watercress.

Cook's Tip

Follow the timings above but until you know your microwave well keep a close watch on the eggs so you know exactly how long it takes for your particular oven. The timing is crucial to success.

Cook's Tip

A bay tree, grown in a tub, is very attractive if you encourage it to grow on a central stem with the top shaped to a glossy ball. Use the leaves straight from the tree or dry and store in an airtight jar.

217 | Pasta Ring

Preparation time
15 minutes

Cooking time
14 minutes, plus 8
minutes to cook pasta

Setting
Full power

Serves 4

Calories
600 per portion

You will need
225 g/8 oz noodles or macaroni
1 teaspoon salt
225 g/8 oz Cheddar cheese, grated

For the filling
350–450 g/12 oz–1 lb frozen
   mixed vegetables
2 tablespoons water
1 packet Cheese Sauce Mix or
   300 ml/½ pint coating cheese
   sauce
50 g/2 oz salted peanuts

Line a 1.15-litre/2-pint ring mould with cling film. Cook the pasta in a large pan of boiling salted water for 8 minutes. Drain and immediately stir in the cheese. Spoon into the mould and press firmly with a spoon. Cool.

To make the filling, cook the frozen vegetables in the water, covered, on Full power for about 8 minutes, stirring once or twice, or until tender but still firm. Stand for 2–3 minutes. Make the Cheese Sauce according to packet directions (using a glass measuring jug) and cook for about 3 minutes, stirring every minute. Mix together the sauce, vegetables and peanuts.

Invert a serving plate over the pasta mould and turn out. Remove film. Spoon sauce mixture into the centre, cover and cook for 3 minutes, until heated through.

218 | Macaroni Cheese

Preparation time
5 minutes

Cooking time
11 minutes, plus 8
minutes to cook pasta

Setting
Full power

Serves 4

Calories
525 per portion

You will need
225 g/8 oz macaroni
1 small onion, chopped
2 tablespoons butter
225 g/8 oz Cheddar cheese, grated
175 ml/6 fl oz milk
½ teaspoon salt
black pepper

For the garnish
tomato lily (optional)
parsley sprig (optional)

Cook the macaroni in a large pan of boiling salted water for 8 minutes. Drain well.

Place onion and butter in a glass dish, cover and cook on Full power for 3 minutes. Stir in macaroni, cheese, milk, salt and pepper to taste. Cover and cook for 4 minutes. Stir, cover and cook for a further 4 minutes. Stand for 4 minutes. Serve hot, garnished as shown, if you like.

Cook's Tip

Take care when removing the cling film from the pasta ring so as not to spoil the shape.

Cook's Tip

Chopped ham makes a delicious addition to this dish. Stir in about 75 g/3 oz just before the final 4 minutes' cooking time.

219 | Lasagne

Preparation time
10 minutes

Cooking time
25–29 minutes, plus
10–12 minutes to cook
pasta

Setting
Full power

Serves 4

Calories
735 per portion

You will need
225 g/8 oz lasagne
salt
1 aubergine, sliced
25 g/1 oz butter
1 tablespoon oil
350 g/12 oz minced beef
scant tablespoon plain flour
1 (397-g/14-oz) can tomatoes
300 ml/½ pint dry white wine or
chicken stock, or a mixture
175 g/6 oz Gruyère cheese, thinly
sliced
paprika

Cook the lasagne conventionally in a large pan of boiling salted water for 10–12 minutes or until just cooked. Drain. Separate sheets.

Place the aubergine, butter and oil in a glass dish. Cover and cook on Full power for 4 minutes or until soft. Add the minced beef, cover, and cook for 5 minutes. Add the flour, tomatoes and their juices, and wine or stock. Cover and cook for 8–10 minutes until cooked.

Layer the meat mixture and lasagne in a serving dish, finishing with a layer of lasagne. Cover with slices of cheese. Cook for 8–10 minutes to melt cheese. Stand for 4 minutes. Sprinkle a little paprika on top.

Cook's Tip

For a tasty vegetarian lasagne, substitute Ratatouille (recipe 151) for the meat sauce, then proceed as in the recipe.

220 | Quick Pizza Baps

Preparation time
15–20 minutes

Cooking time
9 minutes

Setting
Full power

Serves 4

Calories
305 per portion

You will need
1 small onion, finely chopped
1 small green pepper, cored,
deseeded and finely chopped
3 tablespoons water
4 tablespoons concentrated
tomato purée
1 teaspoon brown sugar (optional)
½ teaspoon dried mixed herbs
freshly ground black pepper
4 wholemeal baps
4 slices lean ham, cut in half
2 tomatoes, very thinly sliced
175 g/6 oz Mozzarella cheese,
sliced
1 teaspoon oregano

Place the onion and green pepper in an ovenproof bowl with the water and cook on Full power for 4 minutes, stirring halfway through the cooking time. Stir in the tomato purée, brown sugar, if using, and the dried herbs and season to taste with pepper. Cut each bap in half horizontally and toast the cut sides. Divide the onion and pepper mixture between the halves. Top each with a slice of ham and divide the tomato and cheese slices between the baps to make eight miniature pizzas. Sprinkle them with oregano and arrange them on absorbent kitchen paper on the base of the microwave cooker.

Cook for 5 minutes, rearranging the baps halfway through the cooking time. Brown under a conventional grill preheated to hot, if liked. Serve immediately.

Cook's Tip

Other cheeses can be substituted for the Mozzarrella cheese used above: try using thinly sliced or grated Edam or Cheddar cheese instead.

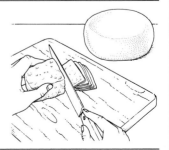

221 | Pizzas

Preparation time
15–20 minutes

Cooking time
21–22 minutes

Setting
Full power

Serves 4

Calories
500 per portion

You will need
50 g/2 oz All-bran cereal
6–7 tablespoons milk
1 egg, beaten
100 g/4 oz self-raising flour
1½ teaspoons baking powder
3 tablespoons margarine
175 g/6 oz Cheddar cheese, grated
3 slices cooked ham, cut into strips
6 button mushrooms, sliced

For the topping
1 tablespoon oil
1 small onion, chopped
1 clove garlic, crushed
1 (397-g/14-oz) can chopped
   tomatoes
1 tablespoon concentrated tomato
   purée
½ teaspoon dried mixed herbs
salt and pepper

For the topping cook the oil, onion and garlic on Full power for 4 minutes, then stir in the remaining ingredients. Cook for 10 minutes, stirring twice.

Mix the All-bran, 3 tablespoons milk and egg. Set aside for 10 minutes. Combine the flour and baking powder. Rub in the margarine, mix in 75 g/3 oz of the cheese and season. Mix in the All-bran and enough of the remaining milk to make a soft dough. Divide into four and pat into 11.5-cm/4½-inch rounds. Spread with topping, add the ham, mushrooms and remaining cheese. Cook, two at a time, for 3½–4 minutes.

222 | Tacos

Preparation time
10 minutes

Cooking time
7–10 minutes

Setting
Full power

Serves 4

Calories
360 per portion

You will need
2 tablespoons grapeseed or
   sunflower oil
225 g/8 oz lean minced beef
1 teaspoon chilli powder
2 tablespoons concentrated
   tomato purée
pinch of salt
freshly ground black pepper
2 onions, finely chopped
2 large tomatoes, finely chopped
1 lettuce heart, shredded
50 g/2 oz Edam cheese, coarsely
   grated
8 taco shells

Place the oil and the beef in a bowl with the chilli powder. Cover and cook on Full power for 3 minutes. Stir the beef thoroughly with a fork to break it up. Replace the cover and cook for a further 2–3 minutes.

Stir in the tomato purée and season with salt and pepper to taste, cover again and cook for a further 1–2 minutes until well cooked. Transfer the mixture to a warmed serving bowl and set aside, covered.

Place the vegetables and cheese in separate bowls. Arrange the taco shells on the base of the microwave cooker and cook for 1–2 minutes or until warm. To serve allow each guest to spoon a little of the chilli mixture into a taco shell and top with a little onion, tomato, lettuce, and cheese.

Cook's Tip

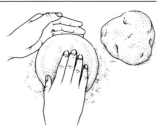

The secret of successful scones, and scone pizzas, is to handle the dough as little as possible. Mix lightly and swiftly and do not roll the dough heavily; simply pat it out to form the four pizzas.

Cook's Tip

Shredded Chinese leaves may be used in place of the lettuce heart, and Cheddar cheese instead of Edam, if preferred.

223 | Tomato, Onion and Salami Flan

Preparation time
10 minutes

Cooking time
27 minutes

Setting
Full power, Defrost

Serves 4—6

Calories
390—260 per portion

You will need
100 g/4 oz salami
500 g/18 oz onions
2 tablespoons oil
1 (225-g/8-oz) can tomatoes
1 teaspoon dried mixed herbs
salt and pepper
1 (20-cm/8-in) pre-baked pastry
 flan case

Thinly slice the salami into 12 thin circles and chop the remainder. Set aside. Slice the onions thinly and place in a bowl with the oil. Cover and cook on Full power for 10 minutes. Add the tomatoes, seasonings and herbs. Re-cover. Cook for another 2 minutes. Add the chopped salami.

Pour the filling into the pastry case. Arrange the salami slices around the perimeter, overlapping each one. Cook on Defrost for about 15 minutes. Leave to stand for 3—4 minutes before serving, or serve cold.

224 | Pasta Pronto

Preparation time
10 minutes

Cooking time
5 minutes, plus 15
minutes to cook pasta

Setting
Full power

Serves 4

Calories
400 per portion

You will need
225 g/8 oz pasta spirals
salt and freshly ground black
 pepper
100 g/4 oz ham, chopped
15 g/½ oz butter
100 g/4 oz frozen peas
225 g/8 oz cottage cheese, sieved
4 tablespoons single cream

Cook the pasta in boiling salted water for about 15 minutes, until tender. While the pasta is boiling, place the ham and butter in a dish with the peas. Cook on Full power for 5 minutes. Drain the pasta and add to the peas and ham. Stir well and arrange in four dishes. Beat cottage cheese and cream, spoon over pasta and serve immediately.

Cook's Tip

To remove the skin on salami, first slice into rounds, then cut off the skin on each using kitchen scissors.

Cook's Tip

If the pasta is to be truly pronto, you need to be able to vary the recipe to utilize whatever you have in refrigerator or store-cupboard. Try substituting sliced grilled sausage or cooked chicken for the ham, or use a small **drained can of shrimps or prawns.**

Sauces and Preserves

A microwave oven can only cope with relatively small quantities of ingredients, so this is not the method to use if you want to turn gluts of fruit into jams, jellies and chutneys. However, small quantities can be made in minutes and it is a marvellous way of experimenting with unusual combinations of ingredients. When it comes to making sauces your microwave will revolutionise your approach. Recipes for all the most popular basic sauces are here.

225 | Plum Jam

(Illustrated on back jacket)

Preparation time
5 minutes

Cooking time
30 minutes

Setting
Full power

Makes about 1 kg/ 2 lb

Total calories
1,940

You will need
675 g/1½ lb plums, stoned and quartered
450 g/1 lb caster sugar

Place the plums in a large mixing bowl and cook on Full power for 5 minutes, stirring once. Stir in the sugar until dissolved. Cook for a further 25 minutes or until the jam has reached setting point, stirring several times during cooking. Cool slightly. Pour into sterilised jars, cover with circles of waxed paper, seal and label.

226 | Apple Jelly

Preparation time
3–4 minutes

Cooking time
17–21 minutes

Setting
Full power

Makes 1 kg/2 lb jelly

Calories
335 per 100 g/4 oz

You will need
475 ml/16 fl oz unsweetened apple juice
800 g/1¾ lb sugar
5 tablespoons commercial pectin
few drops green food colouring (optional)

Place the apple juice and sugar in a 3-litre/5-pint bowl. Mix well, cover and cook on Full power for 12–14 minutes, stirring after 6 minutes.

Carefully stir in the pectin and mix thoroughly. Cover and cook on Full power for 4–6 minutes until the mixture boils. Boil the jelly in the microwave for 1 minute. Stir and remove any foam.

Colour with green food colouring, if desired. Ladle into clean, warmed jars, cover, seal and label.

Cook's Tip

You can sterilise jars in a microwave. Half-fill each jar with water and heat until boiling. Remove carefully because the jars will be hot, pour away the water and drain upside-down before filling.

Cook's Tip

This jelly is particularly good over gingerbread cake, topped with double cream, or to delight children serve on its own with gingerbread men.

227 | Lemon Curd

Preparation time
5 minutes

Cooking time
19–20 minutes

Setting
Full power

**Makes about 1 kg/
2¼ lb**

Total calories
2,365

You will need
3 eggs
grated rind and juice of 3 large
  lemons
100 g/4 oz butter
350 g/12 oz sugar

Sterilise two 450-g/1-lb pots (see Cook's Tip 225). Keep warm. Beat the eggs in a large bowl with the lemon rind. Pour the lemon juice into a basin with the butter and sugar. Cook this mixture on Full power for 6 minutes. Gradually pour the butter mixture on to the eggs, whisking continuously. Place the bowl in the microwave and cook for 13–14 minutes, whisking after 2 and 4 minutes of cooking and then every minute to prevent any part over-cooking. Strain the curd and pour it into the prepared pots. Cover at once with waxed paper discs. Cool. Top with lids, label and store in the refrigerator for up to 1 month.

Cook's Tip

**Use 3 juicy oranges and their
rind to make an orange curd.**

228 | Redberry Jam

Preparation time
10 minutes

Cooking time
17 minutes

Setting
Full power

**Makes about
750 g/1½ lb**

Total calories
1,905

You will need
450 g/1 lb mixed red fruits such as
  strawberries, raspberries,
  redcurrants, blackcurrants etc.
1 tablespoon lemon juice
450 g/1 lb granulated or preserving
  sugar

Wash and prepare the fruits. Put into a large ovenproof bowl. Add the lemon juice.
  Cook on Full power for 5 minutes or until the fruit is soft. Add the sugar and stir until dissolved. Cook for 12 minutes, and check for set. If setting point has not been reached, return to the microwave oven for a further 2 minutes, and check again. Continue this, if necessary, until setting point is reached. Cool slightly, and then put into clean warm jars. Cover and label.

Cook's Tip

**Lemon juice helps this soft
fruit jam to set. Pectin or
tartaric acid works in the same
way. Blackberries or stoned
damsons may also be included
in the jam. Use as filling for a
sponge cake or jam tarts, or
for a cream tea.**

229 | Tomato Relish

Preparation time
20 minutes

Cooking time
3 minutes

Setting
Full power

Makes about
750 ml / 1¼ pints

Total calories
170

You will need
2 teaspoons mustard powder mixed to a paste with water
1 tablespoon dark brown sugar
2 teaspoons white vinegar
½ teaspoon salt
6 firm tomatoes, peeled and chopped
2 sticks celery, chopped
1 green pepper, cored, deseeded and chopped
1 bunch spring onions, trimmed and finely chopped

Place the mustard, sugar, vinegar and salt in a large bowl and cook on Full power for 1 minute. Add the tomatoes, celery, pepper and onions and cook for 2 minutes, stirring well at the end of the cooking time. Cool and chill before serving. Leftovers can be stored in the refrigerator for up to 1 week.

230 | Corn Relish

Preparation time
5 minutes

Cooking time
20 minutes

Setting
Full power

Makes about
1.5 kg / 3 lb

Total calories
1,965

You will need
225 g / 8 oz sugar
2 tablespoons cornflour
1 small onion, chopped
1 tablespoon white mustard seeds
1 teaspoon celery seeds
¼ teaspoon turmeric
250 ml / 8 fl oz vinegar
150 ml / ¼ pint hot water
3 (362-g / 11½-oz) cans sweetcorn with peppers, drained

Place the sugar, cornflour, onion, mustard seeds, celery seeds and turmeric in a large bowl and mix well. Add the vinegar and water and stir thoroughly. Cover and cook on Full power for 5 minutes. Add the sweetcorn with peppers and stir thoroughly. Cover and cook for a further 15 minutes, stirring halfway through the cooking time. Ladle into three cleaned and scalded 450-g / 1-lb pots, cover immediately and label. Cool and keep for at least a week before eating.

Cook's Tip

Peel tomatoes by placing them in a large bowl and pouring boiling water over them. Leave for 30–60 seconds (depending on how ripe they are), drain and peel at once. Slit the skins with a sharp knife and slip them off.

Cook's Tip

Whole mustard seeds are nutty to the bite with a mild flavour. They are perfect in pickles and relishes and also taste good with potato salad, steamed cabbage and cheese dishes. Try using sparingly when cooking pork, veal or fish.

231 | *Cranberry Sauce*

Preparation time
2 minutes

Cooking time
3 minutes

Setting
Full power

Serves 4

Calories
115 per portion

You will need
100 g/4 oz cranberries
100 g/4 oz sugar
2 tablespoons port

Place the cranberries in a large basin with the sugar and cover. Cook on Full power for 3 minutes, stir thoroughly while adding the port. Cover until cool then serve.

232 | *Apple Sauce*

Preparation time
6 minutes

Cooking time
7 minutes

Setting
Full power

Serves 4

Calories
180 per portion

You will need
450 g/1 lb cooking apples,
*   peeled and cored*
100 g/4 oz sugar
25 g/1 oz butter

Slice the apple into a large basin and stir in the sugar. Cover and cook on Full power for 7 minutes. Add the butter and beat the apples until smooth. Cool.

Cook's Tip

An orange flavour goes well with cranberries, so either substitute the grated rind and juice of 1 orange for the port or use 1 tablespoon of an orange-flavoured liqueur.

Cook's Tip

Stir 2 tablespoons of chopped fresh herbs, such as sage, parsley, thyme, rosemary and/ or tarragon, in to the sauce and serve with chicken, lamb or ham, not just pork.

233 | Béchamel Sauce

Preparation time
5 minutes

Cooking time
10 minutes

Setting
Full power

Serves 4–6

Calories
180–120 per portion

You will need
40 g/1½ oz plain flour
1 bay leaf
blade of mace
600 ml/1 pint milk
salt and freshly ground white
   pepper
25 g/1 oz butter

Place the flour, bay leaf and mace in a large basin, gradually pour in the milk, whisking all the time, to make a smooth mixture. Add salt and pepper to taste, and the butter. Cook on Full power for 10 minutes, whisking twice during cooking and again at the end of the cooking time. Discard the bay leaf and mace. Check seasoning before serving.

Variations

Cheese: add 100–175 g/4–6 oz grated Cheddar cheese to the sauce, whisking until it melts. Cook for 1 minute.
Mushroom: add 225 g/8 oz thinly sliced button mushrooms to the sauce and cook for 2 minutes.
Parsley: chop a large handful of fresh parsley and add it to the sauce, stir well and serve.
Onion: finely chop 1 large onion or 2 small onions and cook in 25 g/1 oz butter for 5 minutes on Full power. Then add the flour and milk, stir in the bay leaf and mace and cook as in the main recipe.

Cook's Tip

Mace, the outer covering of the whole nutmeg, adds character to both savoury and sweet dishes. It is stronger than nutmeg in flavour.

234 | Bread Sauce

Preparation time
5 minutes

Cooking time
10–10½ minutes

Setting
Full power

Serves 4

Calories
155 per portion

You will need
1 large onion
6 cloves
1 bay leaf
600 ml/1 pint milk
100 g/4 oz fresh white
   breadcrumbs
salt and freshly ground white
   pepper
¼ teaspoon freshly grated nutmeg

Stud the onion with the cloves and stand it in a 1.15-litre/2-pint basin. Cover and cook on Full power for 2 minutes. Add the bay leaf and pour in the milk, cover and cook for a further 6–6½ minutes. Stir in the breadcrumbs, salt and pepper and nutmeg, and cook for a further 2 minutes uncovered. Remove the onion and bay leaf and whisk the sauce. Check the seasoning before serving.

Cook's Tip

Cooked in a microwave this traditional sauce has a very good flavour. So don't just serve it with turkey, but try it with boiled ham or roast chicken.

235 | Hollandaise Sauce

Preparation time
5 minutes

Cooking time
5 minutes

Setting
Full power

Serves 4

Calories
220 per portion

You will need
2 tablespoons lemon juice
1 tablespoon water
salt and freshly ground white
    pepper
100 g/4 oz butter
2 large egg yolks

Pour the lemon juice and water into a 1.15-litre/2-pint basin, stir in a little seasoning. Cook on Full power for 2 minutes. Place the butter in a heatproof measuring jug or small basin. When the lemon juice and water are hot, whisk in the egg yolks immediately. Heat the butter for 2½ minutes. Slowly pour it on to the egg yolk mixture, whisking continuously. Cook the sauce for 30 seconds, stir well, check seasoning, and serve at once.

236 | Tomato Sauce

Preparation time
10 minutes

Cooking time
18 minutes

Setting
Full power

Serves 4–6

Calories
180–120 per portion

You will need
2 sticks celery, finely chopped
1 large onion, chopped
1–3 cloves garlic, crushed
50 g/2 oz butter
1 bay leaf
2 tablespoons concentrated
    tomato purée
1 tablespoon plain flour
2 (397-g/14-oz) cans chopped
    tomatoes
150 ml/¼ pint full-bodied red wine
salt and pepper

Place the celery, onion and garlic (to taste) in a 1.15-litre/2-pint basin. Add the butter, cover and cook on Full power for 6 minutes. Stir in the bay leaf, purée, and flour, then the tomatoes and wine, mixing well. Cook for 10 minutes, stirring once during cooking.

Cool slightly. Discard the bay leaf. Blend the sauce in a liquidiser until smooth. Season to taste. Cook for 2 minutes until hot and serve as required. Makes about 600 ml/1 pint of sauce.

Cook's Tip

Use a liquidiser for even quicker results. Heat the lemon juice and water as above. Put the seasoning and egg yolks in the liquidiser and pour the hot liquid into it while working. Process for 1 minute. Heat the butter for 3½ minutes.

While the liquidiser is working, pour in the butter in a slow trickle. Serve straight from the liquidiser.

Cook's Tip

Made with lots of garlic, the sauce turns freshly cooked pasta into a quick meal when served with Parmesan cheese. Use less garlic in a sauce for cooking chicken portions or meat balls.

237 | Barbecue Sauce

Preparation time
5 minutes

Cooking time
8–10 minutes

Setting
Full power

**Makes 300 ml/
½ pint sauce**

Total calories
330

You will need
25 g/1 oz butter
1 teaspoon oil
1 onion, finely chopped
3 tablespoons boiling water
2 tablespoons vinegar
1 tablespoon Worcestershire
  sauce
2 tablespoons lemon juice
2 teaspoons soft brown sugar
2 teaspoons prepared mustard
½ teaspoon salt
½ teaspoon paprika
¼ teaspoon chilli powder

Place the butter and oil in a bowl and cook on Full power for 1 minute. Add the onion and cook for 2 minutes.

Add the remaining ingredients, cover and cook on Full power for 5–7 minutes, stirring after 3 minutes. Serve hot.

238 | Custard Sauce

Preparation time
5 minutes

Cooking time
6½–7 minutes

Setting
Full power

Serves 4–6

Calories
170–115 per portion

You will need
2 tablespoons custard powder
600 ml/1 pint milk
2 egg yolks
2 tablespoons sugar

Mix the custard powder to a smooth paste with a little of the milk in a 1.15-litre/2-pint basin. Beat in the egg yolks and sugar. Heat the remaining milk on Full power for 4 minutes.

Gradually pour the hot milk into the basin, whisking all the time. Cook for 2½–3 minutes, whisking once during cooking time and then again just before the end of the cooking time. Serve at once, or cover the surface with greaseproof paper and allow to cool.

Cook's Tip

This sauce makes a zesty marinade for chicken breasts, lamb or beef kebabs, and steak. Leave the meat in the marinade for at least an hour before barbecuing.

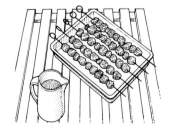

Cook's Tip

Covering the surface of the sauce with greaseproof paper while still hot prevents the formation of a skin. When the custard is cool, remove the paper, scraping off any custard that adheres to it with a palette knife.

239 | *Brandy Sauce*

Preparation time
5 minutes

Cooking time
8 minutes

Setting
Full power

Serves 4–6

Calories
185–125 per portion

You will need
2 tablespoons cornflour
3 tablespoons sugar
600 ml/1 pint milk
4 tablespoons brandy

Mix the cornflour and sugar to a smooth paste with a little of the milk in a 1.15-litre/2-pint basin. Heat the remaining milk on Full power for 4 minutes. Gradually pour the hot milk on to the cornflour mixture, whisking all the time. Cook for a further 4 minutes. Whisk thoroughly at the end of the cooking time, adding the brandy as you do so. Serve at once.

240 | *Fudge Sauce*

Preparation time
3–4 minutes

Cooking time
5–6 minutes

Setting
Full power

**Makes 350 ml/
12 fl oz sauce**

Total calories
1,605

You will need
225 g/8 oz sugar
¼ teaspoon salt
1 (170-g/6-oz) can evaporated milk
50 g/2 oz plain dessert chocolate, broken into pieces
25 g/1 oz butter
1 teaspoon vanilla essence

Place the sugar, salt and milk in a bowl and mix well. Cook on Full power for 5–6 minutes, until the sauce is boiling rapidly.

Carefully add the chocolate, butter and vanilla and stir until the chocolate is melted. Serve warm.

Cook's Tip

For a less expensive sauce, use a medium dry sherry instead of the brandy.

Cook's Tip

This elegant, rich sauce tastes delicious with plain vanilla or coffee ice cream.

Puddings and Desserts

Suet pudding is cooked in minutes rather than hours; simple poached fruit which has a wonderful texture and flavour, and dried fruit compotes that don't need pre-soaking are just a few of the benefits that a microwave oven brings to pudding recipes.

241 | Tropical Shortcake

(Illustrated on front jacket)

Preparation time
Make the double cream at least 3 hours before it's required. 20 minutes

Cooking time
6–8 minutes

Setting
Full power

Serves 6–8

Calories
775–565 per portion

You will need
175 g/6 oz butter, softened
100 g/4 oz dark brown sugar
1 egg, separated
50 g/2 oz desiccated coconut
225 g/8 oz plain flour

For the filling
450 g/1 lb fresh dessert fruit
1 quantity Danish double cream (see Cook's Tip)
150 ml/¼ pint natural yogurt

Beat the butter until smooth, then beat in the sugar and egg yolk. Work in the coconut and flour. Divide the mixture in half. Press one piece on to a plate to make a circle about 20-cm/8-inches in diameter. Cook on Full power for 3–4 minutes, turning the plate once during cooking. Repeat with the remaining shortcake mixture. Cool completely.

   Cut the fruit into pieces and reserve some for decoration. Whisk the egg white until stiff. Whisk the cream until thick and reserve about a quarter. Fold the yogurt into the remaining cream, then fold in the egg white and fruit. Sandwich the shortcake together with this mixture. Top with the reserved cream and decorate with the reserved fruit.

242 | Apricot Crisp

Preparation time
5 minutes

Cooking time
3 minutes

Setting
Full power

Serves 4

Calories
270 per portion

You will need
50 g/2 oz unsalted butter
25 g/1 oz soft brown sugar
1 tablespoon golden syrup
1 tablespoon desiccated coconut
100 g/4 oz cornflakes
1 (425-g/15-oz) can apricot halves in natural juice

Place the butter, sugar and syrup in a basin and cook on Full power for 2 minutes. Stir in the coconut and cornflakes until coated with the butter mixture. Place the apricots, cut sides upwards, with 2 tablespoons of the can juices in a suitable serving dish. Mound the cornflake mixture on top and cook for 1 minute. Serve warm or cold with single cream

---

Cook's Tip

To make the cream place 250 ml/8 fl oz milk in a basin with 175 g/6 oz butter and 1½ teaspoons gelatine. Cook on Full power for 2–2½ minutes, until the butter has melted, stirring once. Blend in a liquidiser for 30 seconds, then chill for at least 3 hours. Use as required. This is a good substitute for fresh double cream.

Cook's Tip

Poach fresh apricot halves in a sugar syrup,* covered, for 4–5 minutes on Full power, stirring once. *Syrup: use 50 g/2 oz sugar 150 ml/¼ pint water and 1 tablespoon lemon juice in a bowl, cover and cook for 5–6 minutes, stirring once.

243 | Fruit Flan

Preparation time
10 minutes, plus 3½
hours to chill

Cooking time
3 minutes, including
preparing Danish cream

Setting
Full power

Serves 6

Calories
580 per portion

You will need
50 g/2 oz unsalted butter, cubed
1 tablespoon liquid honey
175 g/6 oz Nice biscuits, crumbed
450 ml/¾ pint fresh or Danish
    double cream (see Cook's Tip
    241), whipped
175 g/6 oz raspberries
2 tablespoons icing sugar
2 small bananas
2 tablespoons lemon juice
angelica to decorate

Place the butter in a medium bowl and cook on Full power for 1 minute or until melted. Stir in the honey and biscuit crumbs and mix well. Press into a buttered 20-cm/8-inch loose-bottomed flan tin. Chill for 30 minutes.

Set aside 150 ml/¼ pint of the cream. Whip the remaining cream until stiff. Reserve 6 raspberries and mash the remainder. Stir the mashed raspberries into the cream, with sifted icing sugar to taste.

Slice the bananas and coat them in the lemon juice to prevent discoloration. Drain thoroughly, then fold into the cream mixture.

Spoon the raspberry filling into the biscuit crust and chill in the refrigerator for 3 hours or until required. Just before serving, whip the reserved cream, place in a piping bag and decorate the flan with cream rosettes, angelica and reserved raspberries.

Cook's Tip

An easy way to obtain a smooth crumb crust with even sides is to pile the crumb mixture into the tin, then use a small straight-sided pan to flatten the base and press the crumbs into the sides.

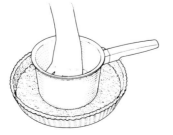

244 | Apricot Rum Caramel

Preparation time
5 minutes, plus 1–2
hours to cool

Cooking time
12 minutes

Setting
Full power

Serves 4

Calories
270 per portion

You will need
1 (411-g/14½-oz) can apricot halves
    in natural juice
225 g/8 oz light brown sugar
150 ml/¼ pint water
2 tablespoons rum
sponge fingers to serve

Drain the apricots, reserving the juice. Place the fruit in a large heatproof bowl and set aside.

Combine the sugar and water in a 1.15-litre/2-pint bowl and stir thoroughly. Cook on Full power for 12 minutes, stirring only once, after 2 minutes, to dissolve the sugar.

As soon as the caramel is a rich brown, remove it from the oven and carefully (see Cook's Tip) trickle in the reserved fruit juice and rum and stir. If necessary, return the bowl to the microwave oven for a few minutes to dissolve the caramel again. Pour the warm syrup over the apricots and set aside for 1–2 hours to cool. Serve in four sundae dishes, with sponge fingers.

Cook's Tip

Hold the bowl with oven mitts and place it on a mat. Add the juice and rum with great care, protecting your hand and standing at arm's length as the mixture will spit violently at first.

245 | Cherry Melba Pie

Preparation time
10–15 minutes, plus about 2–2½ hours to chill

Cooking time
5–5½ minutes

Setting
Full power

Serves 6

Calories
665 per portion

You will need
75 g/3 oz butter
175 g/6 oz digestive biscuits, crumbed
175 g/6 oz cream cheese
75 g/3 oz caster sugar
½ teaspoon vanilla essence
300 ml/½ pint double cream
1 (425-g/15-oz) can black cherries
1 tablespoon arrowroot

Place the butter in a bowl and cook on Full power for 1–1½ minutes or until melted. Stir in the biscuit crumbs and mix well. Press into a buttered 20-cm/8-inch loose-bottomed flan tin. Chill in the refrigerator for 30 minutes.

In a mixing bowl, cream the cheese with the sugar and beat in the vanilla essence. Whip the cream to soft peaks and fold into the cheese mixture, using a metal spoon. Add the cheese filling to the biscuit shell. Chill in the refrigerator for 1–2 hours.

Drain the cherries over a large jug. Remove the stones and set the cherries aside. Add the arrowroot to the cherry syrup, stir until smooth and cook for 4 minutes, stirring once during cooking and again when cooking is complete. Allow to cool completely.

Carefully remove the pie from the tin. Arrange the cherries on top and coat with the cooled sauce. Serve immediately (see Cook's Tip).

Cook's Tip

Do not allow the pie to stand for more than a few minutes after adding the cherries or they may discolour the cream cheese base.

246 | Apricot Flan

Preparation time
20–25 minutes

Cooking time
9–10 minutes, plus 20–25 minutes to bake flan case

Setting
Full power, Medium

Serves 6–8

Calories
470–355 per portion

You will need

For the flan case
175 g/6 oz plain flour
100 g/4 oz butter
2 tablespoons caster sugar
1 egg yolk
1–2 tablespoons water

For the filling
2 egg yolks
50 g/2 oz caster sugar
50 g/2 oz plain flour
300 ml/½ pint milk
2 drops vanilla essence
1 (425-g/15-oz) can apricot halves
3 tablespoons apricot jam
25 g/1 oz flaked almonds, toasted

Sift the flour into a bowl and rub in the butter, stir in the sugar and bind with the yolk and water. Chill, then roll out to line a 20-cm/8-inch flan tin. Line with greaseproof paper and baking beans. Bake blind in a moderately hot oven (200 C, 400 F, gas 6) for 15 minutes, remove the paper and beans and cook for 5–10 minutes.

For the filling, beat the yolks and sugar until creamy. Stir in the flour. Heat the milk on Full power for 4 minutes, then whisk it into the egg. Cook on Medium for 4–5 minutes, stirring frequently, until thick. Stir in the vanilla. Cover the surface with cling film and cool, then spread in the flan. Drain the apricots, reserving 2 tablespoons of the juice, and arrange in the flan. Heat the jam and fruit juice for 1 minute. Use to glaze the apricots and top with almonds.

Cook's Tip

Pastry cases can be cooked in the microwave oven, but it is a fiddly business, requiring the sides of the case to be shielded with foil strips and the base to be lined with absorbent kitchen paper for perfect results. It is far better to cook the pastry conventionally while using the microwave oven to prepare the filling.

247 | Bananas Flambés

Preparation time
5 minutes

Cooking time
8 minutes

Setting
Full power

Serves 4

Calories
245 per portion

You will need
50 g/2 oz unsalted butter
grated rind and juice of 1 orange
½ teaspoon ground cinnamon
50 g/2 oz demerara sugar
4 firm bananas
2–3 tablespoons dark rum
orange segments to decorate
 (optional)
single cream for serving

Place the butter in a basin and cook on Full power for 1 minute or until hot. Stir in the orange rind and juice, cinnamon and sugar until the sugar has dissolved. Cook for 2 minutes or until slightly syrupy. Peel the bananas and cut into 1-cm/½-inch diagonal slices and stir into orange mixture. Cook for 5 minutes. Remove and immediately pour over rum and set alight. Stir gently to mix, decorate with orange segments, if using, and serve with cream.

248 | Peach Blues

Preparation time
10 minutes

Cooking time
3½ minutes

Setting
Full power, Defrost

Serves 6—8

Calories
595–445 per portion

You will need
50 g/2 oz unsalted butter
1 tablespoon golden syrup
¼ teaspoon ground cinnamon
225 g/8 oz digestive or shortcake
 biscuits, crushed
angelica diamonds to decorate

For the filling
1 (425-g/15-oz) can peach halves
 in syrup
175 g/6 oz blue brie
1 tablespoon caster sugar
300 ml/½ pint whipping cream

Place the butter, syrup and cinnamon in a basin and cook on Full power for 2–3 minutes or until the butter has melted. Stir in the crushed biscuits until well mixed and use to line the base and sides of a lightly buttered 20-cm/8-inch flan dish. Chill.

Drain the peaches and reserve 2 tablespoons of the syrup. Remove rind from cheese, place in a basin and soften on Defrost for 20 seconds. Beat in the reserved syrup and the sugar. Whisk the cream until it forms soft peaks. Remove 3 tablespoons, beat until stiff, and place in a piping bag fitted with a large star nozzle. Add remaining cream to cheese mixture and beat thoroughly until mixture thickens slightly. Reserve 1 peach half, chop the remainder and stir into the cheese mixture. Fill the biscuit case. Slice the reserved peach and use to decorate .flan. Pipe reserved cream decoratively round flan and finish with the angelica diamonds.

Cook's Tip

To heat the rum for flaming, pour it into a measuring jug and microwave on Full power for 15 seconds.

Cook's Tip

Brie, a soft cows' milk cheese, should be plump and smooth but not runny. Remove the white floury crust with a sharp knife before softening it in the microwave.

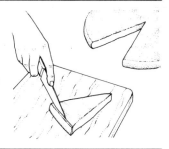

249 | Pear Mould

Preparation time
10 minutes, plus
setting time

Cooking time
2½ minutes

Setting
Full power, Defrost

Serves 6

Calories
110 per portion

You will need
2 (425-g/15-oz) cans pear halves
25 g/1 oz gelatine
grated rind and juice of 1 lemon
about 450 ml/¾ pint milk
yellow food colouring (optional)

Drain the pear juice from one can into a large jug. Heat on Full power for 30 seconds. Sprinkle in the gelatine, leave for 2 minutes, then heat on Defrost for 2 minutes. Stir to dissolve, then stir in the remaining pear juice, lemon rind and juice and milk to make 900 ml/1½ pints. Cool for 15 minutes. Finely chop the pears from one can, stir into the jelly with a little colouring, if liked, and pour into a 1-litre/2-pint mould. Chill until set. Unmould and decorate with pear halves.

250 | Stuffed Peaches

Preparation time
10 minutes

Cooking time
5 minutes

Setting
Full power

Serves 4

Calories
205 per portion

You will need
4 large peaches
6 macaroon biscuits, crushed
1 tablespoon chopped mixed peel
50 g/2 oz nibbed almonds
1 tablespoon Cointreau
3 tablespoons white wine
25 g/1 oz caster sugar

Cut the peaches in half and remove the stones. Scoop out about one-third of the flesh and chop finely. Place the halves in a circle on a large round dish. Mix the chopped peach with the macaroons, peel, almonds and Cointreau. Fill the peach halves with this mixture. Spoon the wine over the tops and sprinkle over the sugar. Cook on Full power for 5 minutes. Serve warm or cold.

Cook's Tip

To unmould, place mould (if not metal) on Full power for 30 seconds or until jelly is loosened from the edge. Alternatively, place mould in hot water for 30 seconds. Invert jelly on to serving plate and remove mould.

Cook's Tip

If you like, substitute the peaches in this recipe with that shiny-skinned member of the same family, the nectarine.

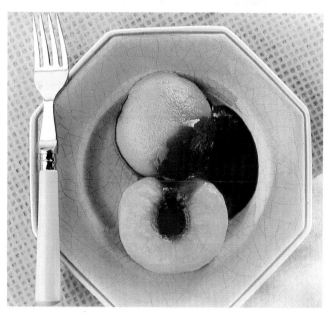

251 | Bananas with Orange and Peanuts

Preparation time
10 minutes

Cooking time
4 minutes

Setting
Full power

Serves 4

Calories
275 per portion

You will need

For the salad
3 oranges
3 bananas
50g/2oz unsalted peanuts

For the sauce
grated rind and juice of 1 orange
25g/1oz butter
50g/2oz light brown soft sugar
generous pinch of ground ginger

Grate the orange rind and cut away the pith. Cut out the segments and place in a serving bowl with the thickly sliced bananas and the peanuts. Place the orange rind, juice, butter, sugar and ginger in a bowl. Heat, un-covered, on Full power for 4 minutes, stirring occasionally, until the sauce is syrupy. Pour the hot sauce over the fruit, cover and cool. Serve chilled with whipped cream.

252 | Poached Peaches

Preparation time
10 minutes

Cooking time
7 minutes

Setting
Full power

Serves 4

Calories
120 per portion

You will need
4 firm, ripe peaches
1 tablespoon lemon juice
300 ml/½ pint unsweetened
 orange juice
2 tablespoons clear honey
fresh mint to decorate (optional)

For the sauce
100g/4oz raspberries, defrosted if
 frozen
2 tablespoons soft light brown
 sugar

Halve, stone and peel the peaches and sprinkle them with lemon juice. Set aside.

Place the orange juice and honey in a shallow oven-proof dish large enough to accommodate the peaches in a single layer. Cover and cook on Full power for 2 minutes. Stir well and add the peach halves, spooning over some of the juice. Re-cover as before and cook on Full power for 2 minutes. Allow to stand, covered, while making the sauce.

Place the raspberries and sugar in a bowl and cover. Cook for 3 minutes, stirring halfway through the cooking time. Place the mixture in a blender or food processor and blend until smooth.

Arrange the peaches on individual serving dishes with a little of the cooking liquid and surround each with some raspberry sauce. Decorate with fresh mint, if using, and serve any remaining raspberry sauce separately.

Cook's Tip

For a special occasion, stir 1 tablespoon of brandy into the sauce before pouring over the fruit.

Cook's Tip

You can substitute fresh or frozen blackberries for the raspberries in the sauce.

253 | Mini Cheesecakes

Preparation time
10–15 minutes, plus
1 hour to set

Cooking time
1½ minutes

Setting
Full power, Defrost

Serves 4

Calories
475 per portion

You will need
25 g / 1 oz butter
2 teaspoons golden syrup
100 g / 4 oz ginger biscuits,
　crumbed
200 g / 7 oz soft cheese with
　pineapple
6 tablespoons whipping cream
4 canned pineapple rings
angelica diamonds to decorate
　(see Cook's Tip)

Place the butter in a bowl and melt on Full power for 45 seconds, then add syrup and biscuit crumbs. Mix well.

Stand a lightly-greased 8-cm/3¼-inch biscuit cutter on a baking sheet lined with non-stick paper. Press a quarter of the mixture into the cutter to form a biscuit base. Carefully lift off the cutter. Repeat to make four biscuit bases. Chill for 1 hour or until set.

Place the cheese in a large bowl and soften on Defrost for 45 seconds. Beat well. Whip the cream to soft peaks and fold into the cheese. Place a third of this mixture in a piping bag fitted with a large star nozzle.

Spread the remaining cheese cream over the prepared biscuit bases and top each with a pineapple ring. Using a palette knife or fish slice, transfer the mini cheesecakes to four dessert plates. Decorate each with a rosette of cheese cream and angelica diamonds.

Cook's Tip

To cut the angelica, use a sharp knife or kitchen scissors, dipping the blades in hot water frequently.

254 | Autumn Crunch

Preparation time
10 minutes, plus 1 hour
to chill

Cooking time
12–14 minutes

Setting
Full power

Serves 4

Calories
315 per portion

You will need
350 g / 12 oz cooking apples
175 g / 6 oz blackberries
25 g / 1 oz caster sugar
50 g / 2 oz Country Store muesli
50 g / 2 oz fresh brown
　breadcrumbs
25 g / 1 oz hazelnuts, roasted
　(Cook's Tip 20)
50 g / 2 oz butter
50 g / 2 oz demerara sugar

Peel, core and slice the apples and place in a large bowl with the blackberries and caster sugar. Cover and cook on Full power for 8–10 minutes. Set aside.

In a second bowl, combine the muesli, breadcrumbs and hazelnuts. Add the butter and cook for 4 minutes (see Cook's Tip), stirring once or twice. Stir in the demerara sugar and set aside.

Layer the fruit and muesli mixture alternately in four individual glass dishes. Chill for at least 1 hour before serving.

Cook's Tip

For a crisper muesli layer, preheat a browning dish according to the manufacturer's instructions. Quickly add the butter to the dish, then the breadcrumbs, muesli and hazelnuts. Cook for 4 minutes, then follow the recipe.

255 | Red Fruit Dessert

Preparation time
5 minutes

Cooking time
7–8 minutes

Setting
Full power

Serves 4–6

Calories
265–180 per portion

You will need
675 g/1½ lb red fruit, such as
　redcurrants, blackcurrants,
　raspberries or strawberries
2 tablespoons water
175 g/6 oz sugar
2 tablespoons arrowroot
25 g/1 oz flaked almonds
caster sugar for sprinkling
single cream to serve

Place the fruit, water and sugar in a bowl, cover and cook on Full power for 5–6 minutes, stirring once. Check the mixture to see if it is sweet enough and stir in a little more sugar, if necessary. Blend the arrowroot to a smooth cream with a little water and stir into the fruit mixture. Cook for a further 2 minutes. Stand for 2 minutes.

　Pour into a serving dish and sprinkle surface with flaked almonds and a little caster sugar to prevent a skin forming. Serve warm, not hot, with single cream.

256 | Pears in Red Wine

Preparation time
15 minutes

Cooking time
11–14 minutes

Setting
Full power

Serves 4

Calories
190 per portion

You will need
8 small firm pears
juice of 1 lemon
75 g/3 oz brown sugar
300 ml/½ pint red wine
1 cinnamon stick
1 tablespoon arrowroot
3 tablespoons water

Peel and core the pears but do not remove the stalks. Sprinkle with the lemon juice. Mix the sugar, wine and cinnamon stick in a casserole, then add the pears. Cover and cook on Full power for 8–10 minutes, or until tender, rearranging once.

　Mix the arrowroot with the water until smooth. Transfer the pears to a serving dish. Stir the arrowroot into the cooking juices and cook for a further 3–4 minutes, or until thickened. Spoon over the pears and serve with cream.

Cook's Tip

Shortbread makes a very good accompaniment to this dish.

Cook's Tip

Stand the pears upright in the casserole for cooking, taking a thin slice off each base so that they do not fall over.

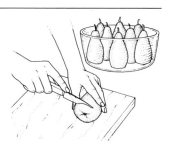

257 | Spiced Apple Charlotte

Preparation time
15 minutes

Cooking time
13–14 minutes, plus grilling time

Setting
Full power

Serves 4–6

Calories
315–210 per portion

You will need

For the topping
50 g/2 oz butter
75 g/3 oz fresh brown breadcrumbs
75 g/3 oz demerara sugar
½ teaspoon ground cinnamon

For the filling
25 g/1 oz sugar
½ teaspoon ground cinnamon
1 kg/2 lb cooking apples, peeled, cored and sliced
4 tablespoons orange juice

Place butter in a large shallow dish and cook on Full power for 1 minute. Add the breadcrumbs, sugar and cinnamon and stir well to coat. Cook, uncovered, on Full power for 5 minutes, stirring occasionally until slightly crisp. Leave to cool. Mix sugar, cinnamon and apples and place in a dish. Add the orange juice and cook, covered, on Full power for 7–8 minutes, stirring once. Top with the crumbs and grill to brown.

258 | Baked Apple Surprise

Preparation time
5 minutes

Cooking time
11 minutes, plus 5 minutes standing time

Setting
Full power

Serves 4

Calories
235 per portion

You will need
50 g/2 oz raisins
1 teaspoon finely grated lemon rind
2 tablespoons golden syrup
50 g/2 oz unsalted peanuts, chopped
4 (275-g/10-oz) cooking apples

Place the raisins, lemon rind and syrup in a small bowl. Cook on Full power for 1 minute. Stir in the peanuts.

Wash and core the apples. Score the skin around the equator of each. Arrange in a circle around the rim of a pie plate. Spoon a quarter of the raisin mixture into each cavity and cook for 10 minutes, rearranging the apples once. Allow to stand for 5 minutes before serving.

Cook's Tip

This topping makes an ideal crumble for any cooked fruit. Try adding chopped nuts or another spice for variety.

Cook's Tip

Don't waste leftover lemon rind. Place it on a glass plate and cook on Full power until all the moisture has evaporated. Cool, crumble and store in an airtight container for future use in cooking and baking.

259 | Minted Apple Snow

Preparation time
10 minutes, plus several hours to chill

Cooking time
10–12 minutes

Setting
Full power

Serves 4

Calories
135 per portion

You will need
1 kg/2 lb cooking apples
finely grated rind and juice of 1 orange
3 tablespoons clear honey
4 large mint sprigs
2 large egg whites

Peel and quarter the apples, then remove their cores and cut them into eighths. Place in a large bowl with the orange rind and juice. Stir in the honey. Set aside a few mint sprigs for decoration and add the rest to the bowl. Cover loosely and cook on Full power for 10–12 minutes, stirring and rearranging the fruit once.

Discard the mint, then beat the pulp vigorously with a wooden spoon to a smooth purée (see Cook's Tip). Set aside until cool.

Whisk the egg whites in a large bowl until stiff. Fold into the apple purée and spoon into a serving bowl or individual glasses. Decorate with the reserved mint leaves. Serve well chilled.

260 | Gooseberry Fool

Preparation time
5 minutes

Cooking time
3 minutes, plus 5 minutes standing time

Setting
Full power

Serves 4

Calories
140 per portion

You will need
225 g/8 oz gooseberries, defrosted if frozen
50 g/2 oz demerara sugar
2 tablespoons clear honey
225 g/8 oz Greek-style (strained) yogurt
mint sprigs to decorate

Place the gooseberries in a large ovenproof bowl with the sugar and honey and cook on Full power for 3 minutes, stirring halfway through the cooking time. Allow to stand for 5 minutes, stirring once. Transfer to a blender or food processor and blend until smooth. Transfer to a bowl.

Reserve 4 tablespoons of the yogurt and beat the remaining yogurt into the gooseberry purée. Divide the mixture between four individual serving dishes or glasses and chill before serving, decorated with mint and yogurt.

Cook's Tip

If preferred, purée the apples in a liquidiser or food processor. Keep some apple purée in a rigid container in the freezer to make a quick dessert. Defrost the purée on Medium for 4–5 minutes and beat well before use.

Cook's Tip

This fool can be made with other fruits such as blackberries, raspberries, blackcurrants or plums. You do not have to strain soft fruits as their seeds (or pips) are very high in dietary fibre. Ordinary natural yogurt may be used although the fool will not be as thick.

261 | Chocolate Supremes

Preparation time
15 minutes, plus 30 minutes to chill

Cooking time
1½–2 minutes

Setting
Full power

Serves 4

Calories
465 per portion

You will need
75 g/3 oz dark chocolate
300 ml/½ pint double cream
2 tablespoons orange liqueur or juice
2 teaspoons grated orange rind
2 egg whites

Break the chocolate into small squares and place in a basin. Cook on Full power for 1½–2 minutes or until melted.

Whip the cream until stiff enough to pipe and place 2 tablespoons in a piping bag fitted with a large star nozzle for decoration. Whisk the chocolate into the remaining cream with the liqueur or juice and orange rind.

Whisk the egg whites until they are stiff but not dry. Fold them into the chocolate mixture and spoon into ramekins or small glass dishes. Pipe a star of cream on top of each. Chill for at least 30 minutes before serving.

262 | Coffee and Ginger Syllabub

Preparation time
10 minutes, plus 4 hours to chill

Cooking time
3 minutes, plus preparing the Danish cream

Setting
Full power

Serves 4—6

Calories
410–275 per portion

You will need
300 ml/½ pint Danish double cream (Recipe 241)
150 ml/¼ pint ginger wine
2 tablespoons strong black coffee
50 g/2 oz caster sugar
dessert biscuits to serve (optional)

Make the Danish double cream in the microwave oven, following the instructions given under Cook's Tip 241.

Combine the ginger wine and coffee in a large bowl. Stir in the sugar. Cover and cook on Full power for 3 minutes, stirring once. Allow to cool.

Whip the chilled cream to soft peaks. Add the ginger wine mixture gradually, continuing to whip. Spoon into four or six glasses and chill lightly before serving with dessert biscuits, if liked.

Cook's Tip

You may like to try a coffee liqueur instead of the orange, in this case omit the orange rind and decorate the cream with an almond paste 'coffee' bean!

Cook's Tip

Use fresh cream in place of Danish, if preferred, and add a little finely chopped crystallised ginger for extra flavour and texture.

263 | Cheshire Cheesecake

Preparation time
10–15 minutes, plus 2 hours to chill

Cooking time
17 minutes

Setting
Full power, Medium

Serves 6

Calories
550 per portion

You will need
40 g/1½ oz butter
75 g/3 oz digestive biscuits, crushed (see Cook's Tip)
100 g/4 oz curd cheese
100 g/4 oz Cheshire cheese, crumbled
2 eggs, separated
3 tablespoons single cream
1 tablespoon cornflour
finely grated rind and juice of 2 lemons
50 g/2 oz caster sugar

For the decoration
icing sugar
150 ml/¼ pint double cream, whipped
crystallised lemon slices

Place the butter in a medium bowl and melt on Full power for 1 minute. Stir in the crushed biscuits and press into the base of a greased 23-cm/9-in flan dish. Chill well.

Mix the cheeses, egg yolks, cream and cornflour in a large bowl and beat thoroughly. Stir in the lemon rind and sugar, then beat in the lemon juice. Whisk the egg whites to soft peaks and gently fold them into the mixture. Spoon the mixture over the base and cook on Medium for 16 minutes or until the cheesecake is firm. Chill then serve, dredged with icing sugar and decorate as shown.

Cook's Tip

To crush the biscuits, break them up roughly and place in a plastic bag. Exclude most of the air (balloons burst!) and crush the biscuits with a rolling pin.

264 | Pear Surprise

Preparation time
5 minutes

Cooking time
1½–2 minutes

Setting
Full power

Serves 4

Calories
285 per portion

You will need
1 (411-g/14½-oz) can pear halves in syrup
100 g/4 oz plain chocolate, in squares
4 scoops vanilla ice cream
25 g/1 oz flaked almonds, toasted
ice cream wafers to decorate

Strain the pears, reserving 6 tablespoons juice. Arrange the pear halves in a heatproof glass serving dish.

Add the chocolate to the pear syrup and cook on Full power for 1½–2 minutes. Stir, cool slightly and pour over the pears.

Serve hot or cold, topped with scoops of ice cream (see Cook's Tip) and sprinkled with toasted almonds. Decorate with ice cream wafers.

Cook's Tip

Ice cream that has just emerged from the freezer is often too hard to scoop successfully. Soften it for a few seconds on Defrost.

265 | Curd Cheese and Raisin Flan

Preparation time
5 minutes, plus 1 hour standing time

Cooking time
22 minutes

Setting
Full power, Low

Serves 6—8

Calories
400—300 per portion

You will need
50 g/2 oz butter
75 g/3 oz digestive biscuits, crushed
pinch of freshly grated nutmeg
450 g/1 lb curd cheese
3 eggs
100 g/4 oz demerara sugar
grated rind of 1 lemon
50 g/2 oz raisins
seasonal fruit to decorate

Place the butter in a medium bowl and melt on Full power for 1 minute. Transfer half the melted butter to the bowl of a liquidiser or food processor. Add the crushed biscuits and nutmeg to the remaining butter and mix well. Press the mixture into the base of a lightly greased 23-cm/9-inch flan dish. Cook on Full power for 1 minute.

Add the cheese, eggs, sugar and lemon rind to the liquidiser or food processor and blend until smooth. Stir in the raisins and pour into the flan case. Cook on Low for 20 minutes until the mixture is set around the edges.

Allow to stand at room temperature for 1 hour, then decorate with any suitable seasonal fruit, such as fresh peaches, kiwi fruit, mandarin oranges, raspberries or cherries. Serve immediately.

Cook's Tip

For a special occasion or treat, soak the raisins in rum before adding them to the filling.

266 | Butterscotch Flan

Preparation time
5 minutes

Cooking time
17 minutes

Setting
Full power

Serves 6

Calories
635 per portion

You will need
1 (20-cm/8-in) shortcrust pastry flan case
175 g/6 oz soft brown sugar
175 g/6 oz margarine
1 (369-g/13-oz) can condensed milk

For the decoration
150 ml/¼ pint double cream, whipped
6 walnut halves

Place the flan case on a serving dish.

Place the sugar, margarine and milk in a large mixing bowl. Cook on Full power for 10 minutes. Stir well and cook for a further 7 minutes or until dark golden. Beat well. Pour into flan case and, when cold, decorate with circles of piped cream stars and the walnut halves.

Cook's Tip

An alternative topping, which adds texture as well as taste, may be provided by browned slivered almonds (Cook's Tip 10) arranged in concentric circles to completely cover the top of the flan. Serve with cream.

267 | *Marbled Pudding*

Preparation time
5 minutes

Cooking time
4 minutes, plus 5
minutes standing time

Setting
Full power

Serves 4

Calories
440 per portion

You will need
100 g/4 oz self-raising flour
¼ teaspoon baking powder
100 g/4 oz soft margarine
100 g/4 oz caster sugar
2 eggs
1 tablespoon water
1 teaspoon vanilla essence
25 g/1 oz walnuts, finely chopped
1 tablespoon strong cold black
  coffee

Sift the flour and baking powder into a mixing bowl. Add the margarine, sugar, eggs and water and beat until smooth.

Place half the mixture in a separate bowl. Add the vanilla essence to the original bowl and the walnuts and coffee to the other.

Drop alternate spoonfuls of the mixture into a greased 1.2-litre/2-pint pudding basin. Smooth the surface, cover loosely and cook on Full power for 4 minutes. Carefully remove the cover and allow to stand for 5 minutes. Invert on a serving plate and serve immediately.

268 | *Topsy-turvy Ring*

Preparation time
5 minutes

Cooking time
6–8 minutes

Setting
Full power

Serves 4–6

Calories
505–335 per portion

You will need
2 tablespoons soft light brown
  sugar
1 (439-g/15½-oz) can pineapple
  rings, drained
6–8 glacé cherries
100 g/4 oz self-raising flour
¼ teaspoon baking powder
100 g/4 oz soft margarine
100 g/4 oz caster sugar
2 eggs

Grease a 1.15-litre/2-pint ring dish. Sprinkle the brown sugar over the base and arrange the pineapple rings on top, placing a cherry in the centre of each.

Sift the flour and baking powder into a bowl. Add the remaining ingredients and beat until smooth. Spoon the mixture into the ring dish, taking care not to disturb the pineapple rings. Cover loosely and cook on Full power for 6–8 minutes. Remove the cover.

Allow to stand for 2 minutes, then invert on a serving plate. Serve immediately, with cream, if liked.

Cook's Tip

Ring the changes. Try adding 1 tablespoon cocoa mixed with 1 tablespoon boiling water to one bowl and 25 g/1 oz chopped hazelnuts to the other. For a pink and cream marble, use red food colouring instead of vanilla and replace the walnuts with finely chopped glacé cherries.

Cook's Tip

Brown sugar that has become hard can easily be softened in the microwave oven. Place 175 g/6 oz sugar in a bowl with a wedge of apple, cover and cook on Full power for about 30 seconds. Allow to stand for 5 minutes.

269 | Apple and Blackberry Crumble

Preparation time
15 minutes

Cooking time
6 minutes, plus 5 minutes standing time

Setting
Full power

Serves 4

Calories
395 per portion

You will need
450 g / 1 lb apples, peeled, cored and sliced
zest of 1 small lemon
2 tablespoons clear honey
225 g / 8 oz blackberries

For the topping
100 g / 4 oz wholemeal flour
50 g / 2 oz rolled oats
25 g / 1 oz butter
3 tablespoons grapeseed or sunflower oil
50 g / 2 oz demerara sugar

Arrange half the apples in a 1.5-litre/2½-pint ovenproof soufflé dish. Sprinkle on half of the lemon zest and drizzle over half of the honey. Reserve a few blackberries and add the remaining apples and honey.

In a large bowl mix together the flour and rolled oats and rub in the butter. Stir in the oil and sugar and spoon this mixture over the fruit. Cook on Full power for 6 minutes. Allow to stand for 5 minutes before decorating with the reserved blackberries and lemon zest.

270 | Fruited Sponge Pudding

Preparation time
10 minutes

Cooking time
4 minutes, plus 5 minutes standing time

Setting
Full power

Serves 2

Calories
470 per portion

You will need
50 g / 2 oz self-raising flour
50 g / 2 oz light soft brown sugar
50 g / 2 oz soft tub margarine
1 egg
2 tablespoons milk
25 g / 1 oz sultanas
25 g / 1 oz currants

Lightly grease a 900-ml/1½-pint pudding basin. Mix together the flour, sugar, margarine and egg and beat until light and creamy. Gradually add enough milk to make a soft, dropping consistency. Stir in the sultanas and currants. Spoon the mixture into the basin and cook on Full power for about 4 minutes, or until the surface is slightly moist.

Leave to stand for 5 minutes. Turn out of basin and serve hot or warm with cream or custard.

Cook's Tip

Wholemeal flour is milled from whole wheat grains and retains most of the original vitamins, salts and minerals. It is a good source of fibre. When sifting wholemeal, always return the contents of the sieve to the bowl.

Cook's Tip

Vary the fruits in this pudding to discover some interesting flavour combinations. Chopped dried figs and no-need-to-soak apricots, for instance, or prunes with glacé cherries.

271 | Spotted Dick

Preparation time
5 minutes

Cooking time
6–7 minutes, plus 4–5
minuts standing time

Setting
Full power

Serves 4–6

Calories
455–305 per portion

You will need
100 g/4 oz butter
75 g/3 oz sugar
½ teaspoon vanilla essence
100 g/4 oz self-raising flour
2 eggs
50 g/2 oz Nutri-grain brown rice
    and rye with raisins
50 g/2 oz currants

Mix the butter, sugar, vanilla essence, flour and eggs in
a bowl and beat thoroughly until pale, soft and light.
Carefully fold in the cereal and currants, using a metal
spoon.

Grease a 1.5-litre/2½-pint pudding basin and spoon
the sponge mixture into it. Cook on Full power for 6–7
minutes.

Allow to stand in the basin for 4–5 minutes, then turn
the pudding out. Cut into individual portions to serve.

272 | Nutty Meringues

Preparation time
10 minutes

Cooking time
1 minute for each batch

Setting
Full power

Makes 36

Calories
70 per meringue

You will need
1 size 4 egg white
pinch of salt
about 275 g/10 oz icing sugar,
    sifted
25 g/1 oz finely chopped walnuts
300 ml/½ pint double or whipping
    cream

Lightly whisk the egg white and salt in a bowl and
gradually stir in the icing sugar and nuts. Knead the
mixture until smooth, adding a little more egg white if
the mixture is too crumbly.

Shape the paste into a roll about 2.5 cm/1 inch in
diameter. Cut into 5-mm/¼-inch slices and roll into
balls. Place four balls on a dish lined with silicone paper.
Cook on Full power for about 1 minute until puffy and
firm. Cool. Repeat with remaining mixture. Whip the
cream until just stiff, and use to sandwich the meringues
together. Decorate with drizzled chocolate (see Cook's
Tip), if preferred.

Cook's Tip

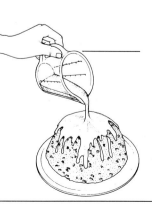

**Sponge puddings cooked in
the microwave do not always
look as wonderful as they
taste. A little apricot jam
(warmed in the microwave
oven until liquid) poured over
looks good and may be topped
with a little extra cereal, if liked.**

Cook's Tip

**For an attractive decoration
place 25 g/1 oz chocolate in a
bowl and melt on Defrost
setting. Place in a greaseproof
paper piping bag and snip off
end. Pipe over meringues.**

Baking

There are not many cakes which are truly successful in a microwave oven, as they do not brown and the cooked cake looks rather insipid. But coloured cake mixtures, such as chocolate, which are iced are good and dark fruit cakes keep beautifully moist. A microwave is also marvellous for softening butter, melting chocolate or heating ingredients for cakes to be made in a conventional oven.

273 | Battenburg Cake

(Illustrated on back jacket)

Preparation time
25 minutes

Cooking time
11 minutes, plus 8 minutes standing time

Setting
Full power

Makes one cake

Total calories
3,475

You will need
For the chocolate mix
65 g/2½ oz self-raising flour
15 g/½ oz cocoa
75 g/3 oz soft tub margarine
75 g/3 oz caster sugar
1 large egg

For the pink mix
75 g/3 oz self-raising flour
75 g/3 oz soft tub margarine
75 g/3 oz caster sugar
1 large egg
2 or 3 drops pink food colouring

For the decoration
2 tablespoons apricot jam
225 g/8 oz almond paste
a little caster sugar

Grease and line two containers each 18 × 11.5 cm/7 × 4½ inches.

To make the chocolate mix, sift the flour and cocoa into a bowl. Beat in the rest of the ingredients until light and fluffy. Make the pink mixture in the same way.

Spoon the cocoa mixture into one container and the pink mixture into the other. Cook cakes on Full power (one at a time) for about 5 minutes or until the surface is slightly moist. Stand for 4 minutes. Cool on a wire rack. Halve each lengthways. Heat the jam on Full power for 1 minute. Sandwich cakes together with the jam to give a Battenburg effect; brush with jam. Roll out the almond paste and cover the cake completely. Dust with sugar.

Cook's Tip

If you have any almond paste left over, decorate the top of the Battenburg with a broad plait, then scallop the edges of the loaf and sift icing sugar over the top.

274 | Date and Bran Loaf

Preparation time
15 minutes

Cooking time
6 minutes, plus 8 minutes standing time

Setting
Full power

Makes one (1-kg/2-lb) loaf

Total calories
2,965 per portion

You will need
3 tablespoons bran
150 g/5 oz wholemeal flour
100 g/4 oz stoned dried dates, chopped
100 g/4 oz sultanas
3 eggs
75 g/3 oz soft brown sugar
150 ml/¼ pint grapeseed or sunflower oil
25 g/1 oz bran
1½ teaspoons baking powder
2 tablespoons milk

Lightly oil an ovenproof 1-kg/2-lb loaf dish and sprinkle the bran all over the base and sides.

Place 2 tablespoons of flour in a plastic bag. Mix in the dates and sultanas, shaking the bag to coat the fruit thoroughly.

In a large bowl, whisk the eggs, sugar and oil together thoroughly. Mix the remaining flour, bran and baking powder together and beat into the egg mixture, a little at a time. Add the milk. Fold in the floured dates and sultanas and pour the mixture into the prepared dish. Cook on Full power for 6 minutes, turning the dish around after 3 minutes. Allow to stand for 8 minutes and test the cake (see Cook's Tip 275).

Turn the cake out on to a wire rack, cover loosely with absorbent kitchen paper or greaseproof paper and cool.

Cook's Tip

Flouring the dates and sultanas prevents them from sinking in the mixture and spoiling the appearance of the sliced loaf.

275 | *Muesli Cake*

Preparation time
10 minutes

Cooking time
6–8 minutes, plus 10 minutes standing time

Setting
Full power

Makes one (15-cm/6-inch) round cake

Total calories
2,550 per portion

You will need
1½ tablespoons soft dark brown sugar
2 tablespoons mixed chopped nuts, toasted
3 eggs
50 g/2 oz demerara sugar
2 tablespoons clear honey
150 ml/¼ pint grapeseed or sunflower oil
75 g/3 oz wholemeal flour
1½ teaspoons baking powder
75 g/3 oz unsweetened muesli
2 tablespoons milk

Lightly oil an ovenproof 15-cm/6-inch soufflé dish and sprinkle the dark brown sugar all over the base. Top with nuts.

In a large bowl, beat the eggs, demerara sugar, honey and oil together thoroughly. Beat in the flour a little at a time. Add the baking powder, muesli and milk and mix well. Spoon into the prepared dish and cook on Full power for 6–8 minutes, turning the dish around halfway through the cooking time.

Allow to stand for 10 minutes. Test the cake (see note below). If ready turn the cake out on to a wire rack, cover lightly with absorbent kitchen paper and leave to cool.

Cook's Tip

To test if a cake is fully cooked, insert a clean skewer into the centre. If it comes out clean, the cake is done. If not, return to the microwave oven for another 1–2 minutes and test again.

276 | *Chocolate and Cherry Gâteau*

Preparation time
15–20 minutes

Cooking time
7–9 minutes

Setting
Full power

Serves 8

Calories
750 per portion

You will need
175 g/6 oz self-raising flour
25 g/1 oz cocoa powder
½ teaspoon baking powder
175 g/6 oz concentrated butter, softened
175 g/6 oz soft light brown sugar
4 eggs, beaten
6 tablespoons milk

For the topping
275 g/10 oz cherries
350 g/12 oz Philadelphia cheese
150 ml/¼ pint natural yogurt
75 g/3 oz soft light brown sugar
75 g/3 oz each white and dark chocolate, grated separately

Beat all the sponge ingredients together until smooth and light. Spoon into a 20-cm/8-inch lined and greased cake dish. Cook on Full power for 7–9 minutes. Leave for 2 minutes, then cool on a wire rack.

Set aside a few cherries; stone the rest. Beat the cheese, yogurt and sugar together. Stir about a quarter into the cherries. Slice the cake in half and sandwich together with the cherry mixture. Reserve about a third of the remaining cheese mixture for piping. Spread the rest on the sides and top of the cake. Mix half the white with half the dark chocolate and press on the sides of the cake. Decorate as shown.

Cook's Tip

Substitute ground carob for the cocoa if liked. It has a similar flavour but contains no caffeine.

277 | No-cook Easter Cake

Preparation time
15 minutes, plus 1 hour to chill

Cooking time
4 minutes

Setting
Medium

Serves 6–8

Calories
545–410 per portion

You will need
75 g/3 oz butter
175 g/6 oz plain chocolate
1 tablespoon clear honey
75 g/3 oz rice crispies
75 g/3 oz raisins
50 g/2 oz crystallised ginger, chopped

For the decoration
250 g/9 oz marzipan
1 egg white, lightly beaten
a little food colouring (optional)

Combine the butter, chocolate and honey in a bowl. Melt on Medium for 4 minutes, stirring halfway thorough. Stir in the cereal, raisins and ginger. Spoon into an 18-cm/7-inch cake tin lined with greaseproof paper. Chill for 1 hour.

Roll out two-thirds of the marzipan to a round measuring 23 cm/9 inches. Roll the remainder of the marzipan to a smaller round, about 13 cm/5 inches. Reserve the marzipan trimmings. Flute the edges of both rounds as shown in the photograph above.

Loosen the uncooked chocolate cake in the tin and invert it in the centre of the larger marzipan round. Centre the smaller round on top of the cake. Roll out the marzipan trimmings, knead in a little food colouring, if liked, and cut out or shape decorations for the top of the cake, fixing them on with egg white (see Cook's Tip).

Cook's Tip

Use a pastry brush to apply the egg white to the marzipan, or keep a child's paint brush especially for this purpose.

278 | Overnight Gâteau

Preparation time
20 minutes, plus overnight to chill

Cooking time
2½ minutes

Setting
Full power

Serves 10–12

Calories
450–375 per portion

You will need
50 g/2 oz glacé cherries
200 g/7 oz plain chocolate, in squares
200 g/7 oz unsalted butter, cubed
grated rind of 1 orange
2 eggs
2 tablespoons caster sugar
50 g/2 oz walnuts, roughly chopped
1 (150-g/5-oz) packet Nice biscuits, roughly broken up

For the decoration
150 ml/¼ pint whipping cream, whipped
1 chocolate flake bar, crumbled

Place the cherries in a strainer and rinse under warm water to remove the syrup coating. Dry on absorbent kitchen paper and cut into quarters.

Combine the chocolate and butter in a large bowl and melt on Full power for 2½ minutes. Add the orange rind and stir thoroughly. Set aside.

In a jug, beat the eggs and sugar together until just mixed (see Cook's Tip). Add to the chocolate mixture a little at a time, mixing thoroughly after each addition. Stir in the walnuts and reserved cherries. Fold in the biscuits and spoon into an 18 × 7.5-cm/7 × 3-inch loaf tin. Level the surface and chill overnight.

Next day, turn out on to a serving dish and remove the lining paper. Decorate with whipped cream and chocolate flake and cut in very thin slices to serve.

Cook's Tip

Try to avoid incorporating too much air when beating the eggs and sugar together, as this would cause bubbles to form in the gâteau.

279 | Butterscotch Traybake

Preparation time
10 minutes, plus 2–3 hours to set

Cooking time
3 minutes

Setting
Full power

Makes 16 squares

Calories
180 per portion

You will need
100 g/4 oz butter
100 g/4 oz golden syrup (see Cook's Tip)
175 g/6 oz no-need-to-soak dried apricots, chopped
100 g/4 oz mixed nuts (hazelnuts, almonds, Brazils), chopped
75 g/3 oz raisins
175 g/6 oz ginger biscuits, crumbed

To make the butterscotch, combine the butter and syrup in a large jug and cook on Full power for 3 minutes, stirring well halfway through cooking. Carefully remove the jug from the microwave oven and set aside.

Mix the apricots, nuts, raisins and biscuit crumbs in a bowl. Pour the butterscotch over and mix well. Press into a greased 18-cm/7-inch square cake tin and allow to set in the refrigerator for 2–3 hours. Cut into squares or triangles to serve.

280 | Chocolate Bakewell Tart

Preparation time
25 minutes, plus 30 minutes to chill

Cooking time
8–8½ minutes

Setting
Full power

Serves 6–8

Calories
320–240 per portion

You will need
50 g/2 oz margarine
100 g/4 oz self-raising flour
1 tablespoon caster sugar
1 egg, beaten
a little cold water

For the filling
50 g/2 oz margarine
50 g/2 oz caster sugar
1 egg
40 g/1½ oz self-raising flour
1 tablespoon cocoa powder
40 g/1½ oz cake crumbs or ground almonds
2 tablespoons jam or honey

Rub the margarine into the flour. Stir in the sugar and about half the egg with enough water to make a soft, not sticky, dough. Roll out to line an 18-cm/7-inch flan dish. Prick the sides and base with a fork and chill for 30 minutes. Reroll trimmings and cut into long strips for the lattice top. Beat the margarine and sugar until creamy then beat in the egg and any left over. Fold in the flour and cocoa, add the crumbs or almonds and fold in until just mixed. Cook the pastry case on Full power for 4 minutes, turning the dish 2 or 3 times. Cool slightly, then fill and top with a pastry lattice. Bake for about 3½–4 minutes or until just cooked, turning the dish 2 or 3 times. Leave to cool. Warm the jam or honey for 30 seconds and brush over the top of the tart.

Cook's Tip

To measure the syrup, weigh the jug with the butter, then spoon in the syrup until the scale registers an additional 100 g/4 oz. Use a spoon dipped in boiling water to ladle out the syrup – it will slide off easily.

Cook's Tip

Use a spoon dipped in boiling water to measure the jam or honey for the filling – it will slide off easily.

Combination Microwave Recipes

With a combination microwave oven you really do have the best of both worlds, the speed of microwave cooking, with the browning and crisping qualities of convected hot air. These recipes have been tested in different ovens but do get to know your own particular cooker and if in doubt err on the side of undercooking.

281 | Piquant Pork

(Illustrated on title page)

Preparation time
10 minutes

Cooking time
17 minutes

Setting
Medium

Oven temperature
250 C

Serves 4

Calories
250 per portion

You will need
1 onion, finely chopped
1 (100-g/4-oz) dessert apple, finely chopped
50 /2 oz fresh breadcrumbs
salt and freshly ground black pepper
pinch of ground cinnamon
2 teaspoons grated orange rind
100 ml/4 fl oz milk
4 (225-g/8-oz) thick pork chops
watercress sprigs to garnish

Put the onion in a basin and cook on Full power for 3 minutes. Stir in all the remaining ingredients, apart from the chops. Heat the oven to 250 C.

Trim excess fat from the chops, then make a horizontal slit into each one as far as the bone but without slitting the ends. Divide the stuffing between what should be good-sized pockets in the chops, using a teaspoon to press it in.

Arrange the chops in a flan dish and roast at 250 C using Medium setting for 7 minutes. Turn the chops over and cook for a further 7 minutes. Serve garnished with watercress sprigs.

Serve with fantail potatoes and French beans, if liked.

282 | Salmon and Prawn Quiche

Preparation time
30 minutes

Cooking time
16 minutes

Oven temperature
250 C

Setting
Medium, Full power

Serves 4

Calories
545 per portion

You will need
75 g/3 oz margarine
175 g/6 oz plain flour
1 egg yolk
2 teaspoons water

For the filling
20 g/¾ oz plain flour
1 bay leaf
1 blade of mace
300 ml/½ pint milk
salt and pepper
15 g/½ oz butter
1 egg, plus egg yolk
1 (213-g/7½-oz) can salmon
100 g/4 oz peeled cooked prawns

Rub the margarine into the flour, stir in the egg yolk and enough water to make a stiff dough. Roll out to line a 20-cm/8-inch flan dish. Prick the base and chill for 10 minutes. Place the flour in a large bowl with the bay leaf and mace. Whisk in the milk, seasoning and butter and cook on Full power for 6 minutes, whisking twice. Remove bay leaf and mace. Place greaseproof paper and some baking beans in the pastry case and bake at 250 C using Medium setting for 5 minutes. Remove the beans and paper and cook for a further 3 minutes. Stir the egg and yolk, salmon and prawns into the sauce. Pour into the pastry case. Cook on Full power for 2 minutes.

Cook's Tip

Combination microwave ovens are very versatile, enabling the cook to use both microwave and convection energy, either separately or (and this is where they differ from convection microwaves) in tandem. The latest models are highly sophisticated; some automatically assess the cooking time, provided the weight of the food is programmed into the memory of the appliance.

Cook's Tip

Special baking beans – made of china – are very useful for baking blind. If you do not have any of these, improvise by using chick peas, dried beans or rice.

283 | Fish Flan

Preparation time
30 minutes

Cooking time
23 minutes

Setting
Full power, Medium

Oven temperature
250 C, 200 C

Serves 6

Calories
420 per portion

You will need
1 onion, sliced
25 g/1 oz butter
2 eggs
150 ml/¼ pint single cream
salt and pepper
75 g/3 oz margarine
175 g/6 oz plain flour
3 tablespoons water
3 tomatoes, peeled, deseeded and
   sliced
1 (198-g/7-oz) can tuna, drained
50 g/2 oz Lancashire cheese,
   grated
25 g/1 oz fresh breadcrumbs

Place the onion and butter in a basin and cook using microwaves only on Full power for 3 minutes. Beat in the eggs, cream and seasoning. Rub the margarine into the flour until the mixture resembles fine breadcrumbs. Stir in the water to make a short dough. Roll out to line a 20-cm/8-inch flan dish. Prick all over and bake blind at 250 C using a Medium microwave setting for 5 minutes.

Arrange the tomatoes and tuna in the flan, pour in the egg mixture and top with the cheese and breadcrumbs, mixed together. Bake at 200 C using Medium microwave setting for 15 minutes, until set and golden.

284 | Fishermans Puff Pie

Preparation time
15 minutes

Cooking time
16 minutes

Oven temperature
220 C

Setting
Full power, Medium

Serves 6

Calories
415 per portion

You will need
50 g/2 oz butter
50 g/2 oz plain flour
600 ml/1 pint milk
salt and pepper
3 tablespoons chopped parsley
350 g/12 oz cod, skinned and
   cubed
225 g/8 oz haddock, skinned and
   cubed
225 g/8 oz shrimps or prawns
1 (250-g/8¾-oz) packet puff pastry,
   defrosted if frozen
beaten egg to glaze

Place the butter in a pie dish and cook on Full power for 1 minute. Stir in the flour until well mixed, then add the milk gradually and stir well. Add the seasoning to taste and cook for 5 minutes, whisking or stirring well twice during the cooking time. Add the parsley, mixing in well. Mix in the cod, haddock and shrimps or prawns, coating well with the sauce. Roll out the puff pastry on a lightly floured surface and use to cover the pie dish. Glaze the pastry with a little beaten egg. Bake at 220 C using a Medium setting for 10 minutes until puffed and golden.

Cook's Tip

A quick way to drain a can of tuna is to cut around two-thirds of the can, then stand the can on its side in the kitchen sink until all the oil or brine has run out. Open the can fully and remove the tuna.

Cook's Tip

To defrost a 250-g/8¾-oz packet of puff pastry, allow 1½–2 minutes on Defrost, then allow to defrost completely at room temperature.

285 | Danish Fish Cobbler

Preparation time
20 minutes

Cooking time
14½–15½ minutes

Oven temperature
250 C

Setting
Full power, Medium

Serves 4

Calories
555 per portion

You will need
25 g/1 oz butter
25 g/1 oz flour
150 ml/¼ pint milk
salt and pepper
¼ teaspoon freshly grated nutmeg
450 g/1 lb cod or haddock fillets, skinned and cut into chunks
50 g/2 oz peeled cooked prawns (optional)
dill sprig to garnish (optional)

For the topping
25 g/1 oz butter
225 g/8 oz plain flour
2 teaspoons baking powder
100 g/4 oz Danish blue cheese
150 ml/¼ pint milk
milk for glazing

Place the butter in a casserole dish and cook on Full power for 30 seconds. Whisk in the flour, milk, seasoning and nutmeg. Cook on Full power for 4–5 minutes, stirring twice. Stir in the fish and prawns, if using. Heat the oven to 250 C. For the topping, rub into the butter the flour and baking powder, then add the cheese and enough milk to form a soft dough. Knead lightly until just smooth, then roll out to 2 cm/¾ inch thick and cut into 5-cm/2-inch rounds. Arrange these scones on top of the fish mixture. Brush with milk and bake at 250 C using Medium setting for about 10 minutes, or until the topping is risen and golden.

Cook's Tip

Combination cooking comes into its own for this dish – the fish is cooked perfectly and the scone topping is light thanks to microwave energy, while simultaneous convection heat gives the dish an attractive golden colour.

286 | Wholemeal Pilchard Flan

Preparation time
20 minutes

Cooking time
17–20 minutes

Oven temperature
250 C, 200 C

Setting
Medium

Serves 4

Calories
525 per portion

You will need
40 g/1½ oz lard
40 g/1½ oz butter
75 g/3 oz plain flour
75 g/3 oz wholemeal flour
pinch of salt
water to mix

For the filling
100 g/4 oz cottage cheese
2 eggs, beaten
salt and pepper
4 tablespoons milk
½ teaspoon dried mixed herbs
1 (425-g/15-oz) can pilchards in brine, drained
4 spring onions, chopped

Rub the lard and butter into the flours and salt. Stir in enough water to make a stiff dough. Roll out on a lightly floured surface to line a 20-cm/8-inch flan dish. Chill the pastry for 10 minutes.

To make the filling, mix together the cottage cheese, eggs, salt and pepper, milk and herbs.

Prick the dough base all over and bake at 250 C (without preheating) using a Medium setting for 5 minutes. Remove from the oven and reduce the temperature to 200 C. Arrange half the pilchards in the pastry case. Sprinkle over the onions and pour over the cottage cheese mixture. Bake at 250 C using Medium setting for 12–15 minutes.

Cook's Tip

If you do not have a rolling pin, use a clean wine bottle to roll out the pastry, either empty or filled with iced water (and tightly corked!).

287 | Haddock and Mushroom Pizza

Preparation time
15 minutes

Cooking time
25–27 minutes

Oven temperature
250 C

Setting
Full power, Medium

Serves 4

Calories
580 per portion

You will need
198 g/7 oz frozen smoked haddock
  fillets with butter (boil-in-the-bag)
25 g/1 oz butter
1 medium onion, finely chopped
100 g/4 oz mushrooms, chopped
15 g/$\frac{1}{2}$ oz flour
150 ml/$\frac{1}{4}$ pint milk
salt and pepper
3 tomatoes, peeled and sliced
100 g/4 oz Cheddar cheese, grated
1 (50-g/2-oz) can anchovies
a few stuffed olives

For the scone base
225 g/8 oz self-raising flour
50 g/2 oz margarine
150 ml/$\frac{1}{4}$ pint milk

Snip the bag containing the fish and place it on a plate, then cook on Full power for 8 minutes. Cook the butter and onion in a basin on Full power for 2 minutes. Add the mushrooms, cover and cook for 2 minutes. Whisk in the flour, milk and seasoning and cook for 5 minutes, whisking twice. Stir in the fish juices. Flake the fish, removing bones and skin, into the sauce. Heat the oven to 250 C. Rub the margarine into the flour, then stir in the milk. Knead lightly then roll out to a 23-cm/9-inch circle; place on a greased flan dish. Top with the fish, tomatoes, cheese, anchovies and olives. Bake at 250 C using Medium setting for 8–10 minutes.

Cook's Tip

Instead of using a scone base, try using a bread mix or packet pizza base mix. Leave the dough to rise in a warm place for 20–30 minutes before cooking.

288 | Stuffed Courgettes

Preparation time
5 minutes

Cooking time
10 minutes

Oven temperature
250 C

Setting
Medium

Serves 4

Calories
85 per portion

You will need
4 large courgettes
1 medium onion, chopped
4 tomatoes, peeled and chopped
2 teaspoons chopped parsley
salt and pepper
1 (198-g/7-oz) can tuna in brine,
  drained
4 teaspoons wholemeal
  breadcrumbs

For the garnish
1 tomato, sliced
2 lemon twists

Cut the courgettes in half and scoop out the middles. Chop these and mix with the onion, tomatoes, parsley, salt and pepper, and tuna. Put the courgette shells in two shallow dishes and press the tuna mixture into the shells. Sprinkle the breadcrumbs on top. Place one dish on the turntable, the second on the wire rack and bake at 250 C using Medium setting for 5 minutes. Swop the dishes and cook for a further 5 minutes and serve on warmed plates. Garnish with sliced tomatoes and lemon twists.

Cook's Tip

Prepare the courgette boats for filling by draining them upside down on absorbent kitchen paper for at least 10 minutes before adding the tuna mixture.

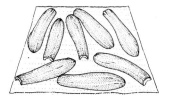

289 | Roast Chicken

Preparation time
5 minutes

Cooking time
35–40 minutes

Oven temperature
220 C

Setting
Medium, Full power

Serves 4

Calories
265 per portion (meat only), 490 per portion with skin

You will need
1 small onion, halved
1 bay leaf
1 (1.5-kg/3½-lb) oven-ready chicken
coriander sprigs to garnish (optional)

For the gravy
600 ml/1 pint stock
salt and pepper
40 g/1½ oz plain flour

Place the halved onion and bay leaf in the body cavity of the chicken. Place in a large flan dish and roast at 220 C using Medium setting for 25–30 minutes, or until the chicken is cooked (see Cook's Tip) and browned.

Place the chicken on a warmed serving plate and cover with foil, shiny side inside. Pour a little of the stock into the cooking dish and scrape off the sediment from the dish. Place the flour in basin, pour in the cooking juices and mix to a smooth paste. Add the remaining stock, whisking well, and cook on Full power (using microwaves only) for 10 minutes, whisking once during cooking and again at the end. Serve with the chicken. Garnish with coriander, if using and serve as shown.

Cook's Tip

The legs of the chicken will move freely when cooked. If you want to make certain the bird is ready, pierce the thickest part of the thigh with a sharp knife. The juices that flow out should be clear.

290 | Chicken 'Carolina' Drumsticks

Preparation time
5 minutes

Cooking time
15–18 minutes

Oven temperature
220 C

Setting
Medium

Serves 8

Calories
120 per portion

You will need
2 tablespoons crunchy peanut butter
1 teaspoon Worcestershire sauce
1 tablespoon clear honey
2 tablespoons lemon juice
1 teaspoon concentrated tomato purée
8 chicken drumsticks

Mix together all the ingredients except the chicken. Brush the chicken drumsticks all over with this mixture and place them in a large dish.

Cook at 220 C using Medium microwave setting for 15–18 minutes, turning once, until the chicken is cooked through and tender. Serve hot or cold with a mixed salad.

Cook's Tip

The best way to eat these tasty drumsticks is in the hand. Wrap the end of each in foil to provide a cool grip and don't forget a big pile of paper napkins.

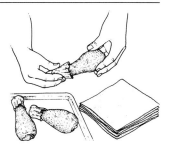

291 | Mushroom-stuffed Chicken

Preparation time
20 minutes

Cooking time
22–25 minutes

Oven temperature
250 C

Setting
Full power, Medium

Serves 4

Calories
355 per portion

You will need
4 chicken quarters with drumsticks
   not wings
1 tablespoon oil
½ small red pepper, cored,
   deseeded and finely chopped
4 spring onions, finely chopped
225 g/8 oz mushrooms, very finely
   chopped
75 g/3 oz curd cheese
1 egg, beaten
1 tablespoon chopped fresh thyme
25 g/1 oz fresh wholemeal
   breadcrumbs
salt and pepper
lettuce or curly endive to garnish

Remove the bones from chicken portions, leaving a neat pocket in place of the leg bones. Place oil, pepper and onions in a basin and cook on Full power (microwaves only) for 2 minutes. Add the mushrooms and cook for 3 minutes. Drain away any juices and stir in the curd cheese, egg, thyme, breadcrumbs and salt and pepper.

Press the stuffing into the chicken pockets. Place the chicken in a well-greased flan dish. Bake at 250 C using Medium setting for 17–20 minutes, or until golden. Turn once during cooking. Leave to cool and serve cold cut into slices with a lettuce or endive garnish.

292 | Lamb Hotpot

Preparation time
20 minutes

Cooking time
38 minutes

Setting
Full power, Medium

Oven temperature
220 C

Serves 4

Calories
550 per portion

You will need
2 potatoes, sliced
1 onion, chopped
1 tablespoon oil
1 clove garlic, crushed
2 courgettes, sliced
4 tomatoes, sliced
1 teaspoon oregano
salt and pepper
8 lamb cutlets
150 ml/¼ pint chicken stock
100 g/4 oz mushrooms, sliced
2 teaspoons flour
2 tablespoons milk
50 g/2 oz low-fat soft cheese (for
   example Shape cheese)
25 g/1 oz butter
watercress to garnish

Place the potatoes in a basin, cover and cook on Full power for 10 minutes, rearranging once. Cook the onion with the oil and garlic in a casserole using microwaves only on Full power for 3 minutes. Stir in the courgettes, tomatoes, oregano and seasoning. Lay the cutlets on top and pour in the stock. Cook at 220 C using Medium microwave setting for 15 minutes. Remove the cutlets, then stir in the mushrooms. Mix the flour, milk and cheese until smooth, then stir into the casserole. Replace the chops, top with the potatoes and dot with butter; cook for a further 10 minutes. Garnish with watercress.

Cook's Tip

A food processor makes short work of the preparation for this dish. Make the breadcrumbs first, adding the thyme when the crumbs are almost ready. Next, chop the pepper and onions, and finally the mushrooms.

Cook's Tip

Use 1 (397-g / 14-oz) can of chopped tomatoes in place of the 4 fresh tomatoes, if preferred.

293 | Savoury Crumble

Preparation time
20 minutes

Cooking time
23 minutes

Setting
Full power, Medium

Oven temperature
200 C

Serves 4

Calories
555 per portion

You will need
1 onion, chopped
1 clove garlic, crushed
2 tablespoons oil
450 g / 1 lb minced lamb
50 g / 2 oz mushrooms, chopped
1 (397-g / 14-oz) can chopped
    tomatoes
salt and pepper
½ teaspoon oregano
50 g / 2 oz margarine
100 g / 4 oz wholemeal flour
50 g / 2 oz low-fat hard cheese,
    grated (for example, Shape
    cheese)
1 carrot, grated
pinch of dried thyme
parsley sprigs to garnish

Mix the onion, garlic and oil in a casserole dish and cook using microwaves only on Full power for 3 minutes. Stir in the lamb, mushrooms, tomatoes, seasoning and oregano. Cover and cook on Full power for 5 minutes, stir well.

Rub the margarine into the flour, stir in the cheese, carrot and thyme. Season, then sprinkle over the meat mixture. Cook at 200 C using Medium microwave setting for 15 minutes, until browned and cooked through. Serve, garnished with parsley, with cooked vegetables or a good mixed salad and baked potatoes as accompaniments.

294 | Asparagus and Ham Rolls

Preparation time
10 minutes

Cooking time
20 minutes

Oven temperature
220 C

Setting
Full power, Medium

Serves 4

Calories
300 per portion

You will need
1 kg / 2 lb asparagus spears,
    trimmed
4 tablespoons water
350 g / 12 oz cooked ham, thickly
    sliced
50 g / 2 oz cheese, grated
chopped parsley to garnish

For the sauce
50 g / 2 oz butter
1 tablespoon flour
300 ml / ½ pint hot chicken or
    vegetable stock
1 egg yolk
salt and pepper
freshly grated nutmeg

Place the asparagus in a roasting bag with the water, close and cook on Full power for 10 minutes, until tender. Reserve the liquid. Place 40 g / 1½ oz butter in a bowl or jug, add the flour and the stock, then gradually stir in the liquid. Cook, stirring twice, for 5 minutes to make a smooth sauce. Stir in the egg yolk. Season with salt and pepper and nutmeg to taste. Heat the oven to 220 C. Place 4–5 asparagus spears on each slice of ham and roll up. Place the rolls in a greased ovenproof dish, pour over the sauce and sprinkle with the cheese. Dot the remaining butter. Bake at 220 C using a Medium setting for 5 minutes. Garnish and serve immediately.

Cook's Tip

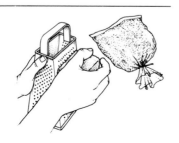

It is a good idea to keep a supply of grated cheese in a sealed plastic bag in the freezer. If the cheese is to be cooked there is seldom any need to defrost it.

Cook's Tip

For a more economical dish, substitute leeks for the asparagus. Slit 8 leeks and wash them thoroughly, then cook exactly as for asparagus.

295 | West Country Pie

Preparation time
30 minutes

Cooking time
20–23 minutes

Setting
Full power, Medium

Oven Temperature
220 C

Serves 6

Calories
695 per portion

You will need
350 g/12 oz plain flour
salt and pepper
175 g/6 oz margarine
4 tablespoons water
beaten egg to glaze

For the filling
450 g/1 lb sausagemeat
100 g/4 oz All-bran, crushed
1½ teaspoons rubbed sage
225 g/8 oz cooking apples, peeled,
    cored and chopped
150 ml/¼ pint medium cider

Mix the flour and a pinch of salt, then rub in the margarine until the mixture resembles fine breadcrumbs. Mix in the water to make a short dough. Use half to line a base-lined and greased, 23-cm/9-inch flan dish. Roll out the rest to make a lid.

Mix all the filling ingredients in a dish, cover and cook on Full power for 5 minutes. Stir well, then press into the pie. Top with the pastry lid, dampening and sealing the edges well. Decorate with pastry trimmings and glaze with egg. Bake at 220 C using Medium microwave setting for 15–18 minutes. Cool, turn out on to a rack, then invert on to a serving plate. Serve with salad.

296 | Ham and Mozzarella Puff

Preparation time
20 minutes

Cooking time
24½–30 minutes

Oven temperature
250 C

Setting
Full power, Medium

Serves 4

Calories
475 per portion

You will need
150 ml/¼ pint water
40 g/1½ oz concentrated butter
40 g/2½ oz plain flour
salt and pepper
3 eggs, beaten
1 tablespoon chopped spring onion
    to garnish

For the filling
20 g/¾ oz concentrated butter
1 medium onion, finely chopped
25 g/1 oz plain flour
450 ml/¾ pint milk
100 g/4 oz Mozzarella cheese,
    grated
175 g/6 oz cooked ham, chopped

Put the water and butter in a large basin and cook on Full power for 2½–3 minutes, until boiling. Immediately tip in the flour and a pinch of salt. Stir quickly to make a smooth thick ball of paste. Cool slightly, then beat in the eggs until smooth and glossy. Place the butter and onion in a basin and cook for 2 minutes. Whisk in the flour and milk. Cook for 5 minutes, whisking twice. Stir in three-quarters of the cheese, the ham and seasoning. Spoon or pipe the paste round the edge of a 23-cm/9-inch flan dish. Pour the sauce into the middle and sprinkle with the remaining cheese. Bake at 250 C using Medium setting for 15–20 minutes. Garnish with spring onion.

Cook's Tip

For a sausage plait, roll the pastry to a rectangle, arrange the filling down the middle, then cut the sides diagonally in strips to fold over the filling as shown. Glaze and bake as in the recipe.

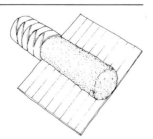

Cook's Tip

Concentrated butter is now available from many supermarkets and grocers and is a relatively inexpensive way of using butter in cooking. If you can't get it use a double quantity of ordinary butter.

297 | Continental Stir-Fry Flan

Preparation time
20 minutes

Cooking time
22–25 minutes

Oven temperature
250 C, 200 C

Setting
Full power, Medium

Serves 4

Calories
505 per portion

You will need
283 g/10 oz frozen Continental
  Stir-Fry vegetables
2 tablespoons water
75 g/3 oz margarine
175 g/6 oz plain flour
salt and pepper
water to mix
100 g/4 oz Cheddar cheese, grated
2 eggs
150 ml/¼ pint milk
2 tablespoons single cream
1 tablespoon chopped parsley

Place the vegetables in a bowl with the water, cover and cook on Full power for 5 minutes. Stand for 2–3 minutes.

Rub the margarine into the flour with a pinch of salt and stir in enough water to make a stiff dough. Roll out to line a 20-cm/8-inch flan dish. Chill the pastry for 10 minutes. Mix together the cheese, eggs, milk, cream, parsley and seasoning. Prick the dough base all over and bake at 250 C using a Medium setting for 5 minutes. Remove from the oven and reduce the temperature to 200 C. Fill the flan case with the drained vegetables and pour over the cheese mixture. Bake using Medium setting for 12–15 minutes.

Cook's Tip

Chilling the pastry case makes it less likely to shrink when cooked.

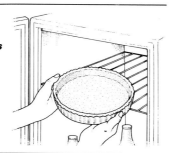

298 | Heavenly Carrot Cake

Preparation time
20 minutes

Cooking time
15–18 minutes, plus 5
minutes standing time

Oven temperature
200 C

Setting
Medium

Makes one (18-cm/7-in) cake

Total calories
4,560

You will need
100 g/4 oz concentrated butter
100 g/4 oz clear honey
75 g/3 oz soft light brown sugar
grated rind and juice of 1 orange
2 eggs, beaten
225 g/8 oz self-raising flour
2 teaspoons baking powder
1 teaspoon ground cinnamon
½ teaspoon freshly grated nutmeg
50 g/2 oz walnut pieces, chopped
100 g/4 oz raisins
175 g/6 oz carrots, finely grated
walnut halves to decorate

For the topping
225 g/8 oz cream cheese
4 teaspoons orange juice
1 tablespoons brown sugar

Line and grease an 18-cm/7-inch deep, round dish bringing the paper about 2.5 cm/1 inch above the rim. Place the butter and honey in a mixing bowl and cook on Full power for 2 minutes or until melted. Beat in the sugar until dissolved. Stir in the orange rind and juice and eggs. Fold in the remaining ingredients, turn into the dish and smooth the top. Bake at 200 C using Medium setting for 13–15 minutes, or until the cake is well risen, lightly browned and set. Stand for 5 minutes. Cool on a wire rack. Beat the topping ingredients together, cover the cake and decorate as shown.

Cook's Tip

If you do not have any self-raising flour, substitute plain, but increase the quantity of baking powder to 4 teaspoons.

299 | *Cherry and Almond Cake*

Preparation time
15 minutes

Cooking time
13–15 minutes

Oven temperature
220C

Setting
Medium

**Makes one
(18-cm/7-in) cake**

Total calories
3,760

You will need
175 g/6 oz margarine
175 g/6 oz soft light brown sugar
3 eggs
50 g/2 oz ground almonds
225 g/8 oz plain flour
1½ teaspoons baking powder
225 g/8 oz glacé cherries, halved, washed and dried

Heat the oven to 220C. Line an 18-cm/7-inch deep, round dish with greased greaseproof paper.

Beat the margarine and sugar together until light and fluffy. Beat in the eggs gradually, mixing well after each addition. Beat in the almonds. Sift in the flour and baking powder, then fold in the cherries. Turn the mixture into the dish and lightly smooth the top. Bake at 220C using Medium setting for 13–15 minutes or until the cake is risen and lightly browned. Leave the cake in the dish for a few minutes, then turn it out on to a wire rack to cool. Remove the paper when cooled completely.

Cook's Tip

An 'oil well' is a boon when it comes to greasing lining paper. It consists of a spill-proof oil container with built-in brush.

300 | *Bread*

Preparation time
20 minutes, plus 2¼ hours proving

Cooking time
9 minutes each loaf

Setting
Medium

Oven temperature
250C

Makes two (450-g /1-lb) loaves

Calories
960 per loaf

You will need
450 g/1 lb strong white flour
1 teaspoon salt
1 teaspoon sugar
50 g/2 oz butter
1 sachet easy-blend dried yeast
300 ml/½ pint lukewarm water

Line two 450-g/1-lb loaf dishes with greaseproof paper, making sure the paper stands 2.5 cm/1 inch above the rim; grease well.

Place the flour in a bowl with the salt and sugar, then rub in the butter and stir in the yeast. Mix in the water to make a stiff dough. Knead for 10 minutes until smooth and elastic. Leave, covered, in a warm place until doubled in size. Turn out and knead briefly, then halve the dough and place one piece in each dish. Cover loosely and leave to rise until doubled in size. Brush with water and bake one at a time at 250C using Medium microwave setting for 9 minutes. Leave for 5 minutes, then cool on a wire rack.

Cook's Tip

Try some different toppings. Brush with egg yolk and add sesame seeds, poppy seeds, grated cheese or a dusting of coarse salt for a variety of interesting effects.

focus on
IRELAND
◆ *inspiring places, beautiful spaces* ◆

Written by Rebecca Snelling
Designed by Kat Mead
Produced by AA Publishing
Text © Automobile Association Developments Limited 2007
For details of photograph copyrights see page 96

Published by AA Publishing (a trading name of Automobile
Association Developments Limited, whose registered office
is Fanum House, Basing View, Basingstoke, Hampshire
RG21 4EA; registered number 1878835).

A03202

ISBN-10: 0-7495-5207-7
ISBN-13: 978-0-7495-5207-7

A CIP catalogue record for this book is available
from the British Library.

Colour reproduction by KDP, Kingsclere, England
Printed in China by C&C Offset Printing

PICTURES FROM TOP TO BOTTOM:
Trees and flowers force their way between limestone ridges
on the rocky upland wilderness of the Burren.

Celtic crosses on Inishmore, one of the Aran Islands,
commemorate islanders who died overseas or at sea.

Surf crashes against the rocks along the rugged Tramore
coastline in the southern county of Waterford.

PAGE 3: The Wicklow Mountains provide a backdrop to the
tree-covered hills near Sally Gap.

PAGE 4: A ride in a jaunting car is a fine way to see the
Muckross Estate in County Kerry.

focus on
IRELAND
◆ *inspiring places, beautiful spaces* ◆

INTRODUCTION

Ireland (Éire) is Europe's third largest island, lying between the Irish Sea and the Atlantic Ocean about 50 miles off the western shores of Britain. Politically, it is divided into the Republic of Ireland, which covers the south, east, west and northwest, and Northern Ireland, the northeast part of the island, which is a state within the United Kingdom. Dublin and Belfast are their respective capitals.

Not for nothing is Ireland known as the 'Emerald Isle'. Its mild, maritime climate and all-too-frequent gentle rainfall (heaviest in the west) produce lush green vegetation all over the island. Within the mountains that girdle much of the coastline lie low, central plains, bisected from north to south by the great River Shannon and its tributaries that form a huge network of navigable inland waterways.

Countless loughs (the Irish equivalent of English lakes or Scottish lochs) – hauntingly beautiful and an angler's dream – and huge tracts of peat bogland are characteristic features of the landscape. So too are patchwork fields and rolling hills, winding country roads, scattered farmsteads, tiny hamlets, whitewashed thatched cottages and traditional fishing villages. Irish beaches, especially in the southwest corner, are second to none.

Natural wonders and must-sees for any visitor to Ireland include the Giant's Causeway – a platform of interlocking hexagonal basalt columns that march into the sea – and the Mountains of Mourne, both in Northern Ireland; the Burren, in the west, a special area of limestone where alpine and Mediterranean plants grow alongside each other; and the Cliffs of Moher, which drop vertically into the sea at the edge of County Clare.

Evidence of Ireland's history can be seen wherever you go. Prehistoric megalithic tombs, stone circles, ring forts and cairns are scattered across the country, many of which are closely associated with Celtic legend and mythology. The Hill of Tara in County Meath was the seat of the High Kings of Ireland, while Newgrange, also in County Meath, was said to be a fairy mound, home of Oenghus, the god of love.

As a result of St Patrick's arrival in the 5th century the island became known as the cradle of Roman Catholic Christianity. Consequently, the island has a rich heritage of monastic architecture ranging from carved high crosses to the ruins of great monasteries and the distinctive, pencil-shaped round towers – found only in Ireland – such as those at Glendalough in County Wicklow or Clonmacnoise in County Offaly. Many fine churches and cathedrals were built at this time too, such as St Mary's Cathedral in Limerick.

Norman and Anglo-Irish castles and fortified tower houses dating mostly from the late 12th to early 16th centuries characterize the west and southwest. One of these, Blarney Castle in County Cork, has gained fame through the Blarney Stone, believed to have special powers. Anyone who kisses the stone is said to acquire the gift of the gab (a way with words) – one of the most charming aspects of so many Irish people.

In the early 18th century Palladian architecture took Ireland by storm, putting its stamp on practically every building of any size. As the century progressed, the style evolved into the elegant Georgian houses, squares and streets for which Dublin is renowned; it is also exemplified in stately homes such as Mount Stewart in County Derry and its magnificent gardens.

The trick of a visit to Ireland is to take things slowly: enjoy what turns up – or doesn't – besides, it's almost a sacrilege to hurry. Explore the country lanes; take time for a chat about nothing in particular; go with the flow. Pervading everyday life is the craic (pronounced crack) – that peculiarly Irish tradition of fun, good conversation and laughter.

Then of course there's Irish music, the lifeblood of the people and the backbone of their culture, celebrated throughout the country in festivals but also in every pub across the country. No matter where you go you'll find musicians, singers and storytellers sharing their talents and enthusiasm with anyone who has the time and inclination to listen. Ireland is a country in which no one is a stranger for long.

*The evening sun casts long shadows over Blackball Head, at Youghal. This resort in the southeast
of County Cork has long been one of Ireland's most popular vacation destinations.
Opposite: the 9th-century stone high cross just outside Moone, in County Kildare. The name Moone comes
from the Gaelic words Maen Colmcille, which means 'Colmcille's property'.
Pages 7–8: St Patrick's Day is celebrated with fireworks in Dublin. Here the 18th-century
Custom House can be seen beside the River Liffey.*

The Killarney mountains and lakes as seen from Ladies' View (a viewpoint named after Queen Victoria's ladies-in-waiting) on the Ring of Kerry in Killarney National Park. Lough Leane is the largest of the lakes, with Muckross Lake and the Upper Lake upstream of it.
Opposite: the tide goes out at Coumeenole Beach at the end of the Dingle Peninsula, the most northerly of the mountainous headlands of County Kerry and the most westerly point of the Republic of Ireland.

A mare with her foal at the Irish National Stud near Kildare. Established in 1946, the stud develops and promotes Irish bloodstock as well as being among Ireland's major tourist attractions.
Opposite: Gougane Barra Forest Park in County Cork. The chapel stands on the site of a hermitage founded by Finbarr, the patron saint of Cork, in the 6th century.

Leenane's fishing harbor is at the head of the natural inlet of Killary Harbour in Connemara.
Previous page: Lismore Castle in County Waterford has been the home of the Dukes of Devonshire since 1753.

Wonderful sandy beaches characterize Inchydoney Island, 3 miles south of the town of Clonakilty (Cloich na Coillte) in County Cork. The island is linked to the mainland by a causeway.

These thatched, whitewashed cottages can be seen at Kilmore Quay, a small fishing village in the southeast.
Top: Mount Errisbeg rises above a ruined building near Roundstone, in the Connemara region.

Pádraic Henry Pearse, poet and leader of the 1916 Easter uprising, made this cottage in Connemara near Ros Muc his summer home. It is now a National Monument/Heritage Site and is open to the public.

These mountains and green patchwork fields lie on the Ring of Kerry, a circular route covering more than
100 miles in County Kerry. It starts from the town of Killarney and heads around the Iveragh Peninsula.

Extensive gardens and ancient parkland surround Blarney Castle and nearby Blarney House,
built in the 19th century. The stone castle is the third to stand on this site in County Cork.

Inside the Gallarus Oratory on the Dingle Peninsula is the Alphabet Stone, a standing pillar carved with Roman and ogham characters. Opposite: this ceiling detail is from the Chester Beatty Library housed in Dublin Castle. The collection comprises artifacts from oriental and western religions, as well as secular items.

*A waterfall in the grounds of Birr Castle, private home of the Parsons family and renowned for its
exotic trees and plants, rivers and lake, formal gardens, terraces, and wildflower meadows.
Opposite: Lough Key in County Roscommon is part of an 800-acre forest park. Legend says that
the fairy king, Tuatha de Danann, drowned when the waters of the lake sprang from the earth.
Pages 24–25: a view towards Blarney Castle, with the house just visible to the right.*

Crosses stand among the ruined buildings of Clonmacnoise in County Offaly. St Ciaran founded the monastery in the 6th century and is believed to be buried in a tiny church on the site.
Opposite: the sun sets over Youghal beach, a 5-mile stretch of sand in the southeast of County Cork. The town is an historic walled seaport at the mouth of the estuary of the River Blackwater.

...the sea the sea crimson sometimes like fire...

The Rock of Cashel ruins high up on the rock that overshadows the town from the west.
Pages 30–31: Ha'Penny Bridge over the River Liffey in Dublin. Its official name is Wellington Bridge,
after the Duke of Wellington. The nickname was given because of the halfpenny toll.

Loughcrew, or the Mountains of the Witch, lies west of Kells in west County Meath. Stretching in a chain over four peaks, the area is scattered with ancient monuments. The sites are dedicated to a witch said to have dropped the stones from her apron as she hopped across the hill.

The resort of Tramore sits on a hillside overlooking Tramore Bay in County Waterford. It has a fine promenade and a 3-mile stretch of beach with high sand dunes. Water-based sports on the beach include surfing, windsurfing, and kitesurfing, and there is an amusement park on the sands.
Opposite: a ruined tower known as the Yellow Steeple is all that remains of the 13th-century Augustinian St Mary's Abbey in Trim, County Meath. It overlooks the town from a ridge opposite Trim Castle.

A marble statue of St Patrick stands on a stone plinth on the summit of the conical peak of Croagh Patrick; it commemorates the legend of the saint banishing all the snakes from Ireland.
Pages 36–37: the monastic remains at Kilmacduagh, in County Galway, show a good example of the distinctive round towers found only in Ireland. St Colman, son of Duagh, founded the monastery.

Belfast's City Hall in Donegall Square is the civic building of the Belfast City Council. Built between 1898 and 1906 from Portland stone with towers at each of the four corners, it features a central copper-coated dome that rises to nearly 174 feet. The building covers an area of one-and-a-half acres and has an enclosed courtyard. There is limited access to the interior, but the surrounding gardens are open to the public.

Mount Baurtregaum in the Slieve Mish Mountain Range overlooks Tralee Bay on the Dingle Peninsula.
The county of Kerry claims Ireland's highest mountains and is its most westerly point.
Opposite: Lough Conn in County Mayo covers about 14,000 acres and is noted for its trout and salmon
fishing. With Lough Cullin just to the south, Conn is linked to the sea by the River Moy.

A simple form of trompe-l'oeil in Kinvara (Kinvarra in English), in the southeast corner of Galway Bay. Customer, shopkeeper, and provisions are all painted onto the shop front: even the bicycle leaning against the wall, and the cat sitting on the doorstep are not what they seem.

Pillars in front of the house and a fanlight above the front door are typical features of Georgian architecture, a period that ran from 1730–1800. This private house in Fitzwilliam Square in Dublin is a classic example.

Enniskillen Castle, beside the River Erne in County Fermanagh, became an English garrison fort in the 17th century and later served as part of a military barracks. It now houses two museums. Opposite: these monastic remains are at Glendalough (Glen of the Two Lakes) in County Wicklow. St Kevin sought solitude here in the 6th century and later set up a large religious settlement. Pages 44–45: dawn breaks over the rushes at the edge of Kylemore Lough, which lies at the foot of the Twelve Bens Mountain range in Connemara in County Galway.

The Chapel of St Kevin is at Glendalough. There are many fanciful and unsubstantiated legends about the saint, but a common theme is his ability to communicate with animals and his preference for their company over that of human beings – especially women's.

Opposite: the Government Buildings in Merrion Street Upper, Dublin. Edward VII laid the foundation stone in 1904 but the building was not finally completed until 1922. It was formerly used by the Royal College of Science and then by University College Dublin.

Horses are exercised at the Curragh, Ireland's flat-racing headquarters in County Kildare. The course hosts all five of the Classic Races, including the Irish Derby. Curragh means 'place of the running horse'.

The Baltimore Beacon (also known as Lot's Wife – in a biblical story, Lot's wife is turned into a pillar of salt) stands at the entrance to Baltimore Harbour in County Cork. The town's long tradition of boat-building is celebrated in the annual Wooden Boat Festival, held in May.

Glenarm village takes its name from the glen in which it lies, one of the nine Glens of Antrim in Northern Ireland that radiate inward from the coast towards Lough Neagh. Its limestone harbor has been restored and attractions nearby include Glenarm Forest Park, Glenarm Castle, and a salmon fishery.

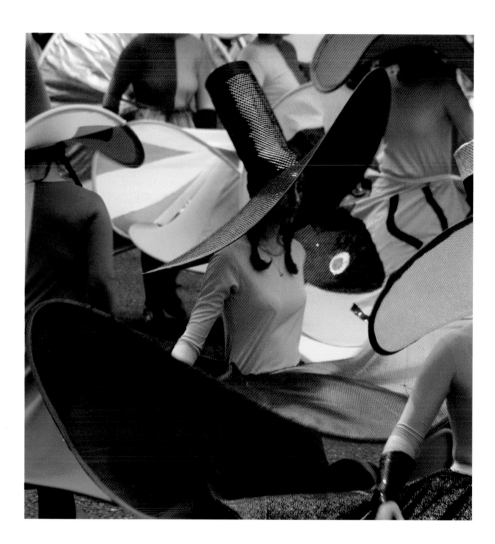

The annual St Patrick's Day parade in Dublin is just one of hundreds of celebrations that takes place among the Irish diaspora around the world on March 17, Patrick's religious feast day. Opposite: traditional Irish dancing is a highlight of the Galway International Oyster Festival, a three-day round of parties, music, entertainment, and gourmet feasting held every September.

Looking out over the River Shannon off Clonmacnois as the sun sets over the village, casting a golden glow over the waters.
Opposite: around 40,000 hexagonal-shaped basalt columns make up the Giant's Causeway in County Antrim. It was formed about 62 to 65 million years ago by volcanic action – not as legend has it, by the giant Finn MacCool, who was trying to reach the Scottish coast.
Previous page: Lough Gill in County Sligo. One of the lake's many islands, Lake Isle of Innisfree, was made famous by the Irish poet William Butler Yeats (1865–1939) in his poem of the same name. A good view of the whole lake can be seen from Dooney Rock.

The classical-style Mussenden Temple, built in the 18th century as a library by the eccentric Earl Bishop Hervey of Derry, is just one of the attractions on the Downhill Estate in Northern Ireland.

A strange, two-sided Janus figure stands in an ancient Christian graveyard on Boa Island, on the north shore of Lower Lough Earne. The carving stands so that its faces look due east and west and the sun rises and sets directly above it at the vernal equinox.

The circular stone fort of Grianan of Aileach in County Donegal, built in the early Christian era, served as the royal seat of the O'Neill clan from the 5th to the 12th century. It was reconstructed in the 1870s. Opposite: a view of the Blasket Islands off the Dingle Peninsula on the southwest coast. Uninhabited today, the islands were once home to a thriving community. Boats take visitors to and fro across the Sound.

Dozens of ancient dolmens, or portal tombs, are scattered over the Burren in County Clare.
Pages 64–65: the principal buildings of Trinity College, Dublin, were founded in 1592 by Elizabeth I
on the site of an Augustinian monastery. The college is set in its own grounds, known as College Park.

Gallarus Oratory, a very early Christian church on the Dingle Peninsula, is a classic example of the art of dry-stone corbelling, a building technique first developed by Neolithic tomb-makers. The horizontal stones were layed at a slight angle, with the lower edge on the outside, to allow water to run off.

The Parliament Building in Belfast has been the home of the Northern Ireland Assembly since 1998. It was built from English Portland stone and has a granite base quarried from the Mountains of Mourne. Pages 68–69: Sligo Bay on the west coast of Ireland. The town of Sligo (its name means 'place of shells') stands on the bay at the mouth of the Garavogue River.

Dunmanus Bay is one of the deep inlets in western Cork. It is bounded on the northern side by the Sheep's Head Peninsula and on the southern side by the Mizen Peninsula. Bantry Bay lies on the other side of Sheep's Head.

A boat moored by the shore in Lough Leane, part of the Killarney National Park.
Top: lobster pots are stacked on Dooneen Pier on Sheep's Head Peninsula in County Cork.

*Island-studded Clew Bay in County Mayo is overlooked by Croagh Patrick, Ireland's holy mountain, and
the mountains of North Mayo. Clare Island marks the entrance of the bay.*

A row of thatched cottages runs through the small fishing village of Kilmore Quay on the eastern side of Ballyteige Bay, about 12 miles from the international ferryport of Rosslare. Noted for its lobster and deep-sea fishing, the village holds a Seafood Festival in the second week of July.

Cattle graze near Killarney, with the Aghadoe Hills beyond. The national park has the country's only herd of red deer, which are native to Ireland. Japanese Sika deer were introduced in the mid-19th century and they pose a potential threat to the pedigree of the red deer should cross-breeding occur.

Lough Corrib, in the west, is the largest lake in the Republic of Ireland at nearly 42,000 acres and is full of islands. The River Corrib and the Galway River connect it to the sea at Galway.
Opposite: the harbour town of Kinsale in County Cork is one of the oldest towns in Ireland.
Pages 76–77: County Down's Mount Stewart House, with its internationally renowned gardens and Temple of the Four Winds, is one of the National Trust's most popular properties in Northern Ireland.

Around 7,400 acres of blanket bog and four of the Twelve Ben peaks are protected as the Connemara National Park. Pádraic Pearse's Cottage stands on the shores of Lough Oiriúlach near Gortmore.

Peat land (bogland) covers much of rural Ireland.
Top: the Twelve Bens mountains are reflected in the blue water of
Derryclare Lough in Connemara National Park.

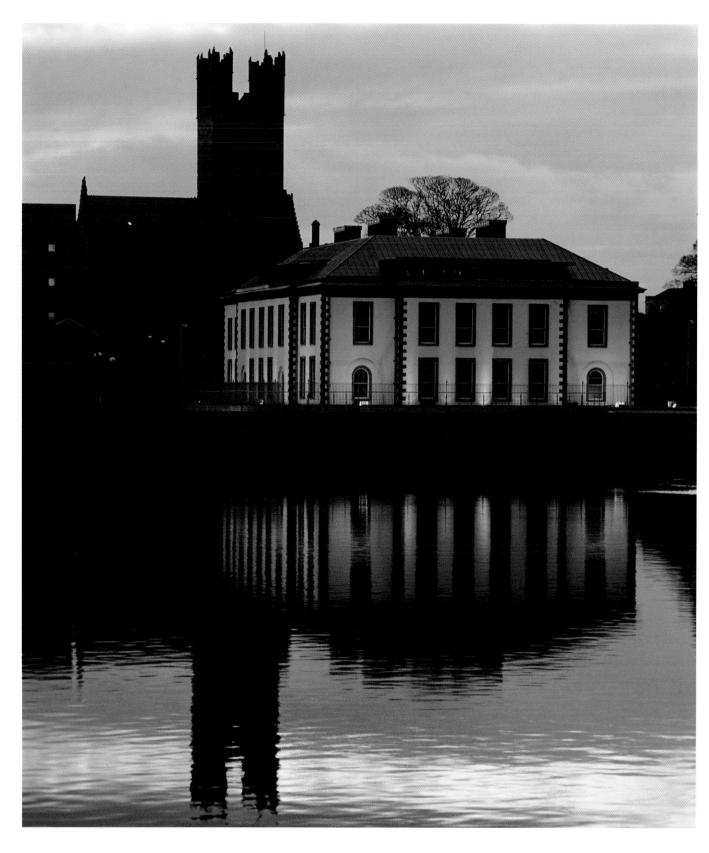

Limerick's Custom House and St Mary's Cathedral can be seen across the River Shannon.
Page 82–83: the remains of fort Dun Aengus are visible on Inishmore Island, largest of the Aran Islands.

*A bronze statue of Lord Edward Carson, Architect of the Northern Ireland State, was erected in 1932
outside the new Parliament Building. It was unveiled by Carson in 1933 two years before his death.*

Stone tomb sculpture and a cloistered arcade are highlights of a visit to the Cistercian Jerpoint Abbey in County Kilkenny.
Opposite: King John's Castle in Limerick stands on King's Island, next to the River Shannon. It dates from the reign of King John of England (1166–1216).

The dome of Dublin's neoclassical Custom House is an unmistakable landmark on the city skyline. It can be seen from both sides of the Liffey thanks to the many bridges.
Opposite: Malahide Castle to the north of Dublin dates largely from the 14th century and houses much of the National Portrait Collection from Dublin's National Gallery.

*This view of Lough Corrib was taken near Oughterard, often referred to as the gateway to Connemara.
The town is a centre for game-fishing on the huge lake, which crosses the border of County Galway into
County Mayo. Boat cruises around the many islands are available.
Pages 90–91: Celtic crosses on Inishmore Island, one of the largest Aran islands.*

Blarney Castle has gained fame through the Blarney Stone, believed to be half of the Stone of Scone over which Scottish Kings were crowned because it was believed to have special powers.

Killarney Lakes (Upper Lakes) with the Macgillycuddy mountain range in the distance.
Opposite: the first lighthouse at Youghal was built in 1190, discontinued in 1542 then taken down in
1848 to make room for the present tower, which was was lit on February 1, 1852. The light was converted
to acetylene in 1939 and electric in 1964.

INDEX

ACKNOWLEDGMENTS

The Automobile Association would like to thank the following photographers, companies and picture libraries for their assistance in the preparation of this book.

Abbreviations for the picture credits are as follows: - (t) top; (b) bottom; (l) left; (r) right; (AA) AA World Travel Library.
2t AA/P Zoeller; 2c AA/S Hill; 2b AA/S Day; 3 AA/M Short; 4 AA/J Blandford; 6/7 AA/S Day; 8 AA/M Short; 9 AA/D Forss; 10 AA/J Blandford; 10/11 AA/C Jones; 12 AA/Slidefile; 13 AA/J Blandford; 14/15 AA/J Blandford; 16 AA/S Day; 17 AA/J Blandford; 18t AA/D Forss; 18b AA/J Blandford; 18/19 AA/C Jones; 20 AA/J Blandford; 21 AA/S McBride; 22 AA/S Hill; 22/23 AA/Slidefile; 24/25 AA/S McBride; 26 AA/C Hill; 27 AA/C Jones; 28 AA/S McBride; 29 AA/D Forss; 30/31 AA/S Whitehorne; 32 AA/S McBride; 33 AA/C Jones; 34 AA; 35 AA/S Day; 36/37 AA/C Coe; 38 AA/L Blake; 39 AA/G Munday; 40 AA/L Blake; 41 AA/M Diggin; 42/43 AA/S Day; 43 AA/S Whitehorne; 44/45 AA/C Hill; 46 AA/G Munday; 47 AA/M Short; 48 AA/C Jones; 49 AA/S Whitehorne; 50/51 AA/S McBride; 52 AA/S Hill; 53 AA/D Forss; 54 AA/S Day; 54/55 AA/S McBride; 56/57 AA/C Hill; 58 AA/S McBride; 59 AA/C Coe; 60/61 AA/G Munday; 61 AA; 62 AA/C Jones; 63 AA/G Munday; 64/65 AA/L Blake; 66 AA/S McBride; 67 AA/C Jones; 68/69 AA/C Coe; 70/71 AA/I Dawson; 71 AA/J Blandford; 72 AA/S McBride; 72/73 AA/L Blake; 74 AA/P Zoeller; 75 AA/S McBride; 76/77 AA/G Munday; 78 AA/D Forss; 79 AA/C Jones; 80/81 AA/C Jones; 81t AA/C Jones; 81b AA/C Jones; 82/83 AA/S Hill; 84 AA/C Jones; 85 AA/I Dawson; 86/87 AA/S Hill; 87 AA/M Short; 88 AA/S Day; 89 AA/Slidefile; 90/91 AA/S Hill; 92 AA/C Jones; 93 AA/S Hill; 94 AA/J Blandford; 95 AA/S Hill.

Every effort has been made to trace the copyright holders, and we apologise in advance for any accidental errors. We would be happy to apply the corrections in the following edition of this publication.

KANDINSKY.

Great Modern Masters

Kandinsky

General Editor: José María Faerna

Translated from the Spanish by Alberto Curotto

CAMEO/ABRAMS

HARRY N. ABRAMS, INC., PUBLISHERS

Kandinsky and Abstraction

Vasily Kandinsky is considered the founder of abstract painting, and any assessment of his importance in the history of modern art must give an account of how that central innovation came about. As often happens with "breakthrough" developments, however, the chronology of specific events is open to debate. For example, most scholars now believe that the small watercolor which is often considered the first abstract (or "non-

Moscow, Zubovsky Square III, *c. 1916.*
Oil on canvas, 13⅜ × 12½" (34 × 32 cm).
Museum Ludwig, Cologne

objective") composition—dated 1910 by Kandinsky—was actually made somewhat later than that. Moreover, there exist a number of isolated examples of nonrepresentational paintings by other artists from before World War I, some as early as 1910. But that is exactly what they are: isolated examples, not the heralds of a radically new aesthetic. For despite the complexities of chronology, it remains clear that Kandinsky was the

4

first painter to "abstract" from the appearance of the objects of the world in a truly programmatic manner—the first to view the renunciation of the representational as a necessary step toward a purer kind of painting.

Varieties of Abstraction

Kandinsky was the principal innovator of abstraction, yet it is important to note that not all modern abstract art can be traced to him. His project was related to other avant-garde movements that emerged in the early decades of the century—Constructivism, Suprematism, Neoplasticism— which also practiced nonrepresentational painting, but often those groups pursued such experiments as part of a larger program, aimed at transforming modern society as well as the visual arts. Nor did the great current of abstraction that dominated modern art between 1945 and 1965, especially in the United States, issue directly from Kandinsky. Indeed, the primary inspiration for artists such as Jackson Pollock, Mark Rothko, Willem de Kooning, or, in Europe, Karel Appel, came not from the first abstract painters at all, but rather from such movements as Surrealism and Cubism, which had, in fact, refused to make the leap into the nonobjective.

This, however, does not diminish Kandinsky's crucial role in the development of modern art. Although not all the varieties of abstract art descend directly from his work, his precedent made them possible. He made it legitimate to sever all ties to the "motif"—the depicted subject—and thereby freed the artist to concentrate on the paint itself, and on how its manipulation in lines, shapes, and forms affected the viewer. To liberate the elements of painting in this way has been one of the great aspirations of modern art, not only since Henri Matisse and Pablo Picasso, but since the time of the Impressionists. It was, in fact, the experience of seeing a work by Claude Monet that profoundly influenced the young Kandinsky and won him over to the cause of modern painting.

The Singer, *1903. During the first decade of the century, Kandinsky made his first woodcuts, executed in a Symbolist idiom.*

The Spiritual in Art

Though Kandinsky's mature work does not seek to imitate the appearance of the physical world, neither does it limit itself to mere decoration. Abstract art was not conceived as a way to produce pretty patterns for their own sake, but as a way to communicate more directly with the soul of the viewer. Kandinsky's art disregards the material world in order to attend more closely to the spiritual one. As with a musical composition, the arrangement of colors in one of his abstract paintings is guided solely by the principles of harmony and contrast, with the intention that this particular combination of elements will strike a resonant chord within the spectator. Kandinsky was in this regard following in the steps of the German and Northern European Romantic tradition, according to which the underlying subject matter of art, despite its many varied material forms, is always the unchanging world of the spirit.

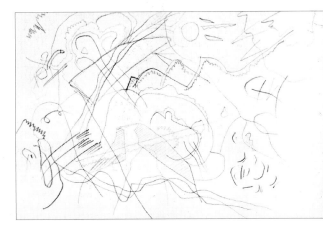

Study for Picture with White Edge, *1913. Kandinsky's studies are diagrams of the distribution of the color masses in the final work.*

Synesthesia

For Kandinsky, the comparison of painting with music was more than simply a metaphor. An awareness of his profound interest in music is crucial

Two Birds, *1907. A clear example of the influence on Kandinsky of Jugendstil in Munich at this time.*

Kandinsky executed this drawing in India ink for the cover of the catalogue of the first Blue Rider exhibition, in 1911, a year before the publication of the famous almanac The Blue Rider.

Little Worlds VI, *1922. Kandinsky re-created the world of his paintings in graphic works such as this.*

to any understanding of his work. The use of musical terms in the titles of his paintings, such as the groups called Improvisations or Compositions, is not gratuitous: instead, it conforms to the notion of "synesthesia," the idea that there are interconnections between the different bodily senses, such as hearing and vision, whereby colors are associated with specific sounds and musical harmonies on the one hand, and with particular emotional states on the other.

Kandinsky wrote about such phenomena in *On the Spiritual in Art* (1911), a brief treatise that defines the equivalencies between colors and concepts that are the basis of his painting. Spiritualistic ideas, derived from theosophy and occultism, also played an important role in reinforcing his ideas about sound and vision. But most of all, Kandinsky's understanding of the connection between painting and music derived from the Romantic operas of Richard Wagner. With his unusual interest in coordinating the effects of scenery and stage lighting with the performance of the score, Wagner conceived of his music dramas as a "total" aesthetic experience, one in which the visual and the auditory components would coalesce into a single, unified experience that would deeply affect the viewer's innermost being. As a result of Wagner's widespread influence, the notion of synesthesia became important for many artists, composers, and poets in the late nineteenth and early twentieth centuries.

The Aims of Art

Possibly because of his academic background, Kandinsky always had a penchant for theory, which led him to try to systematize his thinking about the ultimate goals of art through a number of discursive writings. Moreover, the awareness that he was establishing a new kind of painting increased his need to develop an intellectual rationale for his work. His years as a professor at the Bauhaus—the German school that in the 1920s and 1930s tried to apply the ideas of the avant-garde to architecture and industrial design—witnessed an even more thorough systemization of his theory of painting, notably in the volume *Point and Line to Plane* (1926), a sort of textbook for his classes. His more rigorous way of thinking at that time was not unrelated to the ideas of his Bauhaus colleague Josef Albers concerning the interactions of colors, and Kandinsky's work as an artist also became more disciplined in those years, pursuing a rigorously geometric style. Yet Kandinsky continued to seek the final significance of his paintings in the musical and emotional qualities that he ascribed to color. "Color," he said, "is the medium by which one can affect the soul directly….The soul is a piano with many strings, and the artist is the hand that, by striking one particular key, causes the human soul to vibrate."

In this, Kandinsky strove to fulfill the old aspiration of the Romantic movement for a "total" art, one capable of transforming how we understand the world around us. Therefore, his aims were indeed related to the larger project shared by much of the twentieth-century avant-garde—to rejuvenate a broad range of human endeavor, beginning with the visual arts. Kandinsky's utopia, however, was neither social nor political, but spiritual. His ultimate goal was to facilitate what he called the "inner gaze," that is, a personal vision revealing the hidden soul of things.

Vasily Kandinsky / 1866–1944

andinsky was born in Moscow of a well-to-do family, and although he spent most of his life in Germany and France, he always retained strong emotional ties to his homeland and its culture. During the first thirty years of his life, in Russia, painting remained only a kind of passionate diversion for this seemingly conventional young man, who was actually of a deeply Romantic disposition. After he completed his studies in law, his brilliant academic record earned him a professional position, but he gave it up in 1896 to move to Munich and devote himself entirely to painting.

The Early Years in Munich

The Bavarian capital, where the style known as Jugendstil was developing, was one of Europe's busiest artistic centers. Kandinsky studied painting at the Munich Academy and met Alexei von Jawlensky and Paul Klee, two of the artists with whom he would be closely associated. He also met the painter Gabriele Münter (see plate 14). The intense relationship between them, which lasted from 1902 until 1914, precipitated Kandinsky's separation from his first wife.

In Munich, Kandinsky organized a number of artists' associations designed to promote exhibitions. Phalanx, the first of these groups, was founded in 1901 and showed works by the Impressionists and the Symbolists, artists who had a visible influence on Kandinsky's early paintings. In the same years, Kandinsky began experimenting with woodcuts, a medium with a tradition in Germany going back to the Middle Ages.

This photograph was taken around 1871, when Kandinsky's parents separated and his aunt took charge of his upbringing.

Developing a Personal Style

During 1906–8, Kandinsky traveled in Europe with Münter, exhibited at the Salon d'Automne and the Salon des Indépendants in Paris, and saw works by the Fauvists and the emerging Cubists. The influence of Fauve color can be seen in the works that he painted in 1908 and 1909 after settling in the German city of Murnau. At that time, with Alfred Kubin, Jawlensky, Münter, and others he founded the New Coalition of Munich Artists—known by its German acronym, NKVM. The ideas that would give rise to abstraction were beginning to form: in particular, Kandinsky pursued his interests in theosophy and occultism through the writings of Rudolf Steiner and Madame Blavatsky, which were extremely popular in European cultural circles at the time.

This period also marked the beginning of his friendship with the pioneer of atonal musical composition, Arnold Schoenberg. Schoenberg's development of a kind of music liberated from traditional harmony may have contributed to Kandinsky's development of a kind of painting freed from traditional representation. The composer may also have encouraged Kandinsky's thinking about synesthesia and the interconnections between music and painting.

During this time, the NKVM exhibitions presented works by some of the most important of the Parisian painters, including Picasso, André Derain, Georges Braque, and Maurice de Vlaminck. Kandinsky's work of the time, however, such as the study for *Composition II* (plate 22), still had not let go of the conventions of representational painting, although, in a manner somewhat related to Fauvism, its subjects were beginning to dissolve into

Kandinsky in Dresden, 1905. This was a productive period in the artist's life. In 1906, he would travel with Münter to Paris, where he remained until the next year.

Maria and Franz Marc, Bernhard Koehler (père), Heinrich Campendonk, Thomas von Hartmann, and Kandinsky (seated), 1911.

Above: Kandinsky with his son, Vsevdod, in Moscow, 1918. Below: The artist, photographed by Hannes Beckmann in Paris, 1935.

a vortex of colored shapes. Such works exemplify the ambiguous, transitional stage through which his art was passing at that point.

Exploring an Abstract World

Even this partial dismantling of representation was not welcomed by the NKVM. Kandinsky, however, continued to look toward greater abstraction, writing his treatise *On the Spiritual in Art*, published in 1911. In 1912, with Jawlensky and Münter, he left the NKVM and founded his last and best-known Munich group, the Blue Rider. In the process, Kandinsky met Franz Marc, with whom he collaborated both in the group's exhibitions and in the publication of an almanac, in which they expounded their theoretical principles and commented on the art that aroused their interest, from the work of such contemporaries as Picasso and Derain, to African art, to the Russian and German folk traditions. Among the other artists who exhibited with the Blue Rider were August Macke, Schoenberg, and the Parisian painter Robert Delaunay. Kandinsky was by this time working in a truly abstract mode.

At the outbreak of World War I in 1914, Kandinsky returned to Russia. There, the great upheaval surrounding the October Revolution of 1917 was also a time of artistic ferment, with the participation of some of the most advanced artistic movements of the twentieth century. Although his spirituality and his Romanticism were at odds with the prevailing materialism of the government and most of the leading Russian artists, Kandinsky held a number of important artistic and cultural offices in the administration of the new Soviet state. His efforts led to the founding of several museums throughout Russia and to the development of new educational programs. In 1917, Kandinsky married Nina Adreevsky, his second wife. Four years later, the two left for Berlin, and Kandinsky never again returned to Russia.

From Walter Gropius came the offer of a position at the Bauhaus, where Kandinsky led both the Decorative Painting Workshop and the introductory course from 1922 to 1933. At the Bauhaus, he found his old friend Klee, and with him Jawlensky and Lyonel Feininger. During those years, Kandinsky's work became more rigorous in composition. His devotion to color was supplemented by a new appreciation for geometry and by a more controlled interaction of forms, as his painting responded to the various stylistic currents at the Bauhaus.

Later Years

With the closing of the Bauhaus by the Nazis in 1933, Kandinsky was forced to leave Germany—his paintings would be among those included in the exhibition of condemned works called "Degenerate Art" in 1937—and he settled in Neuilly, near Paris. There he hoped to find a climate favorable to his work, but the French artistic scene was not at that time especially well disposed toward abstraction. André Breton unsuccessfully tried to win him over to the Surrealist cause and, although Kandinsky became a French citizen, the last phase of his career unfolded quietly, amid a general lack of critical understanding of his work. In his last paintings, Kandinsky drifted away from Bauhaus geometry and used more organic and biomorphic shapes. He died in 1944, too soon to witness the triumph of abstract art in the postwar era.

Plates

Formative Influences

Two events that shaped Kandinsky's artistic vocation took place in 1895: he attended a performance of Richard Wagner's opera *Lohengrin,* and he saw one of Claude Monet's Haystack paintings at an exhibition of Impressionist art in Moscow. Kandinsky's response to Wagner at this early date already points to the link between painting and music that would inform his work as an artist. And his response to Monet indicates something of his future course toward nonrepresentational painting, for it was precisely the dematerializing of the motif in Monet's painting, the way that objects were beginning to dissolve into color and light, that impressed Kandinsky, who was captivated by the work. "Unknowingly," he wrote many years later, "the inevitability of the object as a pictorial element was being discredited." Not surprisingly, then, his first painted works reveal the influence of Impressionist color, as later on he would be affected by the color experiments of the Fauves. In Paris in 1906–7, Kandinsky was able to expand his knowledge of many of the French artists, including those who had participated in the Phalanx exhibitions from 1901 to 1904—Monet, Paul Signac, Félix Vallotton, Henri de Toulouse-Lautrec—and those who would participate in the exhibitions of the NKVM: Picasso, Braque, Vlaminck, André Derain, Kees van Dongen, Henri Le Fauconnier, and Georges Rouault.

1 The Old City II, *1902. The mellow evening light gives a poetic aura to this view of Rothenburg, but the sharp, clear-cut volumes recall Paul Cézanne's paintings. Kandinsky's minute brushstrokes, heavy with pigment, make tiny tesserae of color. They suggest the perfectionist preciosity typical of many painters of that period, from Lovis Corinth to Gustav Klimt.*

2 Kochel: Waterfall I, *1900. The notion that a landscape betrays "the state of the soul" dates from Romanticism. Kandinsky may have been influenced by nineteenth-century Russian painting or by the landscapists of the Barbizon school. But more than these, the immediacy of this canvas, with its generous brushstrokes, reveals the influence of the late Impressionist manner that had left its mark on the painter at a Moscow exhibition in 1895.*

1

3

4

3 Trees in Bloom at Lana I, *1908. The intensity of the light green, made still brighter by touches of yellow, is a celebration of springtime, exemplified by the blooming trees. The projection of the artist's feelings onto the painted motif, going beyond mere visual description, is one of the most conspicuous differences between French and Northern European painting at the beginning of the twentieth century.*

4 Riegsee: The Town Church, *1908. The arbitrariness of Fauve color is one of the most important innovations that Kandinsky incorporated into his own painterly style upon his return to Germany from France in 1908. By emancipating color from the restraints of fidelity to nature, he took the first step toward pictorial autonomy— toward painting as a chromatic symphony.*

5 Munich: Schwabing with the Church of St. Ursula, *1908. Another striking example of the effect on Kandinsky of his encounter with Fauvism.*

6

7

6 Landscape with a Tower, *1908. In this mysterious nocturnal setting, the pervasive red-yellow color chord of the brick tower, the roofs, and the field in the lower left corner takes on a somewhat spectral character.*

7 Interior (My Dining Room), *1909. The influence of Félix Vallotton, whose works were shown at the tenth Phalanx exhibition in 1910, as well as that of the French Nabi artists, can be seen in this meticulously painted, decorative interior.*

8 Oriental, *1909. Here, the coloristic exuberance of the Fauvists is beginning to overpower the motif, breaking free from it. The drawn shapes can barely contain the brashly vibrant reds and yellows.*

9 Mountain, *1909. The narrative element is downplayed in favor of a pure harmony of colors. Yellow, red, blue, and green—the basis of Kandinsky's chromatic vocabulary—here create a feeling of ascent, as he arranges the color areas with the brighter, lighter hues toward the top of the painting.*

8

9

Developments in Munich

In 1896, at the time of Kandinsky's arrival in Munich, the Bavarian capital was one of Europe's most important modernist centers. In 1892, a group of artists had broken away from the official academy and founded the Secession movement, which included some of the foremost painters of that time, such as Lovis Corinth and Franz von Stuck. The same year saw the first publication of the review *Jugend*, from which the German modernist style called Jugendstil took its name, and whose orbit attracted such figures as Hermann Obrist and August Endell. Their influence is evident in several of Kandinsky's works, such as his poster for the Phalanx exhibitions, but his strongest link to the Munich art world was his devotion to Romantic idealism, which had already emerged while he was in Russia. Kandinsky assimilated the melancholic tone of Symbolism, one of the prevailing currents of the Secession, and its taste for landscape. The inner correspondence of color with the emotions is part of this Romantic heritage, which Kandinsky combined with the influence of Fauvism.

10 Obermarkt with Mountains, *1908. This is one of the earliest works painted in the small Bavarian village where Kandinsky sojourned with Gabriele Münter. The pale yet luminous color confers an air of melancholy on the scene, which is treated with the sharp contrast of light and shade typical of woodcuts. The picture's style may also owe something to Ferdinand Hodler.*

10

11 The Blue Rider, *1903. At this very early date, Kandinsky introduced what would become the emblem of the most famous of the several groups that he belonged to in his career. For the artist, blue was a celestial symbol; he equated this spiritual rider with the mythical St. George, defeating the "dragon" of materialism. His mysterious presence in the landscape, bathed in an eerie raking light, evokes the atmosphere of German folktales.*

12 *Sketch for* Achtyrka: Autumn, *1901. One of Kandinsky's earliest known works attests to the artist's familiarity with Symbolist painting, although its execution also betrays the influence of the French Impressionists, which began while he was still in Russia.*

13 Riding Couple, *1906–7. The ornamental quality of Kandinsky's early pointillism makes it not unlike the work of Gustav Klimt, and, like that Viennese artist, Kandinsky here explores the decorative aspects of painting as they relate to architectural design. Though the subject suggests a Russian folktale, it is depicted against the transfigured silhouette of an imaginary Moscow—a magical skyline of gilded domes—on the opposite bank of the river.*

15

14 Portrait of Gabriele Münter, *1905. The Phalanx group operated an art school, where Kandinsky met Gabriele Münter, a young German painter who shared his life until 1914. In Moscow, Kandinsky had been married to his cousin, Anna Chemiakina, from whom he was amicably divorced in 1911, when his relationship with Münter was already long established. Münter's sensitive, intelligent features appear in several portraits that Kandinsky painted in those years.*

15 Rapallo: Rough Sea, *1906. This picture was painted in Italy, where Kandinsky was traveling with Münter. The technique suggests Monet, but the atmosphere of mystery and melancholy belongs entirely to the Romantic traditions of Northern Europe.*

16 The Farewell, *1903. During his first years in Munich, Kandinsky produced more woodcuts than oil paintings. This printmaking technique had been deeply rooted in German tradition since the late Middle Ages, and at the beginning of the twentieth century it was revived by artists of many different persuasions. Both the legendary subject of this work and Kandinsky's linear and decorative draftsmanship are clearly related to the woodcut tradition.*

17 Winter Landscape I, *1909. The unexpected use of the color yellow, in the sky and on the house at the center of the composition, competes with the blue hues elsewhere in the landscape. This kind of opposition gives the painting an unsettling effect reminiscent of certain pictures that the Norwegian artist Edvard Munch was painting at about the same time.*

18 Blue Mountain, *1908–9. This image of horseback riders before a towering blue mountain—a color symbolizing the spiritual—is clearly allegorical. The blue-red-yellow triad constitutes one of the basic chromatic harmonies of Kandinsky's work in these years.*

Abandoning Representation

The period from 1908 to 1910 was a personally rewarding one for Kandinsky, as reflected in the remarkable artistic progress of those years. With Gabriele Münter, he bought a house in Murnau, where he was able to spend long periods painting. Until at least 1912, recognizable objects continued to appear in some of his works, but the move to abstraction had already been made. The motif was increasingly dissolved into expanses of color, although he said that as yet he dared not discard it entirely for fear of falling into a merely decorative mode, or producing paintings "that resemble, to say it crudely, carpets or neckties. The beauty of color and form is not enough of a goal for art." He therefore sought to endow painting with spiritual values comparable to those he found in music. It was then that Kandinsky began calling his works Improvisations and Compositions, as though they were musical pieces.

19 Murnau: The Garden I, *1910. The ostensible subject is merely a pretext for the painter to weave a pattern of green, yellow, and red, augmenting that color chord with touches of blue and brown.*

20 Murnau: View with Railroad and Castle, *1909. The flattening of depicted objects, turning them into silhouettes, recalls the woodcuts that Kandinsky made during his first years in Munich.*

21 *Study for* Winter II, *1910–11. A complex area of yellows makes up the central triangle of pictorial space, and into it red and blue objects seem to sink as if in a fluid. The other triangular areas, above and below, create a sense of recession.*

19

20

21

22

22 *Sketch for* Composition II, *1910. The final version of this work, Kandinsky's most ambitious up to that time, was lost in World War II. Shortly after its completion, it was shown at the second NKVM exhibition, where it aroused controversy. The welter of seemingly unrelated figures, caught in a whirlpool of color, signals a crucial stage in the painter's artistic development, the beginning of the break with representation.*

23 Improvisation VI, *1909. Kandinsky had visited Tunis with Gabriele Münter, and echoes of that trip can be found in some works from the time. The subtitle "Africana" is sometimes affixed to this painting, in which Kandinsky incorporated his experience of North Africa into his quest for a new artistic idiom.*

24 Improvisation VII, *1910. Along with* Composition II *(see study, plate 22), this is one of the earliest paintings in which Kandinsky discarded representation. The color arrangement, with barely any delimiting linear structure, transforms pictorial space into a zone of chromatic turbulence, a vortex that spirals in to the upper right quadrant of the painting.*

23

25 Improvisation XVIII (with Tombstones), *1911. The absence of hierarchical order in this painting is characteristic of the works of 1910 and 1911, as Kandinsky explored new territory.*

26 Improvisation XI, *1910. Vestigially representational elements can barely be identified here, having become almost ghostly. A bright yellow triangle is once again the center of attention of an entire composition.*

27 Passage by Boat, *1910. The subject of a boat with oarsmen appears frequently in these years, a time when Kandinsky thought of pure abstraction as a "voyage" to the terra incognita of a new world of painting. The oarsmen steer toward unknown waters, as the artist does; like him, they voyage from darkness to light.*

28   Improvisation XIX, *1911. The discontinuity between the figures, who are rendered with rough black brushstrokes, and the background of the painting—a broad, mottled area of variations on blue, and a warm, red border with touches of yellow and green— makes it possible to speak of color and line as two independent, almost unrelated structures. The harmony of the colors would be just as intelligible without the representational sketch: the insubstantial figures are hardly more than a way to emphasize the tension at the edges of the painting.*

29   All Saints' Day I, *1911. The same year, Kandinsky completed a representational version of this painting using a similar chromatic arrangement (see plate 47). In the present version, the areas of color intermingle in a maelstrom of directional tensions that establishes no clear hierarchical order.*

30   Autumn II, *1912. The tenuous diagonal across the lower portion of the painting gives rise to a spectacular image: a diaphanous landscape of soft, autumn hues is reflected in the still waters of a lake. In this case, it is the title that provides the key to the painting's colors, as elsewhere it is given by a reference to music.*

28

Non-Objective Painting

During the years from 1910 to the outbreak of World War I, Kandinsky created his own painterly domain. The openly nonrepresentational nature of his work caused tensions with the NKVM, which in 1911 refused to exhibit his *Composition V* (private collection), claiming that its format did not comply with the mandatory requirements of the association. But as a result, Kandinsky strengthened his friendships with Franz Marc and Arnold Schoenberg, which led to the forming of the Blue Rider. At the same time, Kandinsky pursued his interest in theosophy, which was to become a spiritual resource for his work as an artist. His paintings were already nonrepresentational; only a few spare brushstrokes occasionally still hinted at figures and objects, now more as oblique allusions to the painting's meaning than as its actual subject. Such vestiges of representation only served to demonstrate Kandinsky's awareness of his role as the founder of a new kind of painting: with their traces of such subjects as the Deluge, the Apocalypse, and the voyage to unknown waters, these works are all images of a great ending, but also of regeneration and of arrival in a new, reborn world. The theme of these paintings is not merely the conflict between vibrant masses of color but, as the artist said, "the perception of the spiritual in material and abstract things."

31 Composition IV, *1911. The rainbow that arches between the mountains establishes the basic color harmony, a blue, yellow, and green chord with strokes of red. The black lines are little more than a template laid over the areas of color.*

32 Improvisation XIII, *1910. Paintings like this one, in which representational content has dissolved into color, best exemplify Kandinsky's work during the years before World War I. Here, the masses of color are contained by thick black strokes that might as well be cast shadows.*

33 Impression V (Park), *1911. The black lines that constitute the figurative elements in this painting were developed from an observed motif, but they have little relation to the chord of primary colors that is the true essence of the work.*

31

34 St. George II, *1911. Differently colored angular shapes cluster like vectors around a yellow diagonal. The organization of the painting is reminiscent of certain Cubist ideas of spatial structure; however, both the date of this work and the nature of Kandinsky's aesthetic decisions make it difficult to imagine a direct influence.*

34

35 Deluge I, *1912. Kandinsky's allusion to the biblical Deluge is one of the most frequent metaphors of regeneration at this stage of his career. Here, a downpour of shapes tumbles through a range of colors, from the intense yellows to white to the reddish-greens at the back.*

36 Improvisation XXVIII *(second version), 1912. Kandinsky viewed the painterly process of the Blue Rider years as a way of freeing the spiritual from the world of matter. This may explain the chaotic appearance of certain works, where the artist seems to be releasing powerful forces that he cannot as yet control.*

36

37

38

34

37 Improvisation (Deluge), *1913. Once again, Kandinsky alludes to the biblical Deluge and to the idea of chaos. Here, however, the relatively cool colors and the black background dampen the explosive energy of the scene, and Kandinsky lowers the temperature of the large red shapes by putting layers of calmer colors on top of them. The three rays across the upper part of the painting suggest the symbolic oars in the works that he painted in 1910 (see plate 27).*

38 *Study for* Deluge II, *1912. The entire composition responds to the diagonal current that originates in the lower left corner. The warmest and most vibrant tones—yellows and reds—create the foreground, with blues and browns for the most part restricted to the top and right.*

39 Improvisation XXVI (Rowing), *1912. A wavy red line splits the pictorial surface into two unequal parts. Once again, rowing figures are defined by a few black strokes, here laid over the pattern of color areas. The black lines establish a forceful diagonal that gives the painting its dynamic quality, and they thus impose a certain tension on the more static background. By showing the tension between such wholly different elements, Kandinsky wanted to convey the opposition between the material and spiritual worlds.*

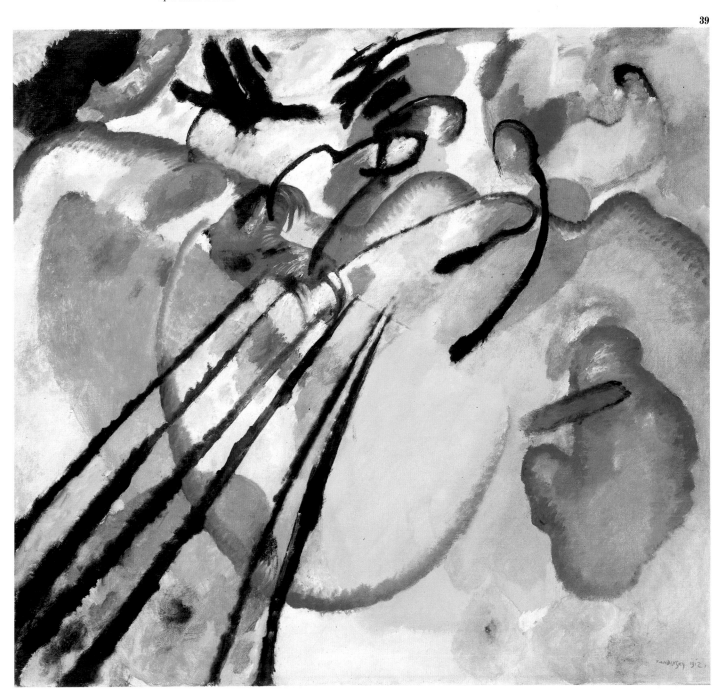

39

40

41

40 Painting with White Form, *1913. The idea of a pictorial core, a vortex upon which all the energies of the painting converge, was one of the earliest organizing principles to appear in Kandinsky's work. Here, the core is the white blot to the left of center.*

41 Composition VI, *1913. Kandinsky called his most complex paintings Compositions, and each was generally preceded by a number of preliminary studies. Works such as this are among his most intricate pictorial structures and can scarcely be appreciated in reproduction.*

42 Fantastic Improvisation, *1913. The dark blot at the center of the painting draws the swirling strokes of color into one central vortex of movement. The more isolated areas in the corners act as a frame for this dominant motion.*

42

43 Moscow II, *1916. This painting was executed after Kandinsky's return to Russia at the outbreak of World War I. It is illuminating to compare it with his written description of sunset in his native city: "The sun dissolves the whole of Moscow into a single spot, which … sets all of one's soul vibrating…. It is the last chord of the symphony, which brings every color vividly to life, which allows, even forces, all of Moscow to resound like the final fortissimo of a gigantic orchestra…. To paint this hour, I thought, must be for an artist the most impossible, the greatest joy."*

44 Black Lines I, *1913. The expansiveness that Kandinsky attributed to the color yellow is here offset by the compact density of the reds and blues, which, with their greater compositional "weight," slip toward the bottom. The graphic lines in the work do not conflict with this underlying painted structure, but instead complement it, giving the viewer a schematic means of reading the picture. With each painting, Kandinsky tested anew the relationship between color and line.*

44

The Folkloric Imagination

During the greater part of his childhood in Russia, Kandinsky was raised by his aunt, Elisabeth Ticheeva, who used to read him Russian and German folktales. In 1889, the Society of Natural Sciences, Ethnography, and Anthropology invited him on a scientific mission to Vologda, in northern Russia, to study agrarian law as well as the surviving traces of pre-Christian religions in the area. These circumstances attest to Kandinsky's early interest in folklore and indigenous culture, among the constants in the Romantic tradition of Northern Europe. In Munich, Kandinsky continued to follow this particular predilection and, as a result, several paintings from his early years depict Russian and German legends and popular figures. It is worth noting his profound interest in the specifically Bavarian tradition, dating from the eighteenth and nineteenth centuries, of depicting naïve, vignette-like religious scenes in the medium of small votive paintings on glass. The almanac published by the Blue Rider in 1912 reproduced works of this kind from the Krötz collection, as well as a series of popular prints of various cultural origins. What Kandinsky looked for in

45 Song of the Volga, *1906. The painter evokes the atmosphere of the Russian folktales of his childhood and the decorative sensibility typical of the German Jugendstil. Although he lingers over such ornamental features as the icons on the masts or the boats' carved figureheads, the whole scene is nonetheless rendered in a vigorous manner.*

45

these sources were signs of a spirituality still uncontaminated by subsequent cultural developments. Kandinsky himself, who never forgot the icons of his native Russia, made paintings on glass as well as woodcuts in the old German tradition.

46

47

46 Glass Painting with Sun, *1910. Bavarian paintings on glass may have put Kandinsky in mind of Russian icons. The idea of painting the frame, however, belongs to a modern tradition according to which a work of art should be a decorative synthesis.*

47 All Saints' Day, *1911. This is Kandinsky's quite straightforward response to the naïve religiosity of the Bavarian paintings on glass from the Krötz collection. However, the same year the artist also painted an abstract version of this scene (plate 29).*

48 Woman in Moscow, *1912. Only rarely did Kandinsky return to figurative art, and when he did it was almost always to deal with memories of his childhood in Russia. The frontal rendition of the central figure here may have been suggested by Russian icons, while the general atmosphere, with mysterious characters floating in midair, is not unlike the fables painted by his countryman Marc Chagall. The choice of colors is quite typical of Kandinsky's other work in those years.*

49 Last Judgment, *1912.*
Apocalyptic imagery
recurs frequently in this
period of transition
toward an abstract art.
In this work, both the
medium of painting on
glass and the decorative
treatment of the frame
suggest ties to folk culture.

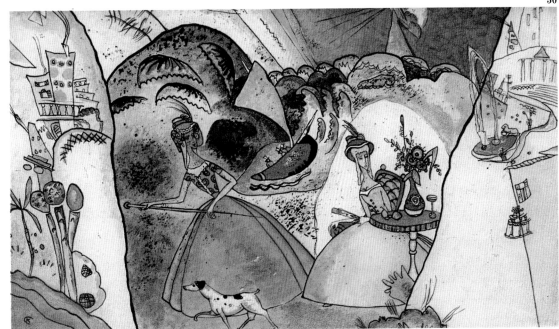

50 Women in Crinoline,
1918. Painted during his
Russian sojourn, this
small work on glass is
so exceptional as to be
accountable only as a
form of private diversion.
Both the theme and the
technique are quite remote
from the artist's central
preoccupations at the
time.

A More Rigorous Style

The years that Kandinsky spent in Russia before again going to Germany, to join the Bauhaus in 1921, were not very productive in terms of the number of works he made. He was kept busy by his responsibilities in the cultural and artistic administration of the new state that had issued from the Revolution. Nonetheless, the paintings that he produced in this period display some significant developments. In spite of his differences with the leading factions of the Russian avant-garde, the influence of their work is clearly felt in the process of systematic analysis that now overtook the flowing chromaticism of the Blue Rider period. Kandinsky wanted to subdue and discipline his masses of color by means of more clearly defined forms. Now, a particular element—an oval or a circle—often became the focus of the composition, and he frequently used the four-sided figure of the trapezoid, and other geometric shapes laid diagonally over the composition, to animate the pictorial surface and define the subject of the painting.

51 In the Gray, *1919. In works like this, previously chaotic compositions begin to become more organized: the placement of the two red areas and the central black one announces the artist's preference for arranging forms along a diagonal. Yet the black strokes and threadlike lines are still reminiscent of Kandinsky's artistic idiom from the Munich period.*

52 White Line, *1920. There is a dynamic tension between the rectangular shape of the canvas itself and the large trapezoid shape that seems to be in front of it and whose corners extend beyond the edges of the painting. This two-layer effect, together with the projecting white arc in the middle, makes the pictorial space seem to bulge outward at the center, as in a relief— a sharp difference from the works of 1910 to 1914.*

51

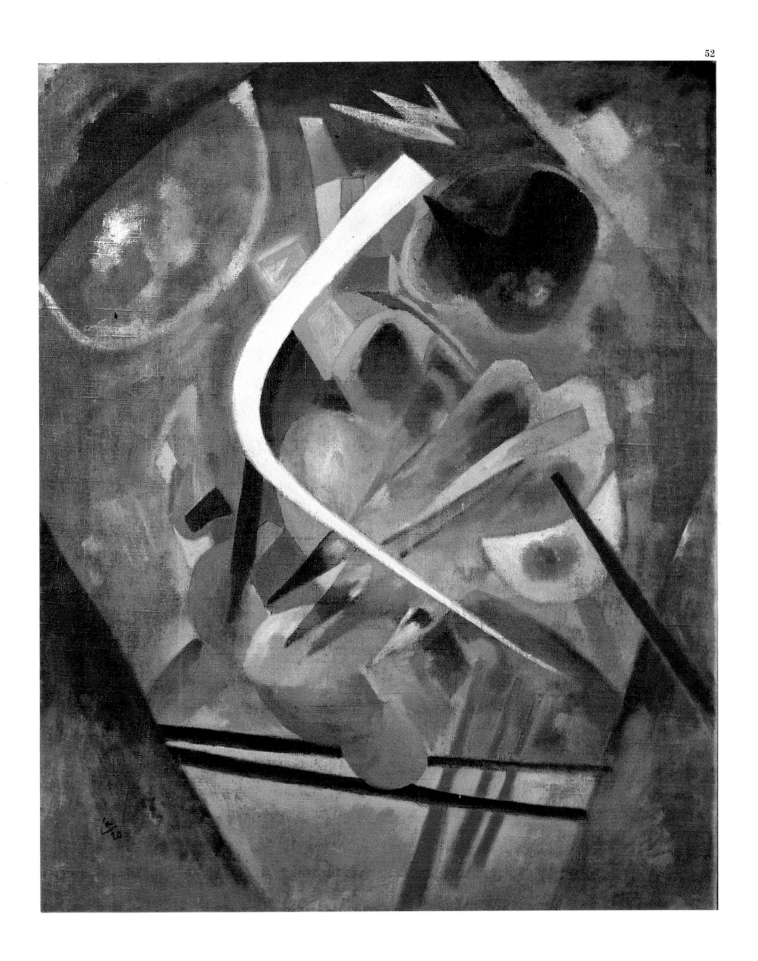

52

53   Red Oval, *1920. The red oval is a variation on the vortex element familiar from Kandinsky's earlier paintings, but the large yellow plane that organizes the picture as a whole heralds a new, increasingly geometric style. Though the elements of Kandinsky's vocabulary had changed little since the Munich period, he was composing with them in a new way.*

54   Maquette of a Mural for the Unjuried Exhibition, *1922. Shortly after returning to Germany, Kandinsky executed a mural painting for the reception hall of the unjuried "Berlin Free Exhibition," one of his few works designed as a decoration. The same year, he took charge of the Decorative Painting Workshop at the Bauhaus.*

55   Black Pattern, *1922. A trapezium divided into tiny cells—to be filled in with colors in later paintings—here becomes the center toward which the other shapes gravitate. The geometrically conceived forms are arranged on overlapping planes. The seeming evocation of ships and fish in the lower left corner is a touch of capricious irony rather than a genuine figurative reference.*

53

Point and Line to Plane

Kandinsky worked for eleven years—from 1922 to 1933—at the Bauhaus, first in Weimar and then in Dessau and Berlin. His experiences led him to systematize his practices as a painter into a body of teaching, most notably in the book *Point and Line to Plane*, published in 1926. The notion of musical and emotional equivalents to color, initially expounded in *On the Spiritual in Art*, continued to be at the core of his painting, but now this idea was combined with a new interaction of forms. Kandinsky had long pursued a theory of color based on an opposition between red and blue. With his increasing reliance on geometric shapes, he could use them to either intensify or reduce the inherent properties of each color, as well as mark directions and points of tension on the pictorial surface. He was careful, however, not to rely too heavily on theory, applying it freely, without falling into the trap of making painting the mechanical implementation of a formula.

56 Composition VIII, *1923. In this period of Kandinsky's career, the circle appears as a symbol of perfection, often carrying cosmic connotations. The vibrant color of the Blue Rider years is now applied more evenly and smoothly. The economy and exactitude of the geometric style establish a new sense of the absolute.*

57 On White II, *1923. Two heavy black lines convey the twisting effect created by the brown trapezoid as it tilts away from the picture plane. The turning of the triangles and quadrilaterals in space reflects this tension, and where they overlap there is a complex mingling of their colors. For Kandinsky, the expressive character of his art, its drama, arose from these dynamic interactions between shapes and colors. "The encounter of a circle with the point of a triangle," he wrote, "is no less affecting than God's finger touching Adam's in the work of Michelangelo."*

56

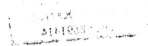

58

58 Still Tension, *1924. As the title
of this painting suggests, its
pictorial structure demonstrates
the balance between opposing
forces. The complex interplay in
the picture between superimposed
forms—a welter of straight lines
set against curves and circles
against rectangles—is resolved by
the equilibrium between the two
principal circles, set in opposite
corners. The strong diagonal
axis that connects the two is
emphasized by an arrow. The
colors, too, are arranged in
accordance with this opposition,
so that the "warmer" reds and
yellows predominate in the upper
left and the "cooler" blues in the
lower right. Within this color
scheme, the two circles serve as
alternatives: a cold vortex and a
hot one. The compositional clarity
sought in this type of painting is
a result both of Kandinsky's
evolution as an artist and his
concurrent experience as a teacher.*

59 Hard But Soft, *1927. Once
again, the structural precision is
reminiscent of the work of the
Russian Constructivists. The
intricate network of straight lines,
circles, and triangles generates a
pattern of small, separate cells,
many of them filled in with color.
The title suggests how the hardness
of this geometric structure is
played off against the softness of
the open, diaphanous background.*

60 Several Circles, *1926. Spheres and disks begin to appear in Kandinsky's work with the 1922 graphic portfolio* Little Worlds *(see page 6), whereby he sought to reconcile the intellectual rigor of the Bauhaus with his own spiritualistic impulses. Thus, in one sense, geometric shapes such as the circle are the products of the rational mind, part of the system of mathematical measurement first developed by the ancient Greeks. Yet at the same time, as Kandinsky said, "a circle ... is a blazing patch of sky"—a solar disk, like the sun, endowed with cosmic overtones and thus a way of picturing, and understanding, the workings of the universe.*

61 Thirteen Rectangles, *1930. As if reversing the course of his development, Kandinsky seems to return to a kind of rigor from which he was actually more distant than he may seem. This work may suggest the Neoplasticist compositions of Piet Mondrian and Theo van Doesburg, but the staircase arrangement of the rectangles, which appears in a number of paintings, also invokes an occult notion of initiation and spiritual progress. As in most works from this period, the entire composition is organized around one element, in this case the large, red square near the center.*

60

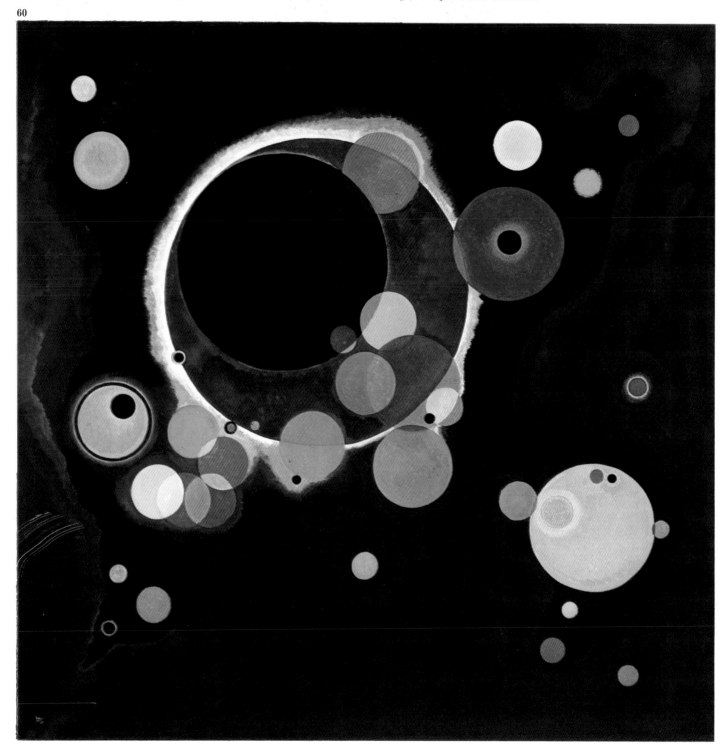

61

A New Freedom

Kandinsky's relation to European abstract painting after he settled in Paris in 1933 was not an easy one. Although, by that time, he was an established artist, his social circle in the French capital was rather restricted. In spite of that, however, his late works are characterized by the special freedom and tranquility sometimes seen in an artist's old age. Kandinsky abandoned the strict geometry that had distinguished the Bauhaus years and started practicing what can be called a "biomorphic" abstraction, on account of its softly organic, sinuous shapes. For some viewers, these images evoke the world revealed by the microscope, an association which may indeed have attracted the artist as an alternative to immediate perception, a fantastic universe concealed from the unaided senses. What the mysterious yet festive lyricism of these paintings really seeks, however, is the "inner gaze," that transcendental goal that Kandinsky had pursued throughout his career. In 1910, writing about the content of his paintings, he said that he wanted "to speak of secrets by means of a secret. Could this be the theme? Is this not the objective, conscious or unconscious, of the urgent creative impulse? With the language of art one can speak to humanity about what is beyond the human."

62

62 Interrelations, *1934. The small, dynamic, and brightly colored organic forms recall the appearance of protozoa, the tiny cells seen through the lens of a microscope. One cannot discount the influence of artists such as Jean Arp and Joan Miró, whom Kandinsky met during his years in Paris, but the principles governing the color relations remain the same as in his own previous works.*

63 Graceful Ascent, *1934. The stepped arrangement of shapes seen in* Thirteen Rectangles *(plate 61) returns here, but now it is presented in a more uninhibited manner, like one of the miniature universes, full of wit, devised by Paul Klee. The suggestion of a spiral, created by the three small crescents above the central square, subtly enhances the sense of upward movement, while also indicating the kind of vortex that Kandinsky had employed in many of his paintings since the Munich years.*

63

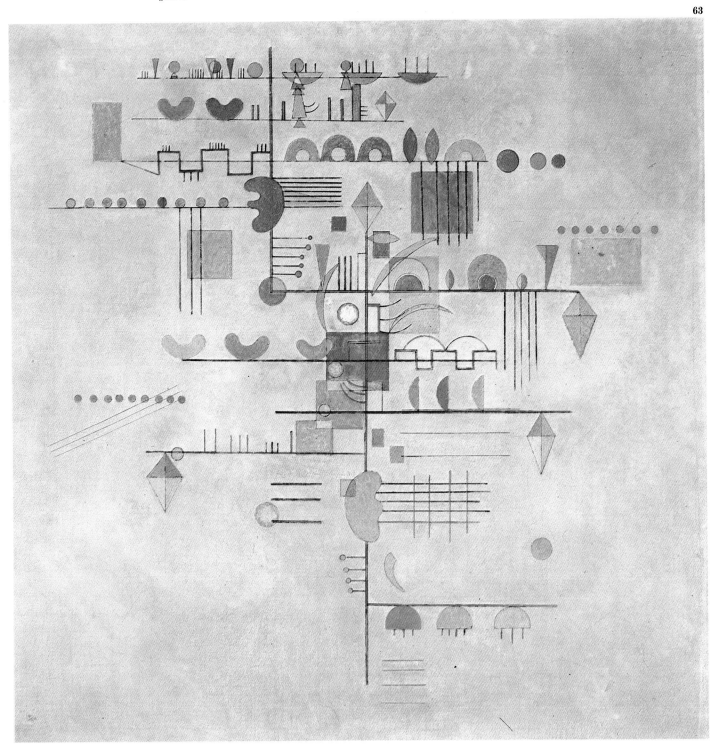

64

64 Dominant Curve, *1936. The symbolic staircase, most evident at the lower right, here incorporates both geometric and organic forms. Though Kandinsky remained indebted to the compositional rigor of the Bauhaus, he also valued the greater freedom of the new idiom that he had now mastered.*

65 Accompanied Milieu, *1937. The familiar symbolism of the circle gives rise to myriad curvilinear shapes, the dominant one resembling the staff of a musical score, all set against a bright yellow field, like the gold background of an icon.*

65

66 The White Line, *1936. Kandinsky here makes use of the distinctively modernist whipping curve, so frequent, for instance, in the decorative works of August Endell, whom Kandinsky met during his first years in Munich. The biomorphic form under the white line, with its related indenting curves, evokes both the contours and the texture of a micro-organism, although recently it has been reinterpreted as a horse and rider.*

67

68

69

67 Unanimity, *1939.
One of the most
distinctive features of
Kandinsky's last phase
is the progressive
lightening of his
palette, which often
became extremely
bright, as well as his
greater use of blended
hues, lessening the
reliance on primary
colors that had
extended through the
Munich and Bauhaus
years.*

68 Composition X,
*1939. For Kandinsky,
abstraction presupposed,
above all, the creation
of an autonomous
artistic universe,
independent of nature,
and yet no less real
and concrete than the
natural world. The
colored shapes floating
before a midnight
background tell of just
such an alternative
and visionary
universe.*

69 Sky Blue, *1940.
The biomorphic forms
seen here, looking like
fantastic animals,
may refer to the world
of children's toys or to
that of Slavic folk art,
although Kandinsky
was usually vexed
when critics made
such associations in
talking about his work.*

70 Accompanied Contrast, *1935. Generally not concerned with purely technical innovation, Kandinsky did nonetheless sometimes experiment with using sand to give texture to the paint.*

71 Delayed Actions, *1941. The freedom and fluidity of paintings such as this can make for quite an elaborate composition. A number of segments throughout the picture could easily have been developed into paintings in their own right. Indeed, many different parts of the canvas carry equal importance, without the focused cores of tension typical of the artist's earlier works.*

70

71

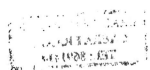

72, 73 Circle and Square, *1943;* The Small Red Circle, *1944. Kandinsky's last works, of which these are two examples, display certain devices from the geometric period, such as circles pierced by triangles, or the interaction between straight lines and curves generating the pictorial space. These are now presented in a different context, of course, but the artist remains loyal to the notion of an alternative painterly universe, only loosely connected to the material world.*

List of Plates

1 The Old City II, *1902. Oil on canvas, 20½ × 30⅞" (52 × 78.5 cm). Musée National d'Art Moderne, Centre Georges Pompidou, Paris*

2 Kochel: Waterfall I, *1900. Oil on canvas over cardboard, 12¾ × 9¼" (32.4 × 23.5 cm). Städtische Galerie, Munich*

3 Trees in Bloom at Lana I, *1908. Oil on canvas over panel, 7 × 10⅛" (17.8 × 25.9 cm). Private collection, New York*

4 Riegsee: The Town Church, *1908. Oil on cardboard, 13 × 17¾" (33 × 45 cm). Von der Heydt-Museum, Wuppertal*

5 Munich: Schwabing with the Church of St. Ursula, *1908. Oil on cardboard, 27 × 19¼" (68.8 × 49 cm). Städtische Galerie im Lenbachhaus, Munich*

6 Landscape with a Tower, *1908. Oil on cardboard, 29⅛ × 38¾" (74 × 98.5 cm). Musée National d'Art Moderne, Centre Georges Pompidou, Paris*

7 Interior (My Dining Room), *1909. Oil on cardboard, 19⅝ × 25⅝" (50 × 65 cm). Städtische Galerie im Lenbachhaus, Munich*

8 Oriental, *1909. Oil on cardboard, 27⅜ × 38" (69.5 × 96.5 cm). Städtische Galerie im Lenbachhaus, Munich*

9 Mountain, *1909. Oil on canvas, 42⅞ × 42⅞" (109 × 109 cm). Städtische Galerie im Lenbachhaus, Munich*

10 Obermarkt with Mountains, *1908. Oil on cardboard, 13 × 16⅛" (33 × 41 cm). Private collection, Germany*

11 The Blue Rider, *1903. Oil on canvas, 21⅝ × 25½" (55 × 65 cm). Private collection, Zurich*

12 *Sketch for* Achtyrka: Autumn, *1901. Oil on canvas over cardboard, 9⅜ × 12⅞" (23.7 × 32.7 cm). Städtische Galerie im Lenbachhaus, Munich*

13 Riding Couple, *1906–7. Oil on canvas, 21⅝ × 19⅞" (55 × 50.5 cm). Städtische Galerie im Lenbachhaus, Munich*

14 Portrait of Gabriele Münter, *1905. Oil on canvas, 17¾ × 17¾" (45 × 45 cm). Städtische Galerie im Lenbachhaus, Munich*

15 Rapallo: Rough Sea, *1906. Oil on canvas over cardboard, 9 × 13" (23 × 33 cm). Musée National d'Art Moderne, Centre Georges Pompidou, Paris*

16 The Farewell, *1903. Woodcut, 12⅜ × 12⅜" (31.3 × 31.2 cm). Musée National d'Art Moderne, Centre Georges Pompidou, Paris*

17 Winter Landscape I, *1909. Oil on cardboard, 28⅛ × 38⅜" (71.5 × 97.5 cm). The State Hermitage Museum, St. Petersburg*

18 Blue Mountain, *1908–9. Oil on canvas, 41¾ × 38" (106 × 96.6 cm). Solomon R. Guggenheim Museum, New York*

19 Murnau: The Garden I, *1910. Oil on canvas, 26 × 32¾" (66 × 82 cm). Städtische Galerie im Lenbachhaus, Munich*

20 Murnau: View with Railroad and Castle, *1909. Oil on cardboard, 14⅛ × 19¼" (36 × 49 cm). Städtische Galerie im Lenbachhaus, Munich*

21 *Study for* Winter II, *1910–11. Oil on cardboard, 13 × 17½" (33 × 44.7 cm). Städtische Galerie im Lenbachhaus, Munich*

22 *Sketch for* Composition II, *1910. Oil on canvas, 38⅜ × 51⅝" (97.5 × 131.2 cm). Solomon R. Guggenheim Museum, New York*

23 Improvisation VI, *1909. Oil on canvas, 42⅛ × 39⅛" (107 × 99.5 cm). Städtische Galerie im Lenbachhaus, Munich*

24 Improvisation VII, *1910. Oil on canvas, 51½ × 38⅛" (131 × 97 cm). Tretyakov Gallery, Moscow*

25 Improvisation XVIII (with Tombstones), *1911. Oil on canvas, 55½ × 47¼" (141 × 120 cm). Städtische Galerie im Lenbachhaus, Munich*

26 Improvisation XI, *1910. Oil on canvas, 38⅜ × 41⅞" (97.5 × 106.5 cm). Russian Museum, St. Petersburg*

27 Passage by Boat, *1910. Oil on canvas, 38½ × 41⅜" (98 × 105 cm). Tretyakov Gallery, Moscow*

28 Improvisation XIX, *1911. Oil on canvas, 47¼ × 55¾" (120 × 141.5 cm). Städtische Galerie im Lenbachhaus, Munich*

29 All Saints' Day I, *1911. Oil on cardboard, 19⅝ × 25⅜" (50 × 64.5 cm). Städtische Galerie im Lenbachhaus, Munich*

30 Autumn II, *1912. Oil on canvas, 23⅝ × 32¼" (60 × 82 cm). The Phillips Collection, Washington, D.C.*

31 Composition IV, *1911. Oil on canvas, 62⅞ × 8′2⅝" (159.5 × 250.5 cm). Kunstsammlung Nordrhein-Westfalen, Düsseldorf*

32 Improvisation XIII, *1910. Oil on canvas, 47¼ × 55⅛" (120 × 140 cm). Staatliche Kunsthalle, Karlsruhe*

33 Impression V (Park), *1911. Oil on canvas, 41¾ × 62" (106 × 157.5 cm). Musée National d'Art Moderne, Centre Georges Pompidou, Paris*

34 St. George II, *1911. Oil on canvas, 42⅛ × 37¾" (107 × 96 cm). Russian Museum, St. Petersburg*

35 Deluge I, *1912. Oil on canvas, 39⅜ × 41⅜" (100 × 105 cm). Kaiser-Wilhelm Museum, Krefeld*

36 Improvisation XXVIII *(second version), 1912. Oil on canvas, 44½ × 62⅛" (113 × 158 cm). Solomon R. Guggenheim Museum, New York*

37 Improvisation (Deluge), *1913. Oil on canvas, 37⅜" × 59" (95 × 150 cm). Städtische Galerie im Lenbachhaus, Munich*

38 *Study for* Deluge II, *1912. Oil on canvas, 37⅜ × 42¼" (95 × 107.5 cm). Collection Harold Diamont, New York*

39 Improvisation XXVI (Rowing), *1912. Oil on canvas, 38⅛ × 42¼" (97 × 107.5 cm). Städtische Galerie im Lenbachhaus, Munich*

40 Painting with White Form, *1913. Oil on canvas, 47⅜ × 55" (120.3 × 139.6 cm). Solomon R. Guggenheim Museum, New York*

41 Composition VI, *1913. Oil on canvas, 6′4¾" × 10′ (195 × 300 cm). The State Hermitage Museum, St. Petersburg*

42 Fantastic Improvisation, *1913. Oil on canvas, 51⅛ × 51⅛"
(130 × 130 cm). Städtische Galerie im Lenbachhaus, Munich*

43 Moscow II, *1916. Oil on canvas, 20½ × 14⅛" (52 × 36 cm).
Private collection*

44 Black Lines I, *1913. Oil on canvas, 51 × 51⅝" (129.4 ×
131.1 cm). Solomon R. Guggenheim Museum, New York*

45 Song of the Volga, *1906. Tempera on cardboard, 19¼ × 26"
(49 × 66 cm). Musée National d'Art Moderne, Centre Georges
Pompidou, Paris*

46 Glass Painting with Sun, *1910. Reverse painting on glass with
painted frame, 12 × 15⅞" (30.6 × 40.3 cm). Städtische Galerie im
Lenbachhaus, Munich*

47 All Saints' Day, *1911. Reverse painting on glass with painted
frame, 13½ × 16" (34.5 × 40.5 cm). Städtische Galerie im
Lenbachhaus, Munich*

48 Woman in Moscow, *1912. Oil on canvas, 42⅞ × 42⅞" (108.8 ×
108.8 cm). Städtische Galerie im Lenbachhaus, Munich*

49 Last Judgment, *1912. Reverse painting on glass with painted
frame, 13¼ × 17⅞" (33.6 × 45.3 cm). Musée National d'Art
Moderne, Centre Georges Pompidou, Paris*

50 Women in Crinoline, *1918. Reverse painting on glass,
9⅞ × 16" (25.1 × 40.8 cm). Tretyakov Gallery, Moscow*

51 In the Gray, *1919. Oil on canvas, 50¾ × 69¼" (129 ×
176 cm). Musée National d'Art Moderne, Centre Georges
Pompidou, Paris*

52 White Line, *1920. Oil on canvas, 38½ × 31½" (98 × 80 cm).
Museum Ludwig, Cologne*

53 Red Oval, *1920. Oil on canvas, 28⅛ × 28" (71.5 × 71.2 cm).
Solomon R. Guggenheim Museum, New York*

54 Maquette of a Mural for the Unjuried Exhibition, *1922.
Gouache on black paper, 13⅝ × 23⅝" (34.7 × 60 cm). Musée
National d'Art Moderne, Centre Georges Pompidou, Paris*

55 Black Pattern, *1922. Oil on canvas, 37¾ × 41¾" (96 ×
106 cm). Musée National d'Art Moderne, Centre Georges
Pompidou, Paris*

56 Composition VIII, *1923. Oil on canvas, 55⅛ × 6'7⅛"
(140 × 201 cm). Solomon R. Guggenheim Museum, New York*

57 On White II, *1923. Oil on canvas, 41⅜ × 38⅝" (105 × 98 cm).
Musée National d'Art Moderne, Centre Georges Pompidou, Paris*

58 Still Tension, *1924. Oil on cardboard, 30⅞ × 21½" (78.5 ×
54.5 cm). Private collection, Paris*

59 Hard But Soft, *1927. Oil on canvas, 39⅜ × 19⅝" (100 ×
50 cm). Museum of Fine Arts, Boston*

60 Several Circles, *1926. Oil on canvas, 55⅛ × 55⅛" (140 ×
140 cm). Solomon R. Guggenheim Museum, New York*

61 Thirteen Rectangles, *1930. Oil on cardboard, 27⅜ × 23⅜"
(69.5 × 59.5 cm). Musée National d'Art Moderne, Centre Georges
Pompidou, Paris*

62 Interrelations, *1934. Mixed mediums on canvas, 35 × 45⅝"
(89 × 116 cm). Collection Mr. and Mrs. David Lloyd Kreeger,
Washington, D.C.*

63 Graceful Ascent, *1934. Oil on canvas, 31½" × 31½" (80 ×
80 cm). Solomon R. Guggenheim Museum, New York*

64 Dominant Curve, *1936. Oil on canvas, 51⅛ × 6'4¾"
(130 × 195 cm). Solomon R. Guggenheim Museum, New York*

65 Accompanied Milieu, *1937. Oil on canvas, 44⅞ × 57½"
(114 × 146 cm). Whereabouts unknown. Formerly collection
Adrien Maeght, Paris*

66 The White Line, *1936. Gouache and tempera on black paper,
19⅝ × 15¼" (49.9 × 38.7 cm). Musée National d'Art Moderne,
Centre Georges Pompidou, Paris*

67 Unanimity, *1939. Oil on canvas, 28¾ × 36¼" (73 × 92 cm).
Collection Jeffrey H. Loria, New York*

68 Composition X, *1939. Oil on canvas, 51⅛ × 6'4¾" (130 ×
195 cm). Kunstsammlung Nordrhein-Westfalen, Düsseldorf*

69 Sky Blue, *1940. Oil on canvas, 39⅜ × 28¾" (100 × 73 cm).
Musée National d'Art Moderne, Centre Georges Pompidou, Paris*

70 Accompanied Contrast, *1935. Oil with sand on canvas,
38⅛ × 63¾" (97 × 162 cm). Solomon R. Guggenheim Museum,
New York*

71 Delayed Actions, *1941. Mixed mediums on canvas, 35 × 45⅝"
(89 × 116 cm). Solomon R. Guggenheim Museum, New York*

72 Circle and Square, *1943. Tempera and oil on cardboard,
16½ × 22⅞" (42 × 58 cm). Musée National d'Art Moderne, Centre
Georges Pompidou, Paris*

73 The Small Red Circle, *1944. Gouache and oil on cardboard,
16½ × 22⅞" (42 × 58 cm). Musée National d'Art Moderne, Centre
Georges Pompidou, Paris*

Selected Bibliography

Avtonomova, Natalia, Vivian Endicott Barnett, et al. *New
    Perspectives on Kandinsky.* Malmö, Sweden: Malmö Konsthall,
    Sydsvenska Dagbladet, 1990.
Dabrowski, Magdalena. *Kandinsky: Compositions.* New York: The
    Museum of Modern Art, 1995.
Grohmann, Will. *Wassily Kandinsky: Life and Work.* New York:
    Harry N. Abrams, Inc., 1958.
Hahl-Koch, Jelena. *Kandinsky.* New York: Rizzoli, 1993.
Lindsay, Kenneth C., and Peter Vergo, eds. *Kandinsky: Complete
    Writings on Art.* Rev. ed., New York: Da Capo Press, 1994.
Roethel, Hans K., and Jean K. Benjamin. *Kandinsky: Catalogue
    Raisonné of the Oil Paintings.* 2 vols. Ithaca, N.Y.: Cornell
    University Press, 1982, 1984.
Washton Long, Rose-Carol. *Kandinsky: The Development of an
    Abstract Style.* Oxford: Clarendon Press, 1980.
Weiss, Peg. *Kandinsky and "Old Russia": The Artist as
    Ethnographer and Shaman.* New Haven, Conn., and London:
    Yale University Press, 1995.

Series Coordinator, English-language edition: Ellen Rosefsky Cohen
Editor, English-language edition: James Leggio
Designer, English-language edition: Judith Michael

Library of Congress Catalog Card Number: 95–78423
ISBN 0–8109–4692–0

Printed and bound in Spain by La Polígrafa, S.L.
Parets del Vallès (Barcelona)
Dep. Leg.: B. 39.912-1995